Jesus of Nazareth

Jesus of Nazareth

From the Baptism in the Jordan to the Transfiguration

by

Joseph Ratzinger
Pope Benedict XVI

Translated from the German by Adrian J. Walker

IGNATIUS PRESS SAN FRANCISCO

Original, hardbound edition published in the United States by Doubleday, an imprint of The Doubleday Broadway Publishing Group, a division of Random House, Inc., New York.

Simultaneously published in Germany as *Jesus von Nazareth.* This edition published by arrangement with RCS Libri S.p.A., Milan.

Interior book design by Maria Carella

Paperback edition published by Ignatius Press, 2008

Front cover art:
Jesus, Salvator Mundi (Savior of the World)
Joos van Cleve (1485–1540)
Réunion des Musée Nationaux/Art Resource, New York

Back cover photograph of Pope Benedict XVI
© Federico Gambarini/Pool/Reuters/Corbis

Cover design adapted by
Roxanne Mei Lum, based on
an original design by Jean Traina

www.ignatius.com

ISBN: 978-1-58617-198-8

Library of Congress Control Number 2006936325

PRINTED IN THE UNITED STATES OF AMERICA

First paper bound edition in the United States of America, 2008

CONTENTS

ABBREVIATIONS

The following abbreviations are used for books of the Bible:

Acts	Acts of the Apostles	Jas	James
Amos	Amos	Jer	Jeremiah
Bar	Baruch	Jn	John
1 Chron	1 Chronicles	1 Jn	1 John
2 Chron	2 Chronicles	2 Jn	2 John
Col	Colossians	3 Jn	3 John
1 Cor	1 Corinthians	Job	Job
2 Cor	2 Corinthians	Joel	Joel
Dan	Daniel	Jon	Jonah
Deut	Deuteronomy	Josh	Joshua
Eccles	Ecclesiastes	Jud	Judith
Eph	Ephesians	Jude	Jude
Esther	Esther	Judg	Judges
Ex	Exodus	1 Kings	1 Kings
Ezek	Ezekiel	2 Kings	2 Kings
Ezra	Ezra	Lam	Lamentations
Gal	Galatians	Lev	Leviticus
Gen	Genesis	Lk	Luke
Hab	Habakkuk	1 Mac	1 Maccabees
Hag	Haggai	2 Mac	2 Maccabees
Heb	Hebrews	Mal	Malachi
Hos	Hosea	Mic	Micah
Is	Isaiah	Mk	Mark
		Mt	Matthew

Nahum	Nahum	1 Sam	1 Samuel
Neh	Nehemiah	2 Sam	2 Samuel
Num	Numbers	Sir	Sirach (Ecclesiasticus)
Obad	Obadiah		
1 Pet	1 Peter	Song	Song of Solomon
2 Pet	2 Peter		
Phil	Philippians	1 Thess	1 Thessalonians
Philem	Philemon	2 Thess	2 Thessalonians
Prov	Proverbs	1 Tim	1 Timothy
Ps	Psalms	2 Tim	2 Timothy
Rev	Revelation (Apocalypse)	Tit	Titus
		Tob	Tobit
Rom	Romans	Wis	Wisdom
Ruth	Ruth	Zech	Zechariah
		Zeph	Zephaniah

The following abbreviations are used from time to time:

ATD: Das Alte Testament Deutsch, ed. Volkmar Herntrich and Artur Weiser, Göttingen, 1949–. This is a famous commentary in German on the Old Testament. The figures that follow the abbreviation indicate the volume number and the page number.

CSEL: Corpus Scriptorum ecclesiasticorum latinorum, Vienna, 1866–. Like the more famous *Patrologia latina,* this is a collection of Christian sources in Latin.

PG: Patrologia Graeca, ed. Jacques-Paul Migne, 161 vols., Paris, 1857–1866. This is a collection of ancient Christian sources in Greek.

RGG: Die Religionen in Geschichte und Gegenwart, Tübingen, 1909–1913; 2nd ed., 1927–1932; 3rd ed., 1956ff. Some articles were contributed to this last edition by the young Professor Ratzinger.

TDNT: Theological Dictionary of the New Testament, ed. G. Kittel and G. Friedrich, 10 vols., Eerdmans, Grand Rapids, 1964–1976.

Publisher's Note

The *Revised Standard Version (RSV)* is the preferred translation for Scriptural quotations within the text. In some instances, however, in order to reflect as clearly as possible the verbal associations emphasized by the author, it has been necessary to translate directly from the original biblical text.

FOREWORD

This book about Jesus, the first part of which I am now presenting to the public, has had a long gestation. When I was growing up—in the 1930s and 1940s—there was a series of inspiring books about Jesus: Karl Adam, Romano Guardini, Franz Michel Willam, Giovanni Papini, and Henri Daniel-Rops were just some of the authors one could name. All of these books based their portrayal of Jesus Christ on the Gospels. They presented him as a man living on earth who, fully human though he was, at the same time brought God to men, the God with whom as Son he was one. Through the man Jesus, then, God was made visible, and hence our eyes were able to behold the perfect man.

But the situation started to change in the 1950s. The gap between the "historical Jesus" and the "Christ of faith" grew wider and the two visibly fell apart. But what can faith in Jesus as the Christ possibly mean, in Jesus as the Son of the living God, if the *man* Jesus was so completely different from the picture that the Evangelists painted of him and that the Church, on the evidence of the Gospels, takes as the basis of her preaching?

As historical-critical scholarship advanced, it led to finer and finer distinctions between layers of tradition in the Gospels, beneath which the real object of faith—the figure [*Gestalt*] of Jesus—became increasingly obscured and blurred. At the same time, though, the reconstructions of this Jesus (who could only be discovered by going behind the traditions and sources used by the Evangelists) became more and more incompatible with one another: at one end of the spectrum, Jesus was the anti-Roman revolutionary working—though finally failing—to overthrow the ruling powers; at the other end, he was the meek moral teacher who approves everything and unaccountably comes to grief. If you read a number of these reconstructions one after the other, you see at once that far from uncovering an icon that has become obscured over time, they are much more like photographs of their authors and the ideals they hold. Since then there has been growing skepticism about these portrayals of Jesus, but the figure of Jesus himself has for that very reason receded even further into the distance.

All these attempts have produced a common result: the impression that we have very little certain knowledge of Jesus and that only at a later stage did faith in his divinity shape the image we have of him. This impression has by now penetrated deeply into the minds of the Christian people at large. This is a dramatic situation for faith, because its point of reference is being placed in doubt: Intimate friendship with Jesus, on which everything depends, is in danger of clutching at thin air.

Rudolf Schnackenburg was probably the most prominent Catholic exegete writing in German during the second half of the twentieth century. It is clear that toward the end of his life, this crisis surrounding the faith made a profound impression on him. In view of the inadequacy of all the portrayals of the "historical" Jesus offered by recent exegesis, he strove to produce one last great work: *Jesus in the Gospels: A Biblical Christology.* The book is intended to help believing Christians "who today have been made insecure by scientific research and critical discussion, so that they may hold fast to faith in the person of Jesus Christ as the bringer of salvation and Savior of the world" (p. x). At the end of the book, Schnackenburg sums up the result of a lifetime of scholarship: "a reliable view of the historical figure of Jesus of Nazareth through scientific effort with historical-critical methods can be only inadequately achieved" (p. 316); "the efforts of scientific exegesis to examine these traditions and trace them back to what is historically credible" draw us "into a continual discussion of tradition and redaction history that never comes to rest" (p. 318).

His own account of the figure of Jesus suffers from a certain unresolved tension because of the constraints of the method he feels bound to use, despite its inadequacies. Schnackenburg shows us the Gospels' image of Christ, but he considers it to be the product of manifold layers of tradition, through which the "real" Jesus can only be glimpsed from afar. He writes: "The historical ground is presupposed but is superseded in the faith-view of the evangelists" (p. 321). Now, no one doubts that; what remains unclear is how far the "historical ground" actually extends. That said, Schnackenburg does clearly throw into relief the decisive point, which he regards as a genuinely historical insight: Jesus' relatedness to

God and his closeness to God (p. 322). "Without anchoring in God, the person of Jesus remains shadowy, unreal, and unexplainable" (p. 322).

This is also the point around which I will construct my own book. It sees Jesus in light of his communion with the Father, which is the true center of his personality; without it, we cannot understand him at all, and it is from this center that he makes himself present to us still today.

To be sure, in the particular contours of my own presentation of Jesus I make a determined effort to go beyond Schnackenburg. The problem with Schnackenburg's account of the relationship between New Testament traditions and historical events stands out very clearly for me when he writes that the Gospels "want, as it were, to clothe with flesh the mysterious Son of God who appeared on earth" (p. 322). I would like to say in response that they did not need to "clothe him with flesh," because he had already truly taken flesh. Of course, the question remains: Can this flesh be accessed through the dense jungle of traditions?

Schnackenburg tells us in the foreword to his book that he feels indebted to the historical-critical method, which had been in use in Catholic theology ever since the door was opened for it by the encyclical *Divino Afflante Spiritu* in 1943 (p. ix). This encyclical was an important milestone for Catholic exegesis. Since then, though, the debate about method has moved on, both inside and outside the Catholic Church. There have been significant new methodological discoveries—both in terms of strictly historical work and in terms of the interplay between theology and historical method in scriptural interpretation. *Dei Verbum,* the Second Vatican

Council's Dogmatic Constitution on Divine Revelation, made a decisive step forward. In addition, two documents of the Pontifical Biblical Commission communicate important insights that have matured in the course of debates among exegetes: *The Interpretation of the Bible in the Church* (Vatican City, 1993) and *The Jewish People and Their Sacred Scriptures in the Christian Bible* (Vatican City, 2001).

I would like to sketch at least the broad outlines of the methodology, drawn from these documents, that has guided me in writing this book. The first point is that the historical-critical method—specifically because of the intrinsic nature of theology and faith—is and remains an indispensable dimension of exegetical work. For it is of the very essence of biblical faith to be about real historical events. It does not tell stories symbolizing suprahistorical truths, but is based on history, history that took place here on this earth. The *factum historicum* (historical fact) is not an interchangeable symbolic cipher for biblical faith, but the foundation on which it stands: *Et incarnatus est*—when we say these words, we acknowledge God's actual entry into real history.

If we push this history aside, Christian faith as such disappears and is recast as some other religion. So if history, if facticity in this sense, is an essential dimension of Christian faith, then faith must expose itself to the historical method—indeed, faith itself demands this. I have already mentioned the conciliar Constitution on Divine Revelation; it makes the same point quite explicitly in paragraph 12 and goes on to list some concrete elements of method that have to be kept in mind when interpreting Scripture. The Pontifical Biblical Commission's document on the interpretation of Holy Scripture develops the same idea much more amply in the chapter entitled "Methods and Approaches for Interpretation."

The historical-critical method—let me repeat—is an indispensable tool, given the structure of Christian faith. But we need to add two points. This method is a fundamental dimension of exegesis, but it does not exhaust the interpretive task for someone who sees the biblical writings as a single corpus of Holy Scripture inspired by God. We will have to return to this point at greater length in a moment.

For the time being, it is important—and this is a second point—to recognize the limits of the historical-critical method itself. For someone who considers himself directly addressed by the Bible today, the method's first limit is that by its very nature it has to leave the biblical word in the past. It is a *historical* method, and that means that it investigates the then-current context of events in which the texts originated. It attempts to identify and to understand the past—as it was in itself—with the greatest possible precision, in order then to find out what the author could have said and intended to say in the context of the mentality and events of the time. To the extent that it remains true to itself, the historical method not only has to investigate the biblical word as a thing of the past, but also has to let it remain in the past. It can glimpse points of contact with the present and it can try to apply the biblical word to the present; the one thing it cannot do is make it into something present *today*—that would be overstepping its bounds. Its very precision in interpreting the reality of the past is both its strength and its limit.

This is connected with a further point. Because it is a historical method, it presupposes the uniformity of the context within which the events of history unfold. It must therefore treat the biblical words it investigates as human words. On painstaking reflection, it can intuit something of the "deeper value" the word contains. It can in some sense catch the sounds of a higher dimension through the human word, and so open up the method to self-transcendence. But its specific object is the human word as human.

Ultimately, it considers the individual books of Scripture in the context of their historical period, and then analyzes them further according to their sources. The unity of all of these writings as one "Bible," however, is not something it can recognize as an immediate historical datum. Of course it can examine the lines of development, the growth of traditions, and in that sense can look beyond the individual books to see how they come together to form the one "Scripture." Nevertheless, it always has to begin by going back to the origin of the individual texts, which means placing them in their past context, even if it goes on to complement this move back in time by following up the process through which the texts were later brought together.

We have to keep in mind the limit of all efforts to know the past: We can never go beyond the domain of hypothesis, because we simply cannot bring the past into the present. To be sure, some hypotheses enjoy a high degree of certainty, but overall we need to remain conscious of the limit of our certainties—indeed, the history of modern exegesis makes this limit perfectly evident.

So far, then, we have said something about the importance of the historical-critical method, on one hand, and we have described its limit, on the other. Something more than just the limit has come into view, though, I hope: the fact that the inner nature of the method points beyond itself and contains within itself an openness to complementary methods. In these words from the past, we can discern the question concerning their meaning for today; a voice greater than man's echoes in Scripture's human words; the individual writings [*Schrifte*] of the Bible point somehow to the living process that shapes the one Scripture [*Schrift*].

Indeed, the realization of this last point some thirty years ago led American scholars to develop the project of "canonical exegesis." The aim of this exegesis is to read individual texts within the totality of the one Scripture, which then sheds new light on all the individual texts. Paragraph 12 of the Second Vatican Council's Constitution on Divine Revelation had already clearly underscored this as a fundamental principle of theological exegesis: If you want to understand the Scripture in the spirit in which it is written, you have to attend to the content and to the unity of Scripture as a whole. The Council goes on to stress the need for taking account of the living tradition of the whole Church and of the analogy of faith (the intrinsic correspondences within the faith).

Let us dwell for the time being on the unity of Scripture. It is a theological datum. But it is not simply imposed from the outside on what is in itself a heterogeneous ensemble of writings. Modern exegesis has brought to light the process of constant rereading that forged the words transmitted in the Bible into Scripture: Older texts are reappropriated, reinterpreted, and read with new eyes in new contexts. They become Scripture by being read anew, evolving in continuity with their original sense, tacitly corrected and given added depth and breadth of meaning. This is a process in which the word gradually unfolds its inner potentialities, already somehow present like seeds, but needing the challenge of new situations, new experiences and new sufferings, in order to open up.

This process is certainly not linear, and it is often dramatic, but when you watch it unfold in light of Jesus Christ, you can see it moving in a single overall direction; you can see that the Old and New Testaments belong together. This Christological hermeneutic, which sees Jesus Christ as the key to the whole and learns from him how to understand the Bible as a unity, presupposes a prior act of faith. It cannot be the conclusion of a purely historical method. But this act of faith is based upon reason—historical reason—and so makes it possible to see the internal unity of Scripture. By the same token, it enables us to understand anew the individual elements that have shaped it, without robbing them of their historical originality.

"Canonical exegesis"—reading the individual texts of the Bible in the context of the whole—is an essential dimension of exegesis. It does not contradict historical-critical interpretation, but carries it forward in an organic way toward becoming theology in the proper sense. There are two further aspects of theological exegesis that I would like to underscore. Historical-critical interpretation of a text seeks to discover the precise sense the words were intended to convey at their time and place of origin. That is good and important. But—aside from the fact that such reconstructions can claim only a relative certainty—it is necessary to keep in mind that any human utterance of a certain weight contains more than the author may have been immediately aware of at the time. When a word transcends the moment in which it is spoken, it carries within itself a "deeper value." This "deeper value" pertains most of all to words that have matured in the course of faith-history. For in this case the author is not simply speaking for himself on his own authority. He is speaking from the perspective of a common history that sustains him and that already implicitly contains the possibilities of its future, of the further stages of its journey. The process of continually rereading and drawing out new meanings from words would not have been possible unless the words themselves were already open to it from within.

At this point we get a glimmer, even on the historical level, of what inspiration means: The author does not speak as a private, self-contained subject. He speaks in a living community, that is to say, in a living historical movement not created by him, nor even by the collective, but which is led forward by a greater power that is at work. There are dimensions of the word that the old doctrine of the fourfold sense of Scripture pinpointed with remarkable accuracy. The four senses of Scripture are not individual meanings arrayed side by side, but dimensions of the one word that reaches beyond the moment.

This already suggests the second aspect I wanted to speak about. Neither the individual books of Holy Scripture nor the Scripture as a whole are simply a piece of literature. The Scripture emerged from within the heart of a living subject—the pilgrim People of God—and lives within this same subject. One could say that the books of Scripture involve three interacting subjects. First of all, there is the individual author or group of authors to whom we owe a particular scriptural text. But these authors are not autonomous writers in the modern sense; they form part of a collective subject, the "People of God," from within whose heart and to whom they speak. Hence, this subject is actually the deeper "author" of the Scriptures. And yet likewise, this people does not exist alone; rather, it knows that it is led, and spoken to, by God himself, who—through men and their humanity—is at the deepest level the one speaking.

The connection with the subject we call "People of God" is vital for Scripture. On one hand, this book—Scripture—is the measure that comes from God, the power directing the people. On the other hand, though, Scripture lives precisely within this people, even as this people transcends itself in Scripture. Through their self-transcendence (a fruit, at the deepest level, of the incarnate Word) they become the people of *God*. The People of God—the Church—is the living subject of Scripture; it is in the Church that the words of the Bible are always in the present. This also means, of course, that the People has to receive its very self from God, ultimately from the incarnate Christ; it has to let itself be ordered, guided, and led by him.

I feel that I owe the reader these remarks about methodology, because they govern my interpretation of the figure of Jesus in the New Testament (cf. the introductory remarks included with the Bibliography). The main implication of this for my portrayal of Jesus is that I trust the Gospels. Of course, I take for granted everything that the Council and modern exegesis tell us about literary genres, about authorial intention, and about the fact that the Gospels were written in the context, and speak within the living milieu, of communities. I have tried, to the best of my ability, to incorporate all of this, and yet I wanted to try to portray the Jesus of the Gospels as the real, "historical" Jesus in the strict sense of the word. I am convinced, and I hope the reader will be, too, that this figure is much more logical and, historically speaking, much more intelligible than the reconstructions we have been presented with in the last decades. I believe that this Jesus—the Jesus of the Gospels—is a historically plausible and convincing figure.

Unless there had been something extraordinary in what happened, unless the person and the words of Jesus radically surpassed the hopes and expectations of the time, there is no way to explain why he was crucified or why he made such an impact. As early as twenty or so years after Jesus' death, the great Christ-hymn of the Letter to the Philippians (cf. Phil 2:6–11) offers us a fully developed Christology stating that Jesus was equal to God, but emptied himself, became man, and humbled himself to die on the Cross, and that to him now belongs the worship of all creation, the adoration that God, through the Prophet Isaiah, said was due to him alone (cf. Is 45:23).

Critical scholarship rightly asks the question: What happened during those twenty years after Jesus' Crucifixion? Where did this Christology come from? To say that it is the fruit of anonymous collective formulations, whose authorship we seek to discover, does not actually explain anything. How could these unknown groups be so creative? How were they so persuasive and how did they manage to prevail? Isn't it more logical, even historically speaking, to assume that the greatness came at the beginning, and that the figure of Jesus really did explode all existing categories and could only be understood in the light of the mystery of God? Admittedly, to believe that, as man, he truly *was* God, and that he communicated his divinity veiled in parables, yet with increasing clarity, exceeds the scope of the historical method. Yet if instead we take this conviction of faith as our starting point for reading the texts with the help of historical methodology and its intrinsic openness to something greater, they are opened up and they reveal a way and a figure that are worthy of belief. Something else comes into clear focus as well: Though the New Testament writings display a many-layered struggle to come to grips with the figure of Jesus, they exhibit a deep harmony despite all their differences.

It is obvious that the way I look at the figure of Jesus goes beyond what much contemporary exegesis, as represented by someone such as Schnackenburg, has to say. I hope it is clear to the reader, though, that my intention in writing this book is not to counter modern exegesis; rather, I write with profound gratitude for all that it has given and continues to give to us. It has opened up to us a wealth of material and an abundance of findings that enable the figure of Jesus to become present to us with a vitality and depth that we could not have imagined even just a few decades ago. I have merely tried to go beyond purely historical-critical exegesis so as to apply new methodological insights that allow us to offer a properly theological interpretation of the Bible. To be sure, this requires faith, but the aim unequivocally is not, nor should be, to give up serious engagement with history.

It goes without saying that this book is in no way an exercise of the magisterium, but is solely an expression of my personal search "for the face of the Lord" (cf. Ps 27:8).

Everyone is free, then, to contradict me. I would only ask my readers for that initial goodwill without which there can be no understanding.

As I said at the beginning of this foreword, the present book has undergone a long gestation. I was able to begin work on it during the 2003 summer holidays. Then, in August 2004, I gave chapters 1–4 their final shape. Since my election to the episcopal see of Rome I have used every free moment to make progress on the book. As I do not know how much more time or strength I am still to be given, I have decided to publish the first ten chapters, covering the period from the Baptism in the Jordan to Peter's confession of faith and the Transfiguration, as Part One of this book.

In Part Two I hope also to be able to include the chapter on the infancy narratives, which I have postponed for now, because it struck me as the most urgent priority to present the figure and the message of Jesus in his public ministry, and so to help foster the growth of a living relationship with him.

Rome, on the Feast of Saint Jerome
30 September 2006

JOSEPH RATZINGER, BENEDICT XVI

INTRODUCTION

An Initial Reflection on the Mystery of Jesus

The Book of Deuteronomy contains a promise that is completely different from the messianic hope expressed in other books of the Old Testament, yet it is of decisive importance for understanding the figure of Jesus. The object of this promise is not a king of Israel and king of the world—a new David, in other words—but a new Moses. Moses himself, however, is interpreted as a prophet. The category "prophet" is seen here as something totally specific and unique, in contrast to the surrounding religious world, something that Israel alone has in this particular form. This new and different element is a consequence of the uniqueness of the faith in God that was granted to Israel. In every age, man's questioning has focused not only on his ultimate origin; almost more than the obscurity of his beginnings, what preoccupies him is the hiddenness of the future that awaits him. Man wants to tear aside the curtain; he wants to know what is going to happen, so that he can avoid perdition and set out toward salvation.

Religions do not aim merely to answer the question about our provenance; all religions try in one way or another to lift the veil of the future. They seem important precisely because they impart knowledge about what is to come, and so show man the path he has to take to avoid coming to grief. This explains why practically all religions have developed ways of looking into the future.

The Deuteronomy text we are considering mentions the different methods used by the peoples surrounding Israel to open a "window" onto the future: "When you come into the land which the LORD your God gives you, you shall not learn to follow the abominable practices of those nations. There shall not be found among you any one who burns his son or his daughter as an offering, any one who practices divination, a soothsayer, or an augur, or a sorcerer, or a charmer, or a medium, or a wizard, or a necromancer. For whoever does these things is an abomination to the LORD" (Deut 18:9–12).

The story of Saul's downfall shows how difficult it was, having renounced these things, to hold firm and to manage without them. Saul himself had tried to enforce this command and to banish sorcery from the land. But faced with the imminent prospect of a perilous battle with the Philistines, he can no longer bear God's silence, and he rides out to Endor, to a woman who conjures the dead, asking her to summon the spirit of Samuel so as to afford him a glimpse into the future. If the Lord will not speak, then someone else will have to tear aside the veil that covers tomorrow (cf. 1 Sam 28).

Chapter 18 of the book of Deuteronomy brands all of these ways of seizing control of the future as an "abomination" in God's eyes. It contrasts this use of soothsaying with the very different way of Israel—the way of faith. It does this in the form of a promise: "The LORD your God will raise up for you a prophet like me from among you . . . him you shall heed" (Deut 18:15). At first glance this seems no more than a declaration that God will establish the prophetic office in Israel and assign its holder the task of interpreting present and future. The harsh critique of false prophets that occurs again and again in the prophetic writings underscores the danger that in practice prophets will assume the role of soothsayers, acting like them and being consulted like them. When this happens, Israel relapses into the very thing that the prophets had been commissioned to prevent.

The conclusion of Deuteronomy returns to the promise and gives it a surprising twist that takes it far beyond the institution of prophecy. In so doing, it gives the figure of the prophet its true meaning. "And there has not arisen a prophet since in Israel like Moses," we read, "whom the LORD knew face to face" (Deut 34:10). A curious melancholy hangs over this conclusion of the fifth Book of Moses. The promise concerning "a prophet like me" has not yet been fulfilled. And it now becomes clear that these words do not refer simply to the institution of prophecy, which in fact already existed, but to something different and far greater: the announcement of a new Moses. It had become evident that taking possession of the land in Palestine did not constitute the chosen people's entry into salvation; that Israel was still awaiting its real liberation; that an even more radical kind of exodus was necessary, one that called for a new Moses.

And now we are told what set the first Moses apart, the unique and essential quality of this figure: He had conversed with the Lord "face to face"; as a man speaks to his friend, so he had spoken with God (cf. Ex 33:11). The most important thing about the figure of Moses is neither all the miraculous deeds he is reported to have done nor his many works and sufferings along the way from the "house of bondage in Egypt" through the desert to the threshold of the Promised Land. The most important thing is that he spoke with God as with a friend. This was the only possible springboard for his works; this was the only possible source of the Law that was to show Israel its path through history.

It now becomes perfectly clear that the prophet is not the Israelite version of the soothsayer, as was widely held at the time and as many so-called prophets considered themselves. On the contrary, the prophet is something quite different. His task is not to report on the events of tomorrow or the next day in order to satisfy human curiosity or the human need for security. He shows us the face of God, and in so doing he shows us the path that we have to take. The future of which he speaks reaches far beyond what people seek from soothsayers. He points out the path to the true "exodus," which consists in this: Among all the paths of history, the path to God is the true direction that we must seek and find. Prophecy in this sense is a strict corollary to Israel's monotheism. It is the translation of this faith into the everyday life of a community before God and on the way to him.

"And there has not arisen a prophet since in Israel like Moses." This judgment gives an eschatological flavor to the promise that "the LORD your God will raise up for you a prophet like me." Israel is allowed to hope for a new Moses, who has yet to appear, but who will be raised up at the appropriate hour. And the characteristic of this "prophet" will be that he converses with God face-to-face, as a friend does with a friend. His distinguishing note will be his immediate relation with God, which enables him to communicate God's will and word firsthand and unadulterated. And that is the saving intervention which Israel—indeed, the whole of humanity—is waiting for.

At this point, though, we need to recall another remarkable story that the Book of Exodus recounts concerning Moses' relationship with God. There we are told that Moses asked God, "I pray thee, show me thy glory" (Ex 33:18). God refuses his request: "You cannot see my face" (Ex 33:20). Moses is placed near God in the cleft of a rock, and God passes by with his glory. As he passes, God covers Moses with his own hand, but he withdraws it at the end: "You shall see my back; but my face shall not be seen" (Ex 33:23).

This mysterious text played an important role in the history of Jewish and Christian mysticism; it served as the basis for attempts to discern how far contact with God can extend in this life and where the boundaries of mystical vision lie. In terms of the present question, the main point is that although Moses' immediate relation to God makes him the great mediator of Revelation, the mediator of the Covenant, it has its limits. He does not behold God's face, even though he is permitted to enter into the cloud of God's presence and to speak with God as a friend. The promise of a "prophet like me" thus implicitly contains an even greater expectation: that the last prophet, the new Moses, will be granted what was refused to the first one—a real, immediate vision of the face of God, and thus the ability to speak entirely from seeing, not just from looking at God's back. This naturally entails the further expectation that the new Moses will be the mediator of a greater covenant than the one that Moses was able to bring down from Sinai (cf. Heb 9:11–24).

This is the context in which we need to read the conclusion of the prologue to John's Gospel: "No one has ever seen God; it is the only Son, who is nearest to the Father's heart, who has made him known" (Jn 1:18). It is in Jesus that the promise of the new prophet is fulfilled. What was true of Moses only in fragmentary form has now been fully realized in the person of Jesus: He lives before the face of God, not just as a friend, but as a Son; he lives in the most intimate unity with the Father.

We have to start here if we are truly to understand the figure of Jesus as it is presented to us in the New Testament; all that we are told about his words, deeds, sufferings, and glory is anchored here. This is the central point, and if we leave it out of account, we fail to grasp what the figure of Jesus is really all about, so that it becomes self-contradictory and, in the end, unintelligible. The question that every reader of the New Testament must ask—where Jesus' teaching came from, how his appearance in history is to be explained—can really be answered only from this perspective. The reaction of his hearers was clear: This teaching does not come from any school. It is radically different from what can be learned in schools. It is not the kind of explanation or interpretation that is taught there. It is different; it is interpretation "with authority." Later we will ponder Jesus' words, and then we will have to return to this judgment on the part of his hearers and delve more deeply into its significance.

Jesus' teaching is not the product of human learning, of whatever kind. It originates from immediate contact with the Father, from "face-to-face" dialogue—from the vision of the one who rests close to the Father's heart. It is the Son's word. Without this inner grounding, his teaching would be pure presumption. That is just what the learned men of Jesus' time judged it to be, and they did so precisely because they could not accept its inner grounding: seeing and knowing face-to-face.

Again and again the Gospels note that Jesus withdrew "to the mountain" to spend nights in prayer "alone" with his Father. These short passages are fundamental for our understanding of Jesus; they lift the veil of mystery just a little; they give us a glimpse into Jesus' filial existence, into the source from which his action and teaching and suffering sprang. This "praying" of Jesus is the Son conversing with the Father; Jesus' human consciousness and will, his human soul, is taken up into that exchange, and in this way human "praying" is able to become a participation in this filial communion with the Father.

Adolf von Harnack famously claimed that Jesus' message was about the Father, not about the Son, and that Christology therefore has no place in it. The fallacy of this argument is evident from what we have been saying. Jesus is only able to speak about the Father in the way he does because he is the Son, because of his filial communion with the Father. The Christological dimension—in other words, the mystery of the Son as revealer of the Father—is present in everything Jesus says and does. Another important point appears here: We have said that in Jesus' filial communion with the Father, his human soul is also taken up into the act of praying. He who sees Jesus sees the Father (cf. Jn 14:9). The disciple who walks with Jesus is thus caught up with him into communion with God. And that is what redemption means: this stepping beyond the limits of human nature, which had been there as a possibility and an expectation in man, God's image and likeness, since the moment of creation.

CHAPTER ONE

The Baptism of Jesus

Jesus' public activity begins with his Baptism in the Jordan by John the Baptist. While Matthew merely gives a formulaic indication of the date of this event—"in those days"—Luke very deliberately puts it in the larger context of secular history, which enables us to assign it a very precise date. That said, Matthew does provide a dating of a sort, in that he places Jesus' family tree at the beginning of his Gospel. This genealogy is arranged to show lineal descent from Abraham and David, and it presents Jesus as the inheritor both of the promise made to Abraham and of God's pledges to David, to whom God had promised—through all of Israel's sins and all of God's chastisements—an eternal kingdom. As this family tree presents it, history is divided into three groups of fourteen generations, fourteen being the numerical value of the name David. The history it recounts breaks down into the period from Abraham to David, the period from David to the Babylonian Exile, and an additional period of fourteen generations. The very fact that yet another fourteen generations have elapsed is an indication that the hour of the definitive David, of the renewal of the kingdom of David that is the establishment of the Kingdom of God himself, has now come.

As one would expect from the Jewish-Christian Evangelist Matthew, this family tree is also a genealogy of Jewish salvation history, which at most offers an oblique perspective on secular history, insofar as the kingdom of the definitive David, being the Kingdom of God, obviously concerns the world as a whole. The actual dating remains therefore vague. This also has to do, of course, with the fact that reckoning of the generations depends less on any historical scheme than on the triple phasing of the promise and so is not intended to establish a precise chronology.

Let us observe here at the outset that Luke does not place his genealogy of Jesus at the beginning of the Gospel, but connects it with the story of Jesus' Baptism, to which it forms a conclusion. He tells us that at this point in time Jesus was about thirty years old, which means he had attained the age that conferred a right to public activity. In contrast to Matthew, Luke uses his genealogy to journey from Jesus back into past history. Abraham and David make their appearance, but without any particular emphasis. The family tree goes back to Adam, and so to creation, for once Luke comes to the name Adam, he adds: "of God." This is a way of underscoring the universal scope of Jesus' mission. He is the son of Adam—the son of man. Because he is man, all of us belong to him and he to us; in him humanity starts anew and reaches its destiny.

Let us return to John the Baptist. Luke has already supplied two important time references in the infancy narratives.

Recounting the beginning of the Baptist's life, Luke tells us that it took place "in the days of Herod, king of Judea" (Lk 1:5). The time reference in the Baptist's case thus remains within the bounds of Jewish history. By contrast, the story of Jesus' infancy begins with the words "in those days a decree went out from Caesar Augustus" (Lk 2:1). The wider history of the world, represented by the Roman Empire, forms the backdrop.

Luke picks up this thread again when he introduces the story of the Baptist, which marks the beginning of Jesus' public activity. At this point he tells us both solemnly and precisely that it was "in the fifteenth year of the reign of Tiberius Caesar, Pontius Pilate being governor of Judea, and Herod being tetrarch of Galilee, and his brother Philip tetrarch of the region of Ituraea and Trachonitis, and Lysanias tetrarch of Abilene, in the high-priesthood of Annas and Caiaphas" (Lk 3:1–2). Once again the mention of the Roman emperor serves to indicate Jesus' chronological place in world history. We are not meant to regard Jesus' activity as taking place in some sort of mythical "anytime," which can mean always or never. It is a precisely datable historical event having the full weight that real historical happenings have; like them, too, it happens once only; it is contemporary with all times, but not in the way that a timeless myth would be.

But the point is not just the chronology: The emperor and Jesus represent two different orders of reality. They are by no means mutually exclusive, but their encounter does have the potential to spark a conflict that has implications for the basic questions facing humanity and human existence. Jesus will later say "render to Caesar the things that are Caesar's, and to God the things that are God's" (Mk 12:17), which is a way of expressing the essential compatibility of the two spheres. But when the imperial power interprets itself as divine, as Augustus' claim to be the bringer of world peace and the savior of humanity already implicitly does, then the Christian has to "obey God more than men" (Acts 5:29). It is then that Christians become "martyrs," witnesses of Christ, who himself was "the faithful witness" who died on the Cross under Pontius Pilate (Rev 1:5). Luke's mention of Pontius Pilate casts the shadow of the Cross over the beginning of Jesus' public activity. The names Herod, Annas, and Caiaphas also foreshadow the Cross.

But a further point comes to light in the fact that Luke lists side by side the emperor and the princes among whom the Holy Land is divided. All these princedoms are dependencies of pagan Rome. The kingdom of David lies broken in pieces, his "hut" in ruins (cf. Amos 9:11f.). His descendant, Jesus' legal father, is a carpenter in the half-paganized province of Galilee. Israel is living once more in the darkness of divine absence; God is silent, seemingly forgetful of the promises to Abraham and David. The old lament is heard once more: We no longer have any prophets, God seems to have abandoned his people. For that very reason, though, the land was full of unrest.

Conflicting movements, hopes, and expectations shaped the religious and political climate. At around the time of Jesus' birth Judas the Galilean had called for an uprising, which was put down by the Romans with a great deal of bloodshed. Judas left behind a party, the Zealots, who were prepared to resort to terror and violence in order to restore Israel's freedom. It is even possible that one or two of Jesus' twelve Apostles—Simon the Zealot and perhaps Judas Iscariot as well—had been partisans of this movement. The Pharisees, whom we are constantly meeting in the Gospels, endeavored to live with the greatest possible exactness according to the instructions of the Torah. They also refused conformity to the hegemony of Hellenistic-Roman culture, which naturally imposed itself throughout the Roman Empire, and was now threatening to force Israel's assimilation to the pagan peoples' way of life. The Sadducees, most of whom belonged to the aristocracy and the priestly class, attempted to practice an enlightened Judaism, intellectually suited to the times, and so also to come to terms with Roman domination. The Sadducees disappeared after the destruction of Jerusalem (A.D. 70), whereas the pattern of life practiced by the Pharisees found an enduring form in the sort of Judaism shaped by the Mishnah and the Talmud. Although we observe sharp antagonism between Jesus and the Pharisees in the Gospels, and although his death on the Cross was the very antithesis of the Zealot program, we must not forget that people came to Christ from every kind of background and that the early Christian community included more than a few priests and former Pharisees.

An accidental discovery after the Second World War led to excavations at Qumran, which brought to light texts that some scholars have associated with yet another movement known until then only from literary references: the so-called Essenes. This group had turned its back on the Herodian temple and its worship to withdraw to the Judean desert. There it created monastic-style communities, but also a religiously motivated common life for families. It also established a productive literary center and instituted distinctive rituals, which included liturgical ablutions and common prayers. The earnest religiosity of the Qumran writings is moving; it appears that not only John the Baptist, but possibly Jesus and his family as well, were close to the Qumran community. At any rate, there are numerous points of contact with the Christian message in the Qumran writings. It is a reasonable hypothesis that John the Baptist lived for some time in this community and received part of his religious formation from it.

And yet the Baptist's appearance on the scene was something completely new. The Baptism that he enjoined is different from the usual religious ablutions. It cannot be repeated, and it is meant to be the concrete enactment of a conversion that gives the whole of life a new direction forever. It is connected with an ardent call to a new way of thinking and acting, but above all with the proclamation of God's judgment and with the announcement that one greater than John is to come. The Fourth Gospel tells us that the Baptist "did not know" (cf. Jn 1:30–33) this greater personage whose way he was to prepare. But he does know that his own role is to prepare a path for this mysterious Other, that his whole mission is directed toward him.

All four Gospels describe this mission using a passage from Isaiah: "A voice cries in the wilderness: 'Prepare the way of the Lord, make straight in the desert a highway for our God'" (Is 40:3). Mark adds a compilation of Malachi 3:1 and Exodus 23:20, which recurs at another point in Matthew (Mt 11:10) and Luke (Lk 1:76, 7:27) as well: "Behold, I send my messenger before thy face, who shall prepare thy way" (Mk

1:2). All of these Old Testament texts envisage a saving intervention of God, who emerges from his hiddenness to judge and to save; it is for this God that the door is to be opened and the way made ready. These ancient words of hope were brought into the present with the Baptist's preaching: Great things are about to unfold.

We can imagine the extraordinary impression that the figure and message of John the Baptist must have produced in the highly charged atmosphere of Jerusalem at that particular moment of history. At last there was a prophet again, and his life marked him out as such. God's hand was at last plainly acting in history again. John baptizes with water, but one even greater, who will baptize with the Holy Spirit and fire, is already at the door. Given all this, there is absolutely no reason to suppose that Mark is exaggerating when he reports that "there went out to him all the country of Judea, and all the people of Jerusalem; and they were baptized by him in the river Jordan, confessing their sins" (Mk 1:5). John's baptism includes the confession of sins. The Judaism of the day was familiar both with more generally formulaic confessions of sin and with a highly personalized confessional practice in which an enumeration of individual sinful deeds was expected (Gnilka, *Matthäusevangelium* I, p. 68). The goal is truly to leave behind the sinful life one has led until now and to start out on the path to a new, changed life.

The actual ritual of Baptism symbolizes this. On one hand, immersion into the waters is a symbol of death, which recalls the death symbolism of the annihilating, destructive power of the ocean flood. The ancient mind perceived the ocean as a permanent threat to the cosmos, to the earth; it was the primeval flood that might submerge all life. The river (Jordan) could also assume this symbolic value for those who were immersed in it. But the flowing waters of the river are above all a symbol of life. The great rivers—the Nile, the Euphrates, the Tigris—are the great givers of life. The Jordan, too, is—even today—a source of life for the surrounding region. Immersion in the water is about purification, about liberation from the filth of the past that burdens and distorts life—it is about beginning again, and that means it is about death and resurrection, about starting life over again anew. So we could say that it is about rebirth. All of this will have to wait for Christian baptismal theology to be worked out explicitly, but the act of descending into the Jordan and coming up again out of the waters already implicitly contains this later development.

The whole of Judea and Jerusalem were making the pilgrimage to be baptized, as we just heard. But now something new happens: "In those days Jesus came from Nazareth of Galilee and was baptized by John in the Jordan" (Mk 1:9). So far, nothing has been said about pilgrims from Galilee; the action seemed limited to the region of Judea. But the real novelty here is not the fact that Jesus comes from another geographical area, from a distant country, as it were. The real novelty is the fact that he—Jesus—wants to be baptized, that he blends into the gray mass of sinners waiting on the banks of the Jordan. We have just heard that the confession of sins is a component of Baptism. Baptism itself was a confession of sins and the attempt to put off an old, failed life and to receive a new one. Is that something Jesus could do? How could he confess sins? How could he separate himself from his previous life in order to start a new one? This is a question that Christians could not avoid asking. The dispute between the Baptist and Jesus that Matthew recounts for us was also an expression of the early Christians' own question to Jesus: "I need to be baptized by you, and do you come to me?" (Mt 3:14). Matthew goes on to report for us that "Jesus answered him, 'Let it be so now; for thus it is fitting for us to fulfill all righteousness.' Then he consented" (Mt 3:15).

It is not easy to decode the sense of this enigmatic-sounding answer. At any rate, the Greek word for "now"—*árti*—implies a certain reservation: This is a specific, temporary situation that calls for a specific way of acting. The key to interpreting Jesus' answer is how we understand the word *righteousness:* The whole of righteousness must be fulfilled. In Jesus' world, righteousness is man's answer to the Torah, acceptance of the whole of God's will, the bearing of the "yoke of God's kingdom," as one formulation had it. There is no provision for John's baptism in the Torah, but this reply of Jesus is his way of acknowledging it as an expression of an unrestricted Yes to God's will, as an obedient acceptance of his yoke.

The act of descending into the waters of this Baptism implies a confession of guilt and a plea for forgiveness in order to make a new beginning. In a world marked by sin, then, this Yes to the entire will of God also expresses solidarity with men, who have incurred guilt but yearn for righteousness. The significance of this event could not fully emerge until it was seen in light of the Cross and Resurrection. Descending into the water, the candidates for Baptism confess their sin and seek to be rid of their burden of guilt. What did

Jesus do in this same situation? Luke, who throughout his Gospel is keenly attentive to Jesus' prayer, and portrays him again and again at prayer—in conversation with the Father—tells us that Jesus was praying while he received Baptism (cf. Lk 3:21). Looking at the events in light of the Cross and Resurrection, the Christian people realized what happened: Jesus loaded the burden of all mankind's guilt upon his shoulders; he bore it down into the depths of the Jordan. He inaugurated his public activity by stepping into the place of sinners. His inaugural gesture is an anticipation of the Cross. He is, as it were, the true Jonah who said to the crew of the ship, "Take me and throw me into the sea" (Jon 1:12). The whole significance of Jesus' Baptism, the fact that he bears "all righteousness," first comes to light on the Cross: The Baptism is an acceptance of death for the sins of humanity, and the voice that calls out "This is my beloved Son" over the baptismal waters is an anticipatory reference to the Resurrection. This also explains why, in his own discourses, Jesus uses the word *baptism* to refer to his death (cf. Mk 10:38; Lk 12:50).

Only from this starting point can we understand Christian Baptism. Jesus' Baptism anticipated his death on the Cross, and the heavenly voice proclaimed an anticipation of the Resurrection. These anticipations have now become reality. John's baptism with water has received its full meaning through the Baptism of Jesus' own life and death. To accept the invitation to be baptized now means to go to the place of Jesus' Baptism. It is to go where he identifies himself with us and to receive there our identification with him. The point where he anticipates death has now become the point where we anticipate rising again with him. Paul develops this inner connection in his theology of Baptism (cf. Rom 6), though without explicitly mentioning Jesus' Baptism in the Jordan.

The Eastern Church has further developed and deepened this understanding of Jesus' Baptism in her liturgy and in her theology of icons. She sees a deep connection between the content of the feast of Epiphany (the heavenly voice proclaiming Jesus to be the Son of God: for the East the Epiphany is the day of the Baptism) and Easter. She sees Jesus' remark to John that "it is fitting for us to fulfill all righteousness" (Mt 3:15) as the anticipation of his prayer to the Father in Gethsemane: "My Father . . . not as I will, but as thou wilt" (Mt 26:39). The liturgical hymns for January 3 correspond to those for Wednesday in Holy Week; the hymns for January 4 to those for Holy Thursday; the hymns for January 5 to those for Good Friday and Holy Saturday.

These correspondences are picked up by the iconographic tradition. The icon of Jesus' Baptism depicts the water as a liquid tomb having the form of a dark cavern, which is in turn the iconographic sign of Hades, the underworld, or hell. Jesus' descent into this watery tomb, into this inferno that envelops him from every side, is thus an anticipation of his act of descending into the underworld: "When he went down into the waters, he bound the strong man" (cf. Lk 11:22), says Cyril of Jerusalem. John Chrysostom writes: "Going down into the water and emerging again are the image of the descent into hell and the Resurrection." The troparia of the Byzantine Liturgy add yet another symbolic connection: "The Jordan was turned back by Elisha's coat, and the waters were divided leaving a dry path. This is a true image of Baptism by which we pass through life" (Evdokimov, *The Art of the Icon,* p. 296).

Jesus' Baptism, then, is understood as a repetition of the whole of history, which both recapitulates the past and anticipates the future. His entering into the sin of others is a descent into the "inferno." But he does not descend merely in the role of a spectator, as in Dante's *Inferno*. Rather, he goes down in the role of one whose suffering-with-others is a transforming suffering that turns the underworld around, knocking down and flinging open the gates of the abyss. His Baptism is a descent into the house of the evil one, combat with the "strong man" (cf. Lk 11:22) who holds men captive (and the truth is that we are all very much captive to powers that anonymously manipulate us!). Throughout all its history, the world is powerless to defeat the "strong man"; he is overcome and bound by one yet stronger, who, because of his equality with God, can take upon himself all the sin of the world and then suffers it through to the end—omitting nothing on the downward path into identity with the fallen. This struggle is the "conversion" of being that brings it into a new condition, that prepares a new heaven and a new earth. Looked at from this angle, the sacrament of Baptism appears as the gift of participation in Jesus' world-transforming struggle in the conversion of life that took place in his descent and ascent.

Has this ecclesiastical interpretation and rereading of the event of Jesus' Baptism taken us too far away from the Bible? It will be helpful to listen to the Fourth Gospel in this context. According to John, when the Baptist first sees Jesus, he says, "Behold, the Lamb of God, who takes away the sin of the world" (Jn 1:29). These words, which are spoken before the distribution of Communion in the Roman Liturgy, have been the occasion of much puzzlement. What does "Lamb of God" mean? Why is Jesus called the Lamb, and why does this Lamb take away the sins of the world, so thoroughly vanquishing them as to rob them of any substance or reality?

Thanks to the work of Joachim Jeremias, we have the key to understand these words correctly and to regard them—even from the historical point of view—as genuine words of the Baptist himself. First of all, they contain two identifiable Old Testament allusions. The Song of the Suffering Servant in Isaiah compares the suffering servant of God with the lamb that is led to the slaughter: "Like a sheep that before its shearers is dumb, so he opened not his mouth" (Is 53:7). Even more importantly, Jesus was crucified on the feast of the Passover, and from that moment on could only appear as the true Passover lamb, in whom is fulfilled the significance of the Passover lamb at the time of the Exodus from Egypt: liberation from the dominion of death in Egypt and release for the Exodus, for the journey into the freedom of the promise. In light of Easter, this lamb symbolism takes on a fundamental importance for understanding Christ. We find it in Paul (cf. 1 Cor 5:7), in John (cf. Jn 19:36), in the First Letter of Peter (cf. 1 Pet 1:19), and in the Book of Revelation (for example, Rev 5:6).

Jeremias makes the further observation that the Hebrew word *talia* means both "lamb" and "boy" or "servant" (*TDNT*, I, p. 339). In the first instance, then, the Baptist may have meant his words as a reference to the Servant of God who bears the sins of the world by his vicarious atonement. But this reference also identifies him as the true Passover lamb who expiates and wipes away the sin of the world: "The Savior, dying on the Cross, went to his vicarious death patiently like a sacrificial lamb. By the expiatory power of his innocent death he blotted out . . . the guilt of all mankind" (*TDNT*, I, p. 340). If at the extreme hour of Israel's oppression in Egypt, the blood of the Paschal lamb had been the key to its liberation, now the Son who became a servant—the shepherd who became a sheep—no longer stands just for Israel, but for the liberation of the world—for mankind as a whole.

This brings us to the great theme of Jesus' universal mission. Israel does not exist for itself; its election is rather the path by which God intends to come to all men. This idea of universality will turn up again and again as the real core of Jesus' mission. By referring to the Lamb of God that takes away the sins of the world, the Fourth Gospel places this idea right at the beginning of Jesus' journey.

The reference to the Lamb of God interprets Jesus' Baptism, his descent into the abyss of death, as a theology of the Cross, if we may so express it. All four Gospels recount in their different ways that, as Jesus came up from the water, heaven was "torn open" (Mk 1:10) or "was opened" (Mt 3:16; Lk 3:21); that the Spirit came down upon him "like a dove"; and that in the midst of all this a voice from heaven resounded. According to Mark and Luke, the voice addresses Jesus with the words "Thou art . . ."; according to Matthew, the voice speaks about him in the third person, saying, "This is my beloved Son, with whom I am well pleased" (Mt 3:17). The image of the dove may be a reminiscence of what the creation account says about the Spirit brooding over the waters (Gen 1:2); the word *like* ("like a dove") suggests that it is "a simile for something that ultimately cannot be described" (Gnilka, *Matthäusevangelium*, I, p. 78). The same heavenly voice sounds out again at the Transfiguration of Jesus, though with the addition of the imperative to "listen to him." When we come to the Transfiguration, we will have to consider the meaning of these words more closely.

At this point I would merely like to underscore briefly three aspects of the scene. The first one is the image of heaven torn open: Heaven stands open above Jesus. His communion of will with the Father, his fulfillment of "all righteousness," opens heaven, which is essentially the place where God's will is perfectly fulfilled. The next aspect is the proclamation of Jesus' mission by God, by the Father. This proclamation interprets not what Jesus does, but who he is: He *is* the beloved Son on whom God's good pleasure rests. Finally, I would like to point out that in this scene, together with the Son, we encounter the Father and the Holy Spirit. The mystery of the Trinitarian God is beginning to emerge, even though its depths can be fully revealed only when Jesus' journey is complete. For this very reason, though, there is an arc joining this beginning of Jesus' journey and the words with which he sends his disciples into the world after his Resurrection: "Go therefore and make disciples of all nations, baptizing them in the name of the Father and of the Son and of the Holy Spirit" (Mt 28:19). The Baptism that Jesus' disciples have been administering since he spoke those words is an entrance into the Master's own Baptism—into the reality that he anticipated by means of it. That is the way to become a Christian.

A broad current of liberal scholarship has interpreted Jesus' Baptism as a vocational experience. After having led a perfectly normal life in the province of Galilee, at the moment of his Baptism he is said to have had an earth-shattering experience. It was then, we are told, that he became aware of his special relationship to God and his religious mission. This mission, moreover, supposedly originated from the expectation motif then dominant in Israel, creatively reshaped by John, and from the emotional upheaval that the event of his Baptism brought about in Jesus' life. But none of this can be found in the texts. However much scholarly erudition goes into the presentation of this reading, it has to be seen as more akin to a "Jesus novel" than as an actual interpretation of the texts. The texts give us no window into Jesus' inner life—Jesus stands above our psychologizing (Guardini, *Das Wesen des Christentums*). But they do enable us to ascertain how Jesus is connected with "Moses and the Prophets"; they do enable us to recognize the intrinsic unity of the trajectory stretching from the first moment of his life to the Cross and the Resurrection. Jesus does not appear in the role of a human genius subject to emotional upheavals, who sometimes fails and sometimes succeeds. If that were the case, he would remain just an individual who lived long ago and so would ultimately be separated from us by an unbridgeable gulf. Instead, he stands before us as the "beloved Son." He is, on one hand, the Wholly Other, but by the same token he can also become a contemporary of us all, "more interior" to each one of us "than we are to ourselves" (Saint Augustine, *Confessions*, III, 6, 11).

CHAPTER TWO

The Temptations of Jesus

The descent of the Holy Spirit upon Jesus, which concludes the baptismal scene, is to be understood as a kind of formal investiture with the messianic office. The Fathers of the Church therefore rightly saw this event as analogous to the anointing by which kings and priests in Israel were installed in office. The words *Messiah* and *Christ* mean "the Anointed": In the Old Testament, anointing was regarded as the visible sign that the person anointed was being invested with the gifts of office, with the Spirit of God. Isaiah 11:1f. develops this theme into a hope for the true "Anointed One," whose "anointing" consists precisely in the fact that the Spirit of the Lord comes down to rest on him: "The spirit of wisdom and understanding, the spirit of counsel and might, the spirit of knowledge and the fear of the LORD" (Is 11:2). According to Saint Luke's account, Jesus presented himself and his mission in the synagogue at Nazareth citing a related passage from Isaiah: "The Spirit of the Lord is upon me, for he has anointed me" (Lk 4:18; cf. Is 61:1). The conclusion of the baptismal scene tells us that Jesus has received this true "anointing," that he is the awaited Anointed One—that at that moment kingly and priestly dignity were formally bestowed on him for all time in the presence of Israel.

From now on he is charged with this commission. The three Synoptic Gospels tell us, much to our surprise, that the Spirit's first command leads him into the desert "to be tempted by the devil" (Mt 4:1). The action is prefaced by interior recollection, and this recollection is also, inevitably, an inner struggle for fidelity to the task, a struggle against all the distortions of the task that claim to be its true fulfillment. It is a descent into the perils besetting mankind, for there is no other way to lift up fallen humanity. Jesus has to enter into the drama of human existence, for that belongs to the core of his mission; he has to penetrate it completely, down to its uttermost depths, in order to find the "lost sheep," to bear it on his shoulders, and to bring it home.

The Apostles' Creed speaks of Jesus' descent "into hell." This descent not only took place in and after his death, but accompanies him along his entire journey. He must recapitulate the whole of history from its beginnings—from Adam on; he must go through, suffer through, the whole of it, in order to transform it. The Letter to the Hebrews is particularly eloquent in stressing that Jesus' mission, the solidarity with all of us that he manifested beforehand in his Baptism, includes exposure to the risks and perils of human existence: "Therefore he had to be made like his brethren in every respect, so that he might become a merciful and faithful high priest in the service of God, to make expiation for the sins of the people. For because he himself has suffered and been tempted, he is able to help those who are tempted" (Heb 2:17–18). "For we have not a high priest who is unable to sympathize with our weaknesses, but one who in every respect has been tempted as we are, yet without sin" (Heb 4:15). The story of the temptations is thus intimately connected with the story of the Baptism, for it is there that Jesus enters into solidarity with sinners. We will see Jesus wrestling once again with his mission during his agony on the Mount of Olives. But the "temptations" are with him every step of the way. In this sense, we can see the story of the temptations—just like the Baptism—as an anticipation that condenses into a single expression the struggle he endured at every step of his mission.

In his short account of the temptations (Mk 1:13), Mark brings into relief the parallels between Adam and Jesus, stressing how Jesus "suffers through" the quintessential human drama. Jesus, we read, "was with the wild beasts; and the angels ministered to him" (Mk 1:13). The desert—the opposite image of the garden—becomes the place of reconciliation and healing. Wild beasts are the most concrete threat that the rebellion of creation and the power of death posed to man. But here they become man's friends, as they once were in paradise. Peace is restored, the peace that Isaiah proclaims for the days of the Messiah: "The wolf shall dwell with the lamb, and the leopard shall lie down with the kid" (Is 11:6). Once sin has been overcome and man's harmony with God restored, creation is reconciled, too. Creation, torn asunder by strife, once more becomes the dwelling place of peace, as Paul expresses it when he speaks of the groaning of creation, which "waits with eager longing for the revealing of the sons of God" (Rom 8:19).

Are not the oases of creation that sprang up, say, around the Benedictine monasteries in the West foreshadowings of this reconciliation of creation brought about by the children of God—just as, conversely, something like Chernobyl is a shocking expression of creation's enslavement in the darkness of God's absence? Mark concludes his brief account of the temptations with a phrase that can be taken as an allusion to Psalm 91:11: "And the angels ministered to him." These words also occur at the close of Matthew's detailed narrative of the temptations, and it is only in that larger context that they can be fully understood.

Matthew and Luke recount three temptations of Jesus that reflect the inner struggle over his own particular mission and, at the same time, address the question as to what truly matters in human life. At the heart of all temptations, as we see here, is the act of pushing God aside because we perceive him as secondary, if not actually superfluous and annoying, in comparison with all the apparently far more urgent matters that fill our lives. Constructing a world by our own lights, without reference to God, building on our own foundation; refusing to acknowledge the reality of anything beyond the political and material, while setting God aside as an illusion—that is the temptation that threatens us in many varied forms.

Moral posturing is part and parcel of temptation. It does not invite us directly to do evil—no, that would be far too blatant. It pretends to show us a better way, where we finally abandon our illusions and throw ourselves into the work of actually making the world a better place. It claims, moreover, to speak for true realism: What's real is what is right there in front of us—power and bread. By comparison, the things of

God fade into unreality, into a secondary world that no one really needs.

God is the issue: Is he real, reality itself, or isn't he? Is he good, or do we have to invent the good ourselves? The God question is the fundamental question, and it sets us down right at the crossroads of human existence. What must the Savior of the world do or not do? That is the question the temptations of Jesus are about. The three temptations are identical in Matthew and Luke, but the sequence is different. We will follow Matthew's sequence, because his arrangement reflects the logic that intensifies from temptation to temptation.

Jesus "fasted forty days and forty nights, and afterward he was hungry" (Mt 4:2). In Jesus' day the number forty was already filled with rich symbolism for Israel. First of all, it recalls Israel's forty years' wandering in the desert, a period in which the people were both tempted and enjoyed a special closeness to God. The forty days and nights also remind us of the forty days that Moses spent on Mount Sinai before he was privileged to receive the word of God, the sacred tablets of the Covenant. They may also serve as a reminder of the rabbinic tale of how Abraham spent forty days and forty nights on the way to Mount Horeb, where he was to sacrifice his son, how during that time he neither ate nor drank anything and nourished himself on the vision and words of the angel who accompanied him.

The Fathers of the Church, stretching number symbolism in an admittedly slightly playful way, regarded forty as a cosmic number, as the numerical sign for this world. The four "corners" encompass the whole world, and ten is the number of the commandments. The number of the cosmos multiplied by the number of the commandments becomes a symbolic statement about the history of this world as a whole. It is as if Jesus were reliving Israel's Exodus, and then reliving the chaotic meanderings of history in general; the forty days of fasting embrace the drama of history, which Jesus takes into himself and bears all the way through to the end.

"If you are the Son of God, command these stones to become loaves of bread" (Mt 4:3)—so the first temptation goes. "If you are the Son of God"—we will hear these words again in the mouths of the mocking bystanders at the foot of the Cross—"If you are the Son of God, come down from the Cross" (Mt 27:40). The Book of Wisdom already foresaw this situation: "If the righteous man is God's son, he will help him" (Wis 2:18). Mockery and temptation blend into each other here: Christ is being challenged to establish his credibility by offering evidence for his claims. This demand for proof is a constantly recurring theme in the story of Jesus' life; again and again he is reproached for having failed to prove himself sufficiently, for having hitherto failed to work that great miracle that will remove all ambiguity and every contradiction, so as to make it indisputably clear for everyone who and what he is or is not.

And we make this same demand of God and Christ and his Church throughout the whole of history. "If you exist, God," we say, "then you'll just have to show yourself. You'll have to part the clouds that conceal you and give us the clarity that we deserve. If you, Christ, are really the Son of God, and not just another one of the enlightened individuals who keep appearing in the course of history, then you'll just have to prove it more clearly than you are doing now. And if the

Church is really supposed to be yours, you'll have to make that much more obvious than it is at present."

We will return to this point in connection with the second temptation, where it is in fact the central issue. The proof of divinity that the tempter proposes at the first temptation consists in changing the stones of the desert into bread. At first it is a question of Jesus' own hunger, which is how Luke sees it: "Command this stone to become bread" (Lk 4:3). Matthew, however, understands the temptation in broader terms, as it would later confront Jesus even during his earthly life and then throughout all of history.

Is there anything more tragic, is there anything more opposed to belief in the existence of a good God and a Redeemer of mankind, than world hunger? Shouldn't it be the first test of the Redeemer, before the world's gaze and on the world's behalf, to give it bread and to end all hunger? During their wandering through the desert, God fed the people of Israel with bread from heaven, with manna. This seemed to offer a privileged glimpse into how things would look when the Messiah came: Did not, and does not, the Redeemer of the world have to prove his credentials by feeding everyone? Isn't the problem of feeding the world—and, more generally, are not social problems—the primary, true yardstick by which redemption has to be measured? Does someone who fails to measure up to this standard have any right to be called a redeemer? Marxism—quite understandably—made this very point the core of its promise of salvation: It would see to it that no one went hungry anymore and that the "desert would become bread."

"If you are the Son of God"—what a challenge! And

should we not say the same thing to the Church? If you claim to be the Church of God, then start by making sure the world has bread—the rest comes later. It is hard to answer this challenge, precisely because the cry of the hungry penetrates so deeply into the ears and into the soul—as well it should. Jesus' answer cannot be understood in light of the temptation story alone. The bread motif pervades the entire Gospel and has to be looked at in its full breadth.

There are two other great narratives concerning bread in Jesus' life. The first is the multiplication of loaves for the thousands who followed the Lord when he withdrew to a lonely place. Why does Christ now do the very thing he had rejected as a temptation before? The crowds had left everything in order to come hear God's word. They are people who have opened their heart to God and to one another; they are therefore ready to receive the bread with the proper disposition. This miracle of the loaves has three aspects, then. It is preceded by the search for God, for his word, for the teaching that sets the whole of life on the right path. Furthermore, God is asked to supply the bread. Finally, readiness to share with one another is an essential element of the miracle. Listening to God becomes living with God, and leads from faith to love, to the discovery of the other. Jesus is not indifferent toward men's hunger, their bodily needs, but he places these things in the proper context and the proper order.

This second narrative concerning bread thus points ahead to, and prepares for, the third: the Last Supper, which becomes the Eucharist of the Church and Jesus' perpetual miracle of bread. Jesus himself has become the grain of wheat that died and brought forth much fruit (cf. Jn 12:24).

He himself has become bread for us, and *this* multiplication of the loaves endures to the end of time, without ever being depleted. This gives us the background we need if we are to understand what Jesus means when he cites the Old Testament in order to repel the tempter: "Man does not live by bread alone, but . . . by everything that proceeds out of the mouth of the LORD" (Deut 8:3). The German Jesuit Alfred Delp, who was executed by the Nazis, once wrote: "Bread is important, freedom is more important, but most important of all is unbroken fidelity and faithful adoration."

When this ordering of goods is no longer respected, but turned on its head, the result is not justice or concern for human suffering. The result is rather ruin and destruction even of material goods themselves. When God is regarded as a secondary matter that can be set aside temporarily or permanently on account of more important things, it is precisely these supposedly more important things that come to nothing. It is not just the negative outcome of the Marxist experiment that proves this.

The aid offered by the West to developing countries has been purely technically and materially based, and not only has left God out of the picture, but has driven men away from God. And this aid, proudly claiming to "know better," is itself what first turned the "third world" into what we mean today by that term. It has thrust aside indigenous religious, ethical, and social structures and filled the resulting vacuum with its technocratic mind-set. The idea was that we could turn stones into bread; instead, our "aid" has only given stones in place of bread. The issue is the primacy of God. The issue is acknowledging that he is a reality, that he is the reality without which nothing else can be good. History cannot be detached from God and then run smoothly on purely material lines. If man's heart is not good, then nothing else can turn out good, either. And the goodness of the human heart can ultimately come only from the One who is goodness, who is the Good itself.

Of course, one can still ask why God did not make a world in which his presence is more evident—why Christ did not leave the world with another sign of his presence so radiant that no one could resist it. This is the mystery of God and man, which we find so inscrutable. We live in this world, where God is not so manifest as tangible things are, but can be sought and found only when the heart sets out on the "exodus" from "Egypt." It is in *this* world that we are obliged to resist the delusions of false philosophies and to recognize that we do not live by bread alone, but first and foremost by obedience to God's word. Only when this obedience is put into practice does the attitude develop that is also capable of providing bread for all.

Let us move on to Jesus' second temptation; of the three it is in many ways the most difficult to understand in terms of the lessons it holds for us. This second temptation has to be interpreted as a sort of vision, which once again represents something real, something that poses a particular threat to the man Jesus and his mission. The first point is the striking fact that the devil cites Holy Scripture in order to lure Jesus into his trap. He quotes Psalm 91:11f., which speaks of the protection God grants to the man who believes: "For he will give his angels charge of you to guard you in all your ways. On their hands they will bear you up, lest you dash your foot against a stone." These words acquire a special significance by virtue of the fact that they are spoken in the holy city and in the holy place. Indeed, the psalm cited here is connected with the Temple; to pray it is to hope for protection in the Temple, since God's dwelling place necessarily means a special place of divine protection. Where should the man who believes in God feel safer than in the sacred precincts of the Temple? (Further details are given in Gnilka, *Matthäusevangelium,* I, p. 88.) The devil proves to be a Bible expert who can quote the Psalm exactly. The whole conversation of the second temptation takes the form of a dispute between two Bible scholars. Remarking on this passage, Joachim Gnilka says that the devil presents himself here as a theologian. The Russian writer Vladimir Soloviev took up this motif in his short story "The Antichrist." The Antichrist receives an honorary doctorate in theology from the University of Tübingen and is a great Scripture scholar. Soloviev's portrayal of the Antichrist forcefully expresses his skepticism regarding a certain type of scholarly exegesis current at the time. This is not a rejection of scholarly biblical interpretation as such, but an eminently salutary and necessary warning against its possible aberrations. The fact is that scriptural exegesis can become a tool of the Antichrist. Soloviev is not the first person to tell us that; it is the deeper point of the temptation story itself. The alleged findings of scholarly exegesis have been used to put together the most dreadful books that destroy the figure of Jesus and dismantle the faith.

The common practice today is to measure the Bible against the so-called modern worldview, whose fundamental dogma is that God cannot act in history—that everything to do with God is to be relegated to the domain of subjectivity.

And so the Bible no longer speaks of God, the living God; no, now *we* alone speak and decide what God can do and what we will and should do. And the Antichrist, with an air of scholarly excellence, tells us that any exegesis that reads the Bible from the perspective of faith in the living God, in order to listen to what God has to say, is fundamentalism; he wants to convince us that only *his* kind of exegesis, the supposedly purely scientific kind, in which God says nothing and has nothing to say, is able to keep abreast of the times.

The theological debate between Jesus and the devil is a dispute over the correct interpretation of Scripture, and it is relevant to every period of history. The hermeneutical question lying at the basis of proper scriptural exegesis is this: What picture of God are we working with? The dispute about interpretation is ultimately a dispute about who God is. Yet in practice, the struggle over the image of God, which underlies the debate about valid biblical interpretation, is decided by the picture we form of Christ: Is he, who remained without worldly power, really the Son of the living God?

The structural question concerning the remarkable scriptural discussion between Christ and the tempter thus leads directly to the question about its content. What is this dispute about? The issue at stake in this second temptation has been summed up under the motif of "bread and circuses." The idea is that after bread has been provided, a spectacle has to be offered, too. Since mere bodily satisfaction is obviously not enough for man, so this interpretation goes, those who refuse to let God have anything to do with the world and with man are forced to provide the titillation of exciting stimuli, the thrill of which replaces religious awe and drives it away.

But that cannot be the point of this passage, since the temptation apparently does not presuppose any spectators.

The point at issue is revealed in Jesus' answer, which is also taken from Deuteronomy: "You shall not put the LORD your God to the test" (Deut 6:16). This passage from Deuteronomy alludes to the story of how Israel almost perished of thirst in the desert. Israel rebels against Moses, and in so doing rebels against God. God has to prove that he is God. The Bible describes this rebellion against God as follows: "They put the LORD to the proof by saying, 'Is the LORD among us or not?'" (Ex 17:7). The issue, then, is the one we have already encountered: God has to submit to experiment. He is "tested," just as products are tested. He must submit to the conditions that we say are necessary if we are to reach certainty. If he doesn't grant us now the protection he promises in Psalm 91, then he is simply not God. He will have shown his own word, and himself too, to be false.

We are dealing here with the vast question as to how we can and cannot know God, how we are related to God and how we can lose him. The arrogance that would make God an object and impose our laboratory conditions upon him is incapable of finding him. For it already implies that we deny God as God by placing ourselves above him, by discarding the whole dimension of love, of interior listening; by no longer acknowledging as real anything but what we can experimentally test and grasp. To think like that is to make oneself God. And to do that is to abase not only God, but the world and oneself, too.

From this scene on the pinnacle of the Temple, though, we can look out and see the Cross. Christ did not cast himself down from the pinnacle of the Temple. He did not leap into the abyss. He did not tempt God. But he did descend into the abyss of death, into the night of abandonment, and into the desolation of the defenseless. He ventured *this* leap as an act of God's love for men. And so he knew that, ultimately, when he leaped he could only fall into the kindly hands of the Father. This brings to light the real meaning of Psalm 91, which has to do with the right to the ultimate and unlimited trust of which the Psalm speaks: If you follow the will of God, you know that in spite of all the terrible things that happen to you, you will never lose a final refuge. You know that the foundation of the world is love, so that even when no human being can or will help you, you may go on, trusting in the One who loves you. Yet this trust, which we cultivate on the authority of Scripture and at the invitation of the risen Lord, is something quite different from the reckless defiance of God that would make God our servant.

We come now to the third and last temptation, which is the climax of the whole story. The devil takes the Lord in a vision onto a high mountain. He shows him all the kingdoms of the earth and their splendor and offers him kingship over the world. Isn't that precisely the mission of the Messiah? Isn't he supposed to be the king of the world who unifies the whole earth in one great kingdom of peace and well-being? We saw that the temptation to turn stones into bread has two remarkable counterparts later on in Jesus' story: the multiplication of the loaves and the Last Supper. The same thing is true here.

The risen Lord gathers his followers "on the mountain" (cf. Mt 28:16). And on this mountain he does indeed say "all authority in heaven and on earth has been given to me" (Mt 28:18). Two details here are new and different. The Lord has power *in heaven* and on earth. And only someone who has this fullness of authority has the real, saving power. Without heaven, earthly power is always ambiguous and fragile. Only when power submits to the measure and the judgment of heaven—of God, in other words—can it become power for good. And only when power stands under God's blessing can it be trusted.

This is where the second element comes in: Jesus has this power in virtue of his Resurrection. This means that it presupposes the Cross, his death. It presupposes that other mountain—Golgotha, where he hangs on the Cross and dies, mocked by men and forsaken by his disciples. The Kingdom of Christ is different from the kingdoms of the earth and their splendor, which Satan parades before him. This splendor, as the Greek word *doxa* indicates, is an illusory appearance that disintegrates. This is not the sort of splendor that belongs to the Kingdom of Christ. His Kingdom grows through the humility of the proclamation in those who agree to become his disciples, who are baptized in the name of the triune God, and who keep his commandments (cf. Mt 28:19f.).

But let us return to the third temptation. Its true content becomes apparent when we realize that throughout history it is constantly taking on new forms. The Christian empire attempted at an early stage to use the faith in order to cement political unity. The Kingdom of Christ was now expected to take the form of a political kingdom and its splendor. The powerlessness of faith, the earthly powerlessness of Jesus Christ, was to be given the helping hand of political and military might. This temptation to use power to secure the faith has arisen again and again in varied forms throughout the centuries, and again and again faith has risked being suffocated in the embrace of power. The struggle for the freedom of the Church, the struggle to avoid identifying Jesus' Kingdom with any political structure, is one that has to be fought century after century. For the fusion of faith and political power always comes at a price: faith becomes the servant of power and must bend to its criteria.

The alternative that is at stake here appears in a dramatic form in the narrative of the Lord's Passion. At the culmination of Jesus' trial, Pilate presents the people with a choice between Jesus and Barabbas. One of the two will be released. But who was Barabbas? It is usually the words of John's Gospel that come to mind here: "Barabbas was a robber" (Jn 18:40). But the Greek word for "robber" had acquired a specific meaning in the political situation that obtained at the time in Palestine. It had become a synonym for "resistance fighter." Barabbas had taken part in an uprising (cf. Mk 15:7), and furthermore—in that context—had been accused of murder (cf. Lk 23:19, 25). When Matthew remarks that Barabbas was "a notorious prisoner" (Mt 27:16), this is evidence that he was one of the prominent resistance fighters, in fact probably the actual leader of that particular uprising.

In other words, Barabbas was a messianic figure. The choice of Jesus versus Barabbas is not accidental; two messiah figures, two forms of messianic belief stand in opposition. This becomes even clearer when we consider that the name Bar-Abbas means "son of the father." This is a typically messianic appellation, the cultic name of a prominent leader of the messianic movement. The last great Jewish messianic war was fought in the year 132 by Bar-Kokhba, "son of the star." The form of the name is the same, and it stands for the same intention.

Origen, a Father of the Church, provides us with another interesting detail. Up until the third century, many manuscripts of the Gospels referred to the man in question here as "Jesus Barabbas"—"Jesus son of the father." Barabbas figures here as a sort of alter ego of Jesus, who makes the same claim but understands it in a completely different way. So the choice is between a Messiah who leads an armed struggle, promises freedom and a kingdom of one's own, and this mysterious Jesus who proclaims that losing oneself is the way to life. Is it any wonder that the crowds prefer Barabbas? (For a fuller discussion of this point, see Vittorio Messori's important book *Patì sotto Ponzio Pilato?* [Turin, 1992], pp. 52–62.)

If we had to choose today, would Jesus of Nazareth, the son of Mary, the Son of the Father, have a chance? Do we really know Jesus at all? Do we understand him? Do we not perhaps have to make an effort, today as always, to get to know him all over again? The tempter is not so crude as to suggest to us directly that we should worship the devil. He merely suggests that we opt for the reasonable decision, that we choose to give priority to a planned and thoroughly organized world, where God may have his place as a private concern but must not interfere in our essential purposes. Soloviev attributes to the Antichrist a book entitled *The Open Way to World Peace and Welfare.* This book becomes something of a new Bible, whose real message is the worship of well-being and rational planning.

Jesus' third temptation proves, then, to be the fundamental one, because it concerns the question as to what sort of action is expected of a Savior of the world. It pervades the entire life of Jesus. It manifests itself openly again at a decisive turning point along his path. Peter, speaking in the name of the disciples, has confessed that Jesus is the Messiah-Christ, the Son of the Living God. In doing so, he has expressed in words the faith that builds up the Church and inaugurates the new community of faith based on Christ. At this crucial moment, where distinctive and decisive knowledge of Jesus separates his followers from public opinion and begins to constitute them as his new family, the tempter appears—threatening to turn everything into its opposite. The Lord immediately declares that the concept of the Messiah has to be understood in terms of the entirety of the message of the Prophets—it means not worldly power, but the Cross, and the radically different community that comes into being through the Cross.

But that is not what Peter has understood: "Peter took him and began to rebuke him, saying, 'God forbid, Lord! This shall never happen to you'" (Mt 16:22). Only when we read these words against the backdrop of the temptation scene—as its recurrence at the decisive moment—do we understand Jesus' unbelievably harsh answer: "Get behind me, Satan! You are a hindrance to me; for you are not on the side of God, but of men" (Mt 16:23).

But don't we all repeatedly tell Jesus that his message leads to conflict with the prevailing opinions, so that there is always a looming threat of failure, suffering, and persecution? The Christian empire or the secular power of the papacy is no longer a temptation today, but the interpretation of Christianity as a recipe for progress and the proclamation of universal prosperity as the real goal of all religions, including Christianity—this is the modern form of the same temptation. It appears in the guise of a question: "What did Jesus bring, then, if he didn't usher in a better world? How can that not be the content of messianic hope?"

In the Old Testament, two strands of that hope are still intertwined without distinction. The first one is the expectation of a worldly paradise in which the wolf lies down with the lamb (cf. Is 11:6), the peoples of the world make their way to Mount Zion, and the prophecy "They shall beat their swords into plowshares, and their spears into pruning hooks" comes true (Is 2:4; Mic 4:1–3). Alongside this expectation, however, is the prospect of the suffering servant of God, of a Messiah who brings salvation through contempt and suffering. Throughout his public ministry, and again in his discourses after Easter, Jesus had to show his disciples that Moses and the Prophets were speaking of him, the seemingly powerless one, who suffered, was crucified, and rose again. He had to show that in *this* way, and no other, the promises were fulfilled. "O foolish men, and slow of heart to believe all that the prophets have spoken!" (Lk 24:25). That is what the Lord said to the disciples on the road to Emmaus and he has to say the same to us repeatedly throughout the centuries, because we too are constantly presuming that in order to make good on his claim to be a Messiah, he ought to have ushered in the golden age.

Jesus, however, repeats to us what he said in reply to Satan, what he said to Peter, and what he explained further to the disciples of Emmaus: No kingdom of this world is the

Kingdom of God, the total condition of mankind's salvation. Earthly kingdoms remain earthly human kingdoms, and anyone who claims to be able to establish the perfect world is the willing dupe of Satan and plays the world right into his hands.

Now, it is true that this leads to the great question that will be with us throughout this entire book: What did Jesus actually bring, if not world peace, universal prosperity, and a better world? What has he brought?

The answer is very simple: God. He has brought God. He has brought the God who formerly unveiled his countenance gradually, first to Abraham, then to Moses and the Prophets, and then in the Wisdom Literature—the God who revealed his face only in Israel, even though he was also honored among the pagans in various shadowy guises. It is this God, the God of Abraham, Isaac, and Jacob, the true God, whom he has brought to the nations of the earth.

He has brought God, and now we know his face, now we can call upon him. Now we know the path that we human beings have to take in this world. Jesus has brought God and with God the truth about our origin and destiny: faith, hope, and love. It is only because of our hardness of heart that we think this is too little. Yes indeed, God's power works quietly in this world, but it is the true and lasting power. Again and again, God's cause seems to be in its death throes. Yet over and over again it proves to be the thing that truly endures and saves. The earthly kingdoms that Satan was able to put before the Lord at that time have all passed away. Their glory, their *doxa,* has proven to be a mere semblance. But the glory of Christ, the humble, self-sacrificing glory of his love, has not passed away, nor will it ever do so.

Jesus has emerged victorious from his battle with Satan. To the tempter's lying divinization of power and prosperity, to his lying promise of a future that offers all things to all men through power and through wealth—he responds with the fact that God is God, that God is man's true Good. To the invitation to worship power, the Lord answers with a passage from Deuteronomy, the same book that the devil himself had cited: "You shall worship the Lord your God and him only shall you serve" (Mt 4:10; cf. Deut 6:13). The fundamental commandment of Israel is also the fundamental commandment for Christians: God alone is to be worshiped. When we come to consider the Sermon on the Mount, we will see that precisely this unconditional Yes to the first tablet of the Ten Commandments also includes the Yes to the second tablet—reverence for man, love of neighbor. Matthew, like Mark, concludes the narrative of the temptations with the statement that "angels came and ministered to him" (Mt 4:11; Mk 1:13). Psalm 91:11 now comes to fulfillment: The angels serve him, he has proven himself to be the Son, and heaven therefore stands open above him, the new Jacob, the Patriarch of a universalized Israel (cf. Jn 1:51; Gen 28:12).

CHAPTER THREE

The Gospel of the Kingdom of God

"Now after John was arrested, Jesus came into Galilee, preaching the Gospel of God, and saying, 'The time is fulfilled, and the Kingdom of God is at hand; repent, and believe in the Gospel'" (Mk 1:14–15). With these words, the Evangelist Mark describes the beginning of Jesus' public activity and at the same time specifies the essential content of his preaching. Matthew, too, sums up Jesus' activity in Galilee in similar terms: "And he went about all Galilee, teaching in their synagogues and preaching the Gospel of the Kingdom and healing every disease and every infirmity among the people" (Mt 4:23, 9:35). Both Evangelists designate Jesus' preaching with the Greek term *evangelion*—but what does that actually mean?

The term has recently been translated as "good news." That sounds attractive, but it falls far short of the order of magnitude of what is actually meant by the word *evangelion*. This term figures in the vocabulary of the Roman emperors, who understood themselves as lords, saviors, and redeemers of the world. The messages issued by the emperor were called in Latin *evangelium*, regardless of whether or not their content was particularly cheerful and pleasant. The idea was that what comes from the emperor is a saving message, that it is not just a piece of news, but a change of the world for the better.

When the Evangelists adopt this word, and it thereby becomes the generic name for their writings, what they mean to tell us is this: What the emperors, who pretend to be gods, illegitimately claim, really occurs here—a message endowed with plenary authority, a message that is not just talk, but reality. In the vocabulary of contemporary linguistic theory, we would say that the *evangelium*, the Gospel, is not just informative speech, but performative speech—not just the imparting of information, but action, efficacious power that enters into the world to save and transform. Mark speaks of the "Gospel of God," the point being that it is not the emperors who can save the world, but God. And it is here that God's word, which is at once word and deed, appears; it is here that what the emperors merely assert, but cannot actually perform, truly takes place. For here it is the real Lord of the world—the living God—who goes into action.

The core content of the Gospel is this: The Kingdom of God is at hand. A milestone is set up in the flow of time; something new takes place. And an answer to this gift is demanded of man: conversion and faith. The center of this announcement is the message that God's Kingdom is at hand. This announcement is the actual core of Jesus' words and works. A look at the statistics underscores this. The phrase "Kingdom of God" occurs 122 times in the New Testament as a whole; 99 of these passages are found in the three Synoptic Gospels, and 90 of these 99 texts report words of Jesus.

In the Gospel of John, and the rest of the New Testament writings, the term plays only a small role. One can say that whereas the axis of Jesus' preaching before Easter is the Kingdom of God, Christology is the center of the preaching of the Apostles after Easter.

Does this mean, then, that there has been a falling away from the real preaching of Jesus? Is the exegete Rudolf Bultmann right when he says that the historical Jesus is not really part of the theology of the New Testament, but must be seen as still essentially a Jewish teacher, who, although certainly to be reckoned as an essential presupposition for the New Testament, ought not to be counted as part of the New Testament itself?

Another variant of this alleged gulf between Jesus and the preaching of the Apostles occurs in the now famous saying of the Catholic modernist Alfred Loisy, who put it like this: Jesus preached the Kingdom of God, and what came was the Church. These words may be considered ironic, but they also express sadness. Instead of the great expectation of God's own Kingdom, of a new world transformed by God himself, we got something quite different—and what a pathetic substitute it is: the Church.

Is this true? Is the form of Christianity that took shape in the preaching of the Apostles, and in the Church that was built on this preaching, really just a precipitous plunge from an unfulfilled expectation into something else? Is the change of subject from "Kingdom of God" to Christ (and so to the genesis of the Church) really just the collapse of a promise and the emergence of something else in its place?

Everything depends on how we are to understand the

expression "Kingdom of God" as used by Jesus, on what kind of relationship exists between the content of his proclamation and his person, as the proclaimer. Is he just a messenger charged with representing a cause that is ultimately independent of him, or is the messenger himself the message? The question about the Church is not the primary question. The basic question is actually about the relationship between the Kingdom of God and Christ. It is on this that our understanding of the Church will depend.

Before we delve more deeply into the words of Jesus in order to understand his message—his action and his suffering—it may be useful to take a brief look at how the word *kingdom* has been understood in the history of the Church. We can identify three dimensions in the Church Fathers' interpretation of this key term.

The first dimension is the Christological one. Origen, basing himself on a reading of Jesus' words, called Jesus the *autobasileia,* that is, the Kingdom in person. Jesus himself is the Kingdom; the Kingdom is not a thing, it is not a geographical dominion like worldly kingdoms. It is a person; it is he. On this interpretation, the term "Kingdom of God" is itself a veiled Christology. By the way in which he speaks of the Kingdom of God, Jesus leads men to realize the overwhelming fact that in him God himself is present among them, that he is God's presence.

There is a second way of looking at the significance of the "Kingdom of God," which we could call the idealistic or mystical interpretation. It sees man's interiority as the essential location of the Kingdom of God. This approach to understanding the Kingdom of God was also inaugurated by

Origen. In his treatise *On Prayer,* he says that "those who pray for the coming of the Kingdom of God pray without any doubt for the Kingdom of God that they contain in themselves, and they pray that this Kingdom might bear fruit and attain its fullness. For in every holy man it is God who reigns [exercises dominion, is the Kingdom of God]. . . . So if we want God to reign in us [his Kingdom to be in us], then sin must not be allowed in any way to reign in our mortal body (Rom 6:12). . . . Then let God stroll at leisure in us as in a spiritual paradise (Gen 3:8) and rule in us alone with his Christ" (*Patrologia Graeca* 11, pp. 495f.). The basic idea is clear: The "Kingdom of God" is not to be found on any map. It is not a kingdom after the fashion of worldly kingdoms; it is located in man's inner being. It grows and radiates outward from that inner space.

The third dimension of the interpretation of the Kingdom of God we could call the ecclesiastical: the Kingdom of God and the Church are related in different ways and brought into more or less close proximity.

This last approach, as far as I can see, has gradually come to dominate the field, especially in modern Catholic theology. To be sure, neither the interpretation in terms of man's interiority nor the connection with Christ ever completely disappeared from sight. But nineteenth- and early-twentieth-century theology did tend to speak of the Church as the Kingdom of God on earth; the Church was regarded as the actual presence of the Kingdom within history. By that time, however, the Enlightenment had sparked an exegetical revolution in Protestant theology, and one of the main results of this revolution was an innovative understanding of Jesus' message concerning the Kingdom of God. This new interpretation immediately broke up into very different trends, however.

One of these was early-twentieth-century liberal theology. Its main spokesman, Adolf von Harnack, saw Jesus' message about the Kingdom of God as a double revolution against the Judaism of Jesus' time. Whereas Judaism focused entirely on the collective, on the chosen people, Harnack held, Jesus' message was strictly individualistic; Jesus addressed the individual, whose infinite value he recognized and made the foundation of his teaching. The second fundamental antithesis, according to Harnack, was this: Whereas ritual worship (and thus the priesthood) had dominated Judaism, Jesus set aside ritual and concentrated his message strictly on morality. Jesus, he argued, was concerned not with ritual purification and sanctification, but with man's soul. The individual's moral action, his works of love, will decide whether he enters into the Kingdom or is shut out of it.

This antithesis between ritual and morality, between the collective and the individual remained influential long after Harnack's time, and it was also widely adopted in Catholic exegesis from about the 1930s on. Harnack himself, though, connected it with his account of the differences between the three major forms of Christianity—the Roman Catholic, the Greek-Slavic, and the Germanic-Protestant—and held that the third of these forms was the one that restored the message of Jesus in its purity. Yet there was also decisive opposition to Harnack within the Protestant world. His opponents insisted that it was not the individual as such who stands under the promise, but the community, and that it is as a member of this community that the individual attains salvation. They pointed out that it is not man's ethical achievement that counts, and they held that the Kingdom of God is, on the contrary, "beyond ethics" and is pure grace, as in their view Jesus' practice of eating with sinners shows particularly clearly (see, for example, K. L. Schmidt, *TDNT*, I, pp. 574ff.).

The great era of liberal theology came to an end with the First World War and the radical change in the intellectual climate that followed it. But there had already been rumblings of a revolution much earlier. The first clear signal of what was to come was a book by Johannes Weiss that appeared in 1892 under the title *Jesus' Proclamation of the Kingdom of God*. Albert Schweitzer's early exegetical works share the same outlook. Jesus' message, it was now claimed, was radically "eschatological"; his proclamation of the imminent Kingdom of God was a proclamation of the imminent end of the world, of the inbreaking of a new world where, as the term *kingdom* suggests, God would reign. The proclamation of the Kingdom of God, it was argued, must therefore be understood as referring strictly to the end times. Even texts that seemingly contradict this interpretation were somewhat violently made to fit it—for example, the growth parables about the sower (cf. Mk 4:3–9), the mustard seed (cf. Mk 4:30–32), the leaven (cf. Mt 13:33/ Lk 13:20), and the spontaneously sprouting seed (cf. Mk 4: 26–29). The point, it was said, is not growth; rather, Jesus is trying to say that while now our world is small, something very different is about to burst suddenly onto the scene. Here, obviously, theory predominated over listening to the text. Various efforts have been made to transpose Jesus' vision of the imminent end times into the language of modern Christian life, since for us it is not immediately intelligible.

Bultmann, for example, tried to do so in terms of the philosophy of Martin Heidegger—arguing that what matters is an existential attitude of "always standing at the ready." Jürgen Moltmann, building on the work of Ernst Bloch, worked out a "theology of hope," which claimed to interpret faith as an active involvement in the shaping of the future.

Since that time, a secularist reinterpretation of the idea of the Kingdom has gained considerable ground, particularly, though not exclusively, in Catholic theology. This reinterpretation propounds a new view of Christianity, religions, and history in general, and it claims that such radical refashioning will enable people to reappropriate Jesus' supposed message. It is claimed that in the pre–Vatican II period "ecclesiocentrism" was the dominant position: The Church was represented as the center of Christianity. Then there was a shift to Christocentrism, to the doctrine that Christ is the center of everything. But it is not only the Church that is divisive—so the argument continues—since Christ belongs exclusively to Christians. Hence the further step from Christocentrism to theocentrism. This has allegedly brought us closer to the community of religions, but our final goal continues to elude us, since even God can be a cause of division between religions and between people.

Therefore, it is claimed, we must now move toward "regnocentrism," that is, toward the centrality of the Kingdom. This at last, we are told, is the heart of Jesus' message, and it is also the right formula for finally harnessing mankind's positive energies and directing them toward the world's future. "Kingdom," on this interpretation, is simply the name for a world governed by peace, justice, and the conservation of creation. It means no more than this. This "Kingdom" is said to be the goal of history that has to be attained. This is supposedly the real task of religions: to work together for the coming of the "Kingdom." They are of course perfectly free to preserve their traditions and live according to their respective identities as well, but they must bring their different identities to bear on the common task of building the "Kingdom," a world, in other words, where peace, justice, and respect for creation are the dominant values.

This sounds good; it seems like a way of finally enabling the whole world to appropriate Jesus' message, but without requiring missionary evangelization of other religions. It looks as if now, at long last, Jesus' words have gained some practical content, because the establishment of the "Kingdom" has become a common task and is drawing nigh. On closer examination, though, it seems suspicious. Who is to say what justice is? What serves justice in particular situations? How do we create peace? On closer inspection, this whole project proves to be utopian dreaming without any real content, except insofar as its exponents tacitly presuppose some partisan doctrine as the content that all are required to accept.

But the main thing that leaps out is that God has disappeared; man is the only actor left on the stage. The respect for religious "traditions" claimed by this way of thinking is only apparent. The truth is that they are regarded as so many sets of customs, which people should be allowed to keep, even though they ultimately count for nothing. Faith and religions are now directed toward political goals. Only the organization of the world counts. Religion matters only insofar as it can serve that objective. This post-Christian vision of faith and religion is disturbingly close to Jesus' third temptation.

Let us return, then, to the Gospel, to the real Jesus. Our main criticism of the secular-utopian idea of the Kingdom has been that it pushes God off the stage. He is no longer needed, or else he is a downright nuisance. But Jesus proclaimed the Kingdom of *God,* not just any kind of kingdom. It is true that Matthew speaks of the "Kingdom of the heavens," but the word *heavens* is an alternative expression for the word *God,* which the Jews, with an eye to the second commandment, largely avoided out of reverence for the mystery of God. Accordingly, the phrase "Kingdom of heaven" is not a one-sided declaration of something "beyond": it speaks of God, who is as much in this world as he is beyond it—who infinitely transcends our world, but is also totally interior to it.

There is another important linguistic observation: The underlying Hebrew word *malkut* "is a *nomen actionis* [an action word] and means—as does the Greek word *basileia* [kingdom]—the regal function, the active lordship of the king" (Stuhlmacher, *Biblische Theologie,* I, p. 67). What is meant is not an imminent or yet to be established "kingdom," but God's actual sovereignty over the world, which is becoming an event in history in a new way.

We can put it even more simply: When Jesus speaks of the Kingdom of God, he is quite simply proclaiming God, and proclaiming him to be the living God, who is able to act concretely in the world and in history and is even now so acting. He is telling us: "God exists" and "God is really God," which means that he holds in his hands the threads of the world. In this sense, Jesus' message is very simple and thoroughly God-centered. The new and totally specific thing about his message is that he is telling us: God is acting now—this is the hour when God is showing himself in history as its Lord, as the living God, in a way that goes beyond anything seen before. "Kingdom of God" is therefore an inadequate translation. It would be better to speak of God's being-Lord, of his lordship.

We must try now, though, to delineate the content of Jesus' "message of the Kingdom" somewhat more precisely in light of its historical context. The announcement of God's lordship is, like Jesus' entire message, founded on the Old Testament. Jesus reads the Old Testament, in its progressive movement from the beginnings with Abraham right down to his own time, as a single whole; precisely when we grasp this movement as a whole, we see that it leads directly to Jesus himself.

In the first place, the so-called throne-accession Psalms proclaim the kingship of God (YHWH)—a kingship that is understood as extending over the whole of the cosmos and that Israel acknowledges through adoration (cf. Ps 47, 93, 96–99). Since the catastrophes that visited the history of Israel in the sixth century B.C., the kingship of God had become an expression of hope for the future. The Book of Daniel—written in the second century before Christ—does speak of God's lordship in the present, but it mainly proclaims to us a hope for the future, for which the figure of the "son of man" now becomes important, as it is he who is charged with ushering in God's lordship. In the Judaism of Jesus' own time, we meet the concept of divine lordship in the context of the

Temple ritual at Jerusalem and in the synagogue liturgy. We meet the same concept in rabbinic literature and in the Qumran writings. The pious Jew prays every day the Shema Israel: "Hear, O Israel: The LORD our God is one LORD; and you shall love the LORD your God with all your heart, and with all your soul, and with all your might" (Deut 6:4–5, 11:13; cf. Num 15:37–41). The recitation of this prayer was understood as the act of taking on one's shoulders the yoke of God's sovereign lordship. This prayer is not just a matter of words: the one who prays it accepts God's lordship, which consequently, through the act of praying, enters into the world. The one who is praying helps to bear it on his shoulders, and through his prayer, God's lordship shapes his way of life, his day-to-day existence, making it a locus of God's presence in the world.

We see, then, that the divine lordship, God's dominion over the world and over history, transcends the moment, indeed transcends and reaches beyond the whole of history. Its inner dynamism carries history beyond itself. And yet it is at the same time something belonging absolutely to the present. It is present in the liturgy, in Temple and synagogue, as an anticipation of the next world; it is present as a life-shaping power through the believer's prayer and being: by bearing God's yoke, the believer already receives a share in the world to come.

From this vantage point, we can see clearly both that Jesus was a "true Israelite" (cf. Jn 1:47) and also that—in terms of the inner dynamic of the promises made to Israel—he transcended Judaism. Nothing of what we have just discovered is lost. And yet something new is here, something that finds expression above all in such statements as "the

Kingdom of God is at hand" (Mk 1:15), it "has already come upon you" (Mt 12:28), it is "in the midst of you" (Lk 17:21). What these words express is a process of coming that has already begun and extends over the whole of history. It was these words that gave rise to the thesis of "imminent expectation" and made this appear as Jesus' specific characteristic. This interpretation, though, is by no means conclusive; in fact, if we consider the entire corpus of Jesus' sayings, it can actually be decisively ruled out. This is evident from the fact that the exponents of the apocalyptic interpretation of Jesus' Kingdom proclamation (i.e., imminent expectation) are simply forced, on the basis of their hypothesis, to ignore a large number of Jesus' sayings on this matter, and to bend others violently in order to make them fit.

We have already seen that Jesus' message of the Kingdom includes statements expressing its meager dimensions within history. It is like a grain of mustard, the tiniest of all seeds. It is like a leaven, a small quantity in comparison to the whole mass of the dough, yet decisively important for what becomes of the dough. It is compared again and again to the seed that is planted in the field of the world, where it meets various fates—it is pecked up by the birds, or it is suffocated among the thorns, or else it ripens into abundant fruit. Another parable tells of how the seed of the Kingdom grows, but an enemy comes and sows weeds in its midst, which for the present grow up with the seed, with the division coming only at the end (cf. Mt 13:24–30).

Yet another aspect of this mysterious reality of "God's lordship" comes to light when Jesus compares it with a treasure that was buried in a field. The finder of the treasure buries it again and sells everything in order to buy the field, so to gain possession of the treasure that can fulfill every desire. There is a parallel to this in the parable of the pearl of great price, whose finder likewise gives away everything in order to attain this good of surpassing value (cf. Mt 13:44ff.). Yet another side of the "lordship of God" (Kingdom) comes to light when Jesus makes the enigmatic statement that "the kingdom of heaven has suffered violence, and men of violence take it by force" (Mt 11:12). It is methodologically illegitimate to admit only one aspect of the whole as attributable to Jesus and then, on the basis of such an arbitrary claim, to bend everything else until it fits. Instead we should say: The reality that Jesus names the "Kingdom of God, lordship of God" is extremely complex, and only by accepting it in its entirety can we gain access to, and let ourselves be guided by, his message.

Let us examine more closely at least one text that typifies how difficult it is to decipher Jesus' mysteriously coded message. Luke 17:20–21 tells us that, "being asked by the Pharisees when the Kingdom of God was coming, he answered them, 'The Kingdom of God is not coming with signs to be observed [by neutral observers], nor will they say, "Lo, here it is!" or "There!" for behold, the Kingdom of God is in the midst of you.'" As the interpreters go to work on this text, they reflect here, too, their different approaches to understanding the "Kingdom of God" in general—according to the prior decisions and the basic worldview that each interpreter brings with him.

There is the "idealistic" interpretation, which tells us that the Kingdom of God is not an exterior structure, but is located in the interiority of man—recall what we heard earlier from Origen. There is truth in this interpretation, but it is not sufficient, even from the linguistic point of view. Then there is the interpretation in the sense of imminent expectation. It explains that the Kingdom of God does not come gradually, so as to be open to observation, but it is suddenly there. This interpretation, however, has no basis in the actual formulation of the text. For this reason, there is a growing tendency to hold that Christ uses these words to refer to himself: He, who is in our midst, is the "Kingdom of God," only we do not know him (cf. Jn 1:30). Another saying of Jesus points in the same direction, although with a somewhat different nuance: "But if it is by the finger of God that I cast out demons, then the Kingdom of God has come upon you" (Lk 11:20). Here (as in the preceding text, for that matter) it is not simply in Jesus' physical presence that the "Kingdom" is located; rather, it is in his action, accomplished in the Holy Spirit. In this sense, it is in and through him that the Kingdom of God becomes present here and now, that it "is drawing near."

Thus the following solution presents itself, albeit in a preliminary way that has to be explored further in the entire course of our attentive listening to Scripture. The new proximity of the Kingdom of which Jesus speaks—the distinguishing feature of his message—is to be found in Jesus himself. Through Jesus' presence and action, God has here and now entered actively into history in a wholly new way. The reason why *now* is the fullness of time (Mk 1:15), why *now* is in a unique sense the time of conversion and penance, as well as the time of joy, is that in Jesus it is God who draws near to us. In Jesus, God is now the one who acts and who rules as Lord—rules in a divine way, without worldly power, rules through the love that reaches "to the end" (Jn 13:1), to the Cross. It is from this center that the different, seemingly contradictory aspects can be joined together. In this context we understand Jesus' statements about the lowliness and hiddenness of the Kingdom; in this context we understand the fundamental image of the seed, which we will be considering again in various ways; in this context we also understand his invitation to follow him courageously, leaving everything else behind. He himself is the treasure; communion with him is the pearl of great price.

This interpretation now also sheds light on the tension between ethics and grace, between the strictest personalism and the call to enter a new family. When we consider the Messiah's Torah in the Sermon on the Mount, we will see several strands coming together: freedom from the Law; the gift of grace; and the "greater righteousness," that is, the "surplus" of righteousness that Jesus demands of his disciples beyond the righteousness of the Pharisees and scribes (cf. Mt 5:20). In the meantime, let us consider just one example: the story of the Pharisee and the tax collector, both of whom pray in the Temple in their very different ways (cf. Lk 18:9–14).

The Pharisee can boast considerable virtues; he tells God only about himself, and he thinks he is praising God in praising himself. The tax collector knows he has sinned, he knows he cannot boast before God, and he prays in full awareness of his debt to grace. Does this mean, then, that the Pharisee represents ethics and the tax collector represents grace without ethics or even in opposition to ethics? The real point is not the question "ethics—yes or no?" but that there are two ways of relating to God and to oneself. The Pharisee does not really look at God at all, but only at himself; he does not really need God, because he does everything right by himself. He has no real relation to God, who is ultimately superfluous—what he does himself is enough. Man makes himself righteous. The tax collector, by contrast, sees himself in the light of God. He has looked toward God, and in the process his eyes have been opened to see himself. So he knows that he needs God and that he lives by God's goodness, which he cannot force God to give him and which he cannot procure for himself. He knows that he needs mercy and so he will learn from God's mercy to become merciful himself, and thereby to become like God. He draws life from being-in-relation, from receiving all as gift; he will always need the gift of goodness, of forgiveness, but in receiving it he will always learn to pass the gift on to others. The grace for which he prays does not dispense him from ethics. It is what makes him truly capable of doing good in the first place. He needs God, and because he recognizes that, he begins through God's goodness to become good himself. Ethics is not denied; it is freed from the constraints of moralism and set in the context of a relationship of love—of relationship to God. And that is how it comes truly into its own.

The "Kingdom of God" is a theme that runs through the whole of Jesus' preaching. We can therefore understand it only in light of that preaching as a whole. In turning our attention now to one of the core elements of Jesus' preaching—the Sermon on the Mount—we will find there a deeper development of the themes that we have barely touched upon here. Above all, what we will see in the next chapter is that Jesus always speaks as the Son, that the relation between Father and Son is always present as the background of his message. In this sense, God is always at the center of the discussion, yet precisely because Jesus himself is God—the Son—his entire preaching is a message about the mystery of his person, it is Christology, that is, discourse concerning God's presence in his own action and being. And we will see that this is the point that demands a decision from us, and consequently this is the point that leads to the Cross and the Resurrection.

CHAPTER FOUR

The Sermon on the Mount

Matthew immediately follows the story of Jesus' temptation with a short account of the beginning of his ministry. In this context, he explicitly presents Galilee as "Galilee of the Gentiles"—as the place where the Prophets (Is 8:23; 9:1) had foretold that the "great light" (cf. Mt 4:15f.) would dawn. In this way Matthew responds to the surprise that the Savior does not come from Jerusalem and Judea, but from a district that was actually regarded as half pagan. The very thing that in the eyes of many tells *against* Jesus' messianic mission—the fact that he comes from Nazareth, from Galilee—is in reality the *proof* of his divine mission. From the start of his Gospel, Matthew claims the Old Testament for Jesus, even when it comes to apparent minutiae. What Luke states as a fundamental principle, without going into detail, in his account of the journey to Emmaus (cf. Lk 24:25ff.)—namely, that all the Scriptures refer to Jesus—Matthew, for his part, tries to demonstrate with respect to all the details of Jesus' path.

There are three elements in this first summary of Jesus' activity (cf. Mt 4:12–25) to which we will have to return later. The first is Matthew's indication of the fundamental content of Jesus' preaching, which is intended to summarize his entire message: "Repent, for the Kingdom [the lordship] of heaven is at hand" (Mt 4:17). The second element is the calling of the twelve Apostles, which is both a symbolic gesture and a totally concrete act by which Jesus announces and initiates the renewal of the twelve tribes, the new assembly of the people of Israel. Finally, this passage already makes it clear that Jesus is not just the teacher, but also the Redeemer of the whole person: The Jesus who teaches is at the same time the Jesus who saves.

With a few strokes of his brush—in fourteen verses (4:12–25)—Matthew presents his audience with an initial portrait of the figure and work of Jesus. Thereupon follow the three chapters of the Sermon on the Mount. What is this Sermon? With this great discourse, Matthew puts together a picture of Jesus as the new Moses in precisely the profound sense that we saw earlier in connection with the promise of a new prophet given in the Book of Deuteronomy.

The opening verse is far more than a casual introduction: "Seeing the crowds, he went up on the mountain, and when he sat down his disciples came to him. And he opened his mouth and taught them" (Mt 5:1–2). Jesus sits down—the expression of the plenary authority of the teacher. He takes his seat on the cathedra of the mountain. Later on he will speak of the rabbis who sit in the cathedra—the chair—of Moses and so have authority (cf. Mt 23:2); for that reason their teaching must be listened to and accepted, even though their lives contradict it, even though they themselves are not authority, but receive authority from another. Jesus takes his seat on the cathedra as the teacher of Israel and as the teacher of people everywhere. For—as we shall see when we consider the text itself—Matthew uses the word *disciple* here not in order to restrict the intended audience of the Sermon on the Mount, but to enlarge it. Everyone who hears and accepts the word can become a "disciple."

What counts from now on is hearing and following, not lineage. Discipleship is possible for everyone; it is a calling for everyone. Hearing, then, is the basis on which a more inclusive Israel is built—a renewed Israel, which does not exclude or revoke the old one, but steps beyond it into the domain of universality.

Jesus sits on the cathedra of Moses. But he does so not after the manner of teachers who are trained for the job in a school; he sits there as the greater Moses, who broadens the Covenant to include all nations. This also explains the significance of the mountain. The Evangelist does not tell us which of the hills of Galilee it was. But the very fact that it is the scene of Jesus' preaching makes it simply "the mountain"—the new Sinai. The "mountain" is the place where Jesus prays—where he is face-to-face with the Father. And that is exactly why it is also the place of his teaching, since his teaching comes forth from this most intimate exchange with the Father. The "mountain," then, is by the very nature of the case established as the new and definitive Sinai.

And yet how different this "mountain" is from that imposing rocky mass in the desert! Tradition has identified a hill north of Lake Genesareth as the Mount of the Beatitudes. Anyone who has been there and gazed with the eyes of his soul on the wide prospect of the waters of the lake, the sky and the sun, the trees and the meadows, the flowers and the sound of birdsong can never forget the wonderful atmosphere of peace and the beauty of creation encountered there—in a land unfortunately so lacking in peace.

Wherever the Mount of the Beatitudes actually was, something of this peace and beauty must have characterized it. Elijah was granted a transformed version of the Sinai experience: He experienced God passing by, not in the storm or in the fire or in the earthquake, but in the still small breeze (1 Kings 19:1–13). That transformation is completed here. God's power is now revealed in his mildness, his greatness in his simplicity and closeness. And yet his power and greatness are no less profound. What formerly found expression in storm, fire, and earthquake now takes on the form of the Cross, of the suffering God, who calls us to step into this mysterious fire, the fire of crucified love: "Blessed are you when men revile you and persecute you" (Mt 5:11). The violence of the Revelation of Sinai so frightened the people that they said to Moses, "You speak to us, and we will hear; but let not God speak to us, lest we die" (Ex 20:19).

Now God speaks intimately, as one man to another. Now he descends into the depth of their human sufferings. Yet that very act prompts, and will continually prompt, his hearers—the hearers who nonetheless think of themselves as disciples—to say, "This is a hard saying; who can listen to it?" (Jn 6:60). This new goodness of the Lord is no sugarplum. The scandal of the Cross is harder for many to bear than the thunder of Sinai had been for the Israelites. In fact, the Israelites were quite right when they said they would die if God should speak with them (Ex 20:19). Without a "dying," without the demise of what is simply our own, there is no communion with God and no redemption. Our meditation on the Baptism has already demonstrated this for us—Baptism cannot be reduced to a mere ritual.

We have already anticipated some points that will emerge fully when we consider the text itself. It should be clear by now that the Sermon on the Mount is the new Torah brought by Jesus. Moses could deliver his Torah only by entering into the divine darkness on the mountain. Jesus' Torah likewise presupposes his entering into communion with the Father, the inward ascents of his life, which are then prolonged in his descents into communion of life and suffering with men.

The Evangelist Luke gives us a shorter version of the Sermon on the Mount with different emphases. Luke writes for Gentile Christians, and so his concern is not so much to portray Jesus as the new Moses whose words constitute the definitive Torah. Hence even the outward framework of the Sermon is differently presented. In Luke's account, the Sermon on the Mount immediately follows the calling of the twelve Apostles, which he presents as the fruit of a night spent watching in prayer. Luke sets the calling of the Twelve on the mountain, the place of Jesus' prayer. After this event, which is of such fundamental importance for Jesus' path, the Lord comes down from the mountain with the Twelve, whom he has just chosen (and whom Luke has just introduced by name), and he stands on the plain. For Luke, this standing is an expression of Jesus' sovereignty and plenitude of authority, and the plain is an expression of the broad scope of his intended audience. Luke goes on to underscore this breadth when he tells us that—apart from the Twelve with whom Jesus had come down from the mountain—a great host of his disciples, as well as a crowd of people from Judea, Jerusalem, and the coastal regions of Tyre and Sidon, had flocked to listen to him and be healed by him (Lk 6:17ff.). The universal significance of the Sermon evident in this scene is further qualified when Luke—like Matthew—goes on to say that "he lifted up his eyes on his disciples, and said . . ." (Lk 6:20). Both elements are true: The Sermon on the Mount is addressed to the entire world, the entire present and future, and yet it demands *discipleship* and can be understood and lived out only by following Jesus and accompanying him on his journey.

The following reflections cannot, of course, aim at a verse-by-verse exegesis of the Sermon on the Mount. I would like to pick out three parts of it, from which it seems to me that the message and the person of Jesus emerge with particular clarity. Firstly, the Beatitudes. Secondly, I would like to reflect on the new version of the Torah that Jesus offers us. Jesus stands here in dialogue with Moses, with the traditions of Israel. There is an important book in which the great Jewish scholar Jacob Neusner takes his place, as it were, among the audience of the Sermon on the Mount and, having listened to Jesus, attempts a dialogue with him under the title *A Rabbi Talks with Jesus*. More than other interpretations known to me, this respectful and frank dispute between a believing Jew and Jesus, the son of Abraham, has opened my eyes to the greatness of Jesus' words and to the choice that the Gospel places before us. In the second section, then, I would like as a

Christian to join in the rabbi's conversation with Jesus, so as to be guided toward a better understanding of the authentic Jewishness and the mystery of Jesus. Finally, an important part of the Sermon on the Mount is devoted to prayer—indeed, how could it be otherwise? This part culminates in the Our Father, by means of which Jesus intends to teach disciples of all times how to pray; he intends to place them before the face of God, thus guiding them along the path to life.

The Beatitudes

The Beatitudes are not infrequently presented as the New Testament's counterpart to the Ten Commandments, as an example of the Christian ethics that is supposedly superior to the commands of the Old Testament. This approach totally misconstrues these words of Jesus. Jesus always presupposed the validity of the Ten Commandments as a matter of course (see, for example, Mk 10:19; Lk 16:17). In the Sermon on the Mount, he recapitulates and gives added depth to the commandments of the second tablet, but he does not abolish them (cf. Mt 5:21–48). To do so would in any case diametrically contradict the fundamental principle underpinning his discussion of the Ten Commandments: "Think not that I have come to abolish the Law and the Prophets; I have come not to abolish them but to fulfill them. For truly, I say to you, till heaven and earth pass away, not an iota, not a dot, will pass from the Law until all is accomplished" (Mt 5:17–18). This statement, which only *appears* to contradict the teaching of Saint Paul, will require further discussion after our examination of the dialogue between Jesus and the rabbi. For the time being, it suffices to note that Jesus has no intention of abrogating the Ten Commandments. On the contrary, he reinforces them.

But what are the Beatitudes? First of all, they are situated within a long tradition of Old Testament teachings, such as we find in Psalm 1 and in the parallel text at Jeremiah 17:7–8: Blessed is the man who trusts in the Lord. These are words of promise. At the same time, though, they are criteria for the discernment of spirits and so they prove to be directions for finding the right path. The setting in which Luke frames the Sermon on the Mount clarifies to whom the Beatitudes of Jesus are addressed: "He lifted up his eyes on his disciples." The individual Beatitudes are the fruit of this looking upon the disciples; they describe what might be called the actual condition of Jesus' disciples: They *are* poor, hungry, weeping men; they *are* hated and persecuted (cf. Lk 6:20ff.). These statements are meant to list practical, but also theological, attributes of the disciples of Jesus—of those who have set out to follow Jesus and have become his family.

Yet the menacing empirical situation in which Jesus sees his followers becomes a promise when his looking upon them is illuminated in the light of the Father. The Beatitudes, spoken with the community of Jesus' disciples in view, are paradoxes—the standards of the world are turned upside down as soon as things are seen in the right perspective, which is to say, in terms of God's values, so different from those of the world. It is precisely those who are poor in worldly terms, those thought of as lost souls, who are the truly fortunate ones, the blessed, who have every reason to rejoice and exult in the midst of their sufferings. The Beatitudes are promises resplendent with the new image of the world and of man inaugurated by Jesus, his "transformation of values." They are eschatological promises. This must not, however, be taken to mean that the joy they proclaim is postponed until some infinitely remote future or applies exclusively to the next world. When man begins to see and to live from God's perspective, when he is a companion on Jesus' way, then he lives by new standards, and something of the *éschaton,* of the reality to come, is already present. Jesus brings joy into the midst of affliction.

The paradoxes that Jesus presents in the Beatitudes express the believer's true situation in the world in similar terms to those repeatedly used by Paul to describe his experience of living and suffering as an Apostle: "We are treated as impostors, and yet are true; as unknown, and yet well known; as dying, and behold we live; as punished, and yet not killed; as sorrowful, yet always rejoicing; as poor, yet making many rich; as having nothing, and yet possessing everything" (2 Cor 6:8–10). "We are afflicted in every way, but not crushed; perplexed, but not driven to despair; persecuted, but not forsaken; struck down, but not destroyed" (2 Cor 4:8–9). What the Beatitudes in Luke's Gospel present as a consolation and a promise, Paul presents as the lived experience of the apostle. He considers that he has been made "last of all," a man under a death sentence, a spectacle to the world, homeless, calumniated, despised (cf. 1 Cor 4:9–13). And yet he experiences a boundless joy. As the one who has been handed over, who has given himself away in order to bring Christ to men, he experiences the interconnectedness of Cross and Resurrection: We are handed over to death "so that the life of Jesus may be manifested in our mortal flesh" (2 Cor 4:11). In his messengers Christ himself still suffers, still hangs on the Cross. And yet he is risen, irrevocably risen. Although Jesus' messenger in this world is still living the story of Jesus' suffering, the splendor of the Resurrection shines through, and it brings a joy, a "blessedness," greater than the happiness he could formerly have experienced on worldly paths. It is only now that he realizes what real "happiness," what true "blessedness" is, and, in so doing, notices the paltriness of what by conventional standards must be considered satisfaction and happiness.

The paradoxes that Saint Paul experienced in his life, which correspond to the paradoxes of the Beatitudes, thus display the same thing that John expresses in yet another way when he calls the Lord's Cross an "exaltation," an elevation to God's throne on high. John brings Cross and Resurrection, Cross and exaltation together in a single word, because for him the one is in fact inseparable from the other. The Cross is the act of the "exodus," the act of love that is accomplished to the uttermost and reaches "to the end" (Jn 13:1). And so it is the place of glory—the place of true contact and union with God, who is love (cf. 1 Jn 4:7, 16). This Johannine vision, then, is the *ne plus ultra* in concentrating the paradoxes of the Beatitudes and bringing them within reach of our understanding.

This reflection upon Paul and John has shown us two things. First, the Beatitudes express the meaning of discipleship. They become more concrete and real the more completely the disciple dedicates himself to service in the way that is illustrated for us in the life of Saint Paul. What the Beatitudes mean cannot be expressed in purely theoretical terms; it is proclaimed in the life and suffering, and in the mysterious joy, of the disciple who gives himself over completely to following the Lord. This leads to the second point: the Christological character of the Beatitudes. The disciple is bound to the mystery of Christ. His life is immersed in communion with Christ: "It is no longer I who live, but Christ who lives in me" (Gal 2:20). The Beatitudes are the transposition of Cross and Resurrection into discipleship. But they apply to the disciple because they were first paradigmatically lived by Christ himself.

This becomes even more evident if we turn now to consider Matthew's version of the Beatitudes (cf. Mt 5:3–12). Anyone who reads Matthew's text attentively will realize that the Beatitudes present a sort of veiled interior biography of Jesus, a kind of portrait of his figure. He who has no place to lay his head (cf. Mt 8:20) is truly poor; he who can say, "Come to me . . . for I am meek and lowly in heart" (cf. Mt 11:28–29) is truly meek; he is the one who is pure of heart and so unceasingly beholds God. He is the peacemaker, he is the one who suffers for God's sake. The Beatitudes display the mystery of Christ himself, and they call us into communion with him. But precisely because of their hidden Christological character, the Beatitudes are also a road map for the Church, which recognizes in them the model of what she herself should be. They are directions for discipleship, directions that concern every individual, even though—according to the variety of callings—they do so differently for each person.

Let us now take a somewhat closer look at each individual link in the chain of the Beatitudes. First of all, we have the much debated saying about the "poor in spirit." This term figures in the Qumran scrolls as the self-designation of the pious. They also call themselves "the poor of grace," "the poor of thy redemption," or simply "the poor" (Gnilka, *Matthäusevangelium,* I, p. 121). By referring to themselves in this way, they express their awareness of being the true Israel, thereby invoking traditions that are deeply rooted in Israel's faith. At the time of the Babylonian conquest of Judea, 90 percent of Judeans would have been counted among the poor; Persian tax policy resulted in another situation of dramatic poverty after the Exile. It was no longer possible to maintain the older vision according to which the righteous prosper and poverty is a consequence of a bad life (the so-called *Tun-Ergehens-Zusammenhang,* or conduct-life correspondence). Now Israel recognizes that its poverty is exactly what brings it close to God; it recognizes that the poor, in their humility, are the ones closest to God's heart, whereas the opposite is true of the arrogant pride of the rich, who rely only on themselves.

The piety of the poor that grew out of this realization finds expression in many of the Psalms; the poor recognize themselves as the true Israel. In the piety of these Psalms, in their expression of deep devotion to God's goodness, in the human goodness and humility that grew from it as men waited vigilantly for God's saving love—here developed that generosity of heart that was to open the door for Christ. Mary and Joseph, Simeon and Anna, Zachariah and Elizabeth, the shepherds of Bethlehem, and the Twelve whom the Lord called to intimate discipleship are all part of this current, which contrasts with the Pharisees and the Sadducees, but also, despite a great deal of spiritual affinity, with Qumran as well. They are the ones in whom the New Testament begins, in full awareness of its perfect unity with the faith of Israel that has been maturing to ever greater purity.

Silently evolving here was the attitude before God that Paul explored in his theology of justification: These are people who do not flaunt their achievements before God. They do not stride into God's presence as if they were partners able to engage with him on an equal footing; they do not lay claim to a reward for what they have done. These are people who know that their poverty also has an interior dimension; they are lovers who simply want to let God bestow his gifts upon them and thereby to live in inner harmony with God's nature and word. The saying of Saint Thérèse of Lisieux about one day standing before God with empty hands, and holding them open to him, describes the spirit of these poor ones of God: They come with empty hands; not with hands that grasp and clutch, but with hands that open and give and thus are ready to receive from God's bountiful goodness.

Because this is the case, there is no opposition between Matthew, who speaks of the poor in spirit, and Luke, in whose Gospel the Lord addresses the "poor" without further qualification. Some have claimed that Matthew took the concept of poverty that Luke originally understood in a totally material and real way, spiritualized it, and so robbed it of its radicalism. Yet anyone who reads the Gospel of Luke knows perfectly well that it is he who introduces us to the "poor in spirit"—the sociological group, one might say, among whom Jesus' earthly journey, and that of his message, could begin. Conversely, it is clear that Matthew remains completely in the tradition of piety reflected in the Psalms and so in the vision of the true Israel expressed in them.

The poverty of which this tradition speaks is never a purely material phenomenon. Purely material poverty does not bring salvation, though of course those who are disadvantaged in this world may count on God's goodness in a particular way. But the heart of those who have nothing can be hardened, poisoned, evil—interiorly full of greed for material things, forgetful of God, covetous of external possessions.

On the other hand, the poverty spoken of here is not a purely spiritual attitude, either. Admittedly, not everyone is called to the radicalism with which so many true Christians—from Anthony, father of monasticism, to Francis of Assisi, down to the exemplary poor of our era—have lived and continue to live their poverty as a model for us. But, in order to be the community of Jesus' poor, the Church has constant need of the great ascetics. She needs the communities that follow them, living out poverty and simplicity so as to display to us the truth of the Beatitudes. She needs them to wake everyone up to the fact that possession is all about service, to contrast the culture of affluence with the culture of inner freedom, and thereby to create the conditions for social justice as well.

The Sermon on the Mount is not a social program per se, to be sure. But it is only when the great inspiration it gives us vitally influences our thought and our action, only when faith generates the strength of renunciation and responsibility for our neighbor and for the whole of society—only then can social justice grow, too. And the Church as a whole must never forget that she has to remain recognizably the community of God's poor. Just as the Old Testament opened itself through God's poor to renewal in the New Covenant, so too any renewal of the Church can be set in motion only through those who keep alive in themselves the same resolute humility, the same goodness that is always ready to serve.

Thus far, we have considered only the first half of the first Beatitude, "Blessed are the poor in spirit." In both Matthew and Luke the promise assigned to them is as follows: "Theirs [yours] is the Kingdom of God [the Kingdom of heaven]" (Mt 5:3; Lk 6:20). "Kingdom of God" is the basic category of Jesus' message; here it becomes part of the Beatitudes. This context is important for a correct understanding of this much disputed term. We have already seen this in our examination of the meaning of the expression "Kingdom of God," and we will need to recall it frequently in the course of our further reflections.

But it may be a good idea—before we continue our meditation on the text—to turn for a moment to the figure whom the history of faith offers us as the most intensely lived illustration of this Beatitude: Francis of Assisi. The saints are the true interpreters of Holy Scripture. The meaning of a given passage of the Bible becomes most intelligible in those human beings who have been totally transfixed by it and have lived it out. Interpretation of Scripture can never be a purely academic affair, and it cannot be relegated to the purely historical. Scripture is full of potential for the future, a potential that can only be opened up when someone "lives through" and "suffers through" the sacred text. Francis of Assisi was gripped in an utterly radical way by the promise of the first Beatitude, to the point that he even gave away his garments and let himself be clothed anew by the bishop, the representative of God's fatherly goodness, through which the lilies of the field were clad in robes finer than Solomon's (cf. Mt 6:28–29). For Francis, this extreme humility was above all freedom for service, freedom for mission, ultimate trust in

God, who cares not only for the flowers of the field but specifically for his human children. It was a corrective to the Church of his day, which, through the feudal system, had lost the freedom and dynamism of missionary outreach. It was the deepest possible openness to Christ, to whom Francis was perfectly configured by the wounds of the stigmata, so perfectly that from then on he truly no longer lived as himself, but as one reborn, totally from and in Christ. For he did not want to found a religious order: He simply wanted to gather the People of God to listen anew to the word—without evading the seriousness of God's call by means of learned commentaries.

By creating the Third Order, though, Francis did accept the distinction between radical commitment and the necessity of living in the world. The point of the Third Order is to accept with humility the task of one's secular profession and its requirements, wherever one happens to be, while directing one's whole life to that deep interior communion with Christ that Francis showed us. "To own goods as if you owned nothing" (cf. 1 Cor 7:29ff.)—to master this inner tension, which is perhaps the more difficult challenge, and, sustained by those pledged to follow Christ radically, truly to live it out ever anew—that is what the third orders are for. And they open up for us what this Beatitude can mean for *all*. It is above all by looking at Francis of Assisi that we see clearly what the words "Kingdom of God" mean. Francis stood totally within the Church, and at the same time it is in figures such as he that the Church grows toward the goal that lies in the future, and yet is already present: The Kingdom of God is drawing near. . . .

Let us pass over for the time being the second Beatitude listed in Matthew's Gospel and go directly to the third, which is closely connected with the first: "Blessed are the meek, for they shall inherit the earth" (Mt 5:5). Some translations render the Greek word *praus* as "nonviolent" rather than "meek." This is a narrowing of the Greek term, which carries a great wealth of tradition. The third Beatitude is practically a Psalm citation: "The meek shall possess the land" (Ps 37:11). The word *praus* in the Greek Bible translates the Hebrew *anawim,* which was used to designate God's poor, of whom we spoke in connection with the first Beatitude. The first and third Beatitudes thus overlap to a large extent; the third Beatitude further illustrates an essential aspect of what is meant by poverty lived from and for God.

The focus is enlarged, though, when we take account of a few other texts in which the same word occurs. In Numbers 12:3 we read: "Now the man Moses was very meek, more than all men that were on the face of the earth." One cannot help thinking of Jesus' saying, "Take my yoke upon you, and learn from me; for I am meek and lowly in heart" (Mt 11:29). Christ is the new, the true Moses (this idea runs through the whole Sermon on the Mount). In him there appears the pure goodness that above all befits the great man, the ruler.

We are led even deeper when we consider another set of interconnections between the Old and New Testaments based around the word *praus,* "meek." In Zech 9:9–10, we read: "Rejoice greatly, O daughter of Zion! Shout aloud, O daughter of Jerusalem! Lo, your king comes to you; triumphant and victorious is he, humble [meek] and riding on an ass, on a colt the foal of an ass. He will cut off the chariot from Ephraim . . .

the battle bow shall be cut off, and he shall command peace to the nations; his dominion shall be from sea to sea, and from the River to the ends of the earth." This passage announces a poor king—a king whose rule does not depend on political and military might. His inmost being is humility and meekness before God and men. In this he is the exact opposite of the great kings of the world. And a vivid illustration is the fact that he rides on an ass—the mount of the poor, the counter-image of the chariot that he rejects. He is the king of peace—and by God's power, not his own.

There is a further element: His kingdom is universal, it embraces the whole earth. "From sea to sea"—behind this expression is the image of a flat earth surrounded on all sides by the waters, and it thus gives us an inkling of the world-spanning extent of his dominion. Karl Elliger is therefore correct when he says that "through all the fog" we do "glimpse with surprising distinctness the figure of the one who has now really brought the whole world the peace that passes all understanding. He has done so in filial obedience: by renouncing violence and accepting suffering until he was released from it by the Father. And so from now on he builds up his kingdom simply by the word of peace" (*Das Alte Testament Deutsch*, 24/25, p. 151). Only against this backdrop do we grasp the full scope of the account of Palm Sunday, only now do we understand what it means when Luke (and, in a similar vein, John) tells us that Jesus ordered his disciples to procure him a she-ass and her foal: "This took place to fulfill what was spoken by the prophet, saying, 'Tell the daughter of Zion, "Behold, your king is coming to you, [meek] and mounted on an ass, and on a colt, the foal of an ass" ' "(Mt 21:4–5; cf. Jn 12:15).

Unfortunately some translations obscure these interconnections by using different words to translate *praus*. Within the wide arc of these texts—from Numbers 12 through Zechariah 9 to the Beatitudes and the account of Palm Sunday—we can discern the vision of Jesus, the king of peace, who throws open the frontiers separating the peoples and creates a domain of peace "from sea to sea." Through his obedience he calls us into this peace and plants it in us. The word *meek* belongs, on one hand, to the vocabulary of the People of God, to the Israel that in Christ has come to span the whole world. At the same time, it is a word related to kingship, which unlocks for us the essence of Christ's new kingship. In this sense, we could say that it is both a Christological word and an ecclesiological one. In any case, it is a word that calls us to follow the one whose entry into Jerusalem mounted on an ass reveals the whole essence of his kingship.

In the text of Matthew's Gospel, this third Beatitude is associated with the promise of the land: "Blessed are the meek, for they shall inherit the land." What does this statement mean? Hope for the land is part of the original content of the promise to Abraham. During Israel's years of wandering in the desert, the promised land is always envisaged as the goal of the journey. In exile Israel waits for the return to the land. We must not overlook, however, that the promise of the land is clearly about something far greater than the mere idea of possessing a piece of ground or a national territory in the sense that every people is entitled to do.

The main issue in the foreground of the struggle for liberation prior to Israel's exodus from Egypt is the right to freedom of worship, the people's right to their own liturgy.

As time went by, it became increasingly clear that the promise of the land meant this: The land was given as a space for obedience, a realm of openness to God, that was to be freed from the abominations of idolatry. The concept of obedience to God, and so of the right ordering of the earth, is an essential component of the concept of freedom and the concept of the land. From this perspective, the exile, the withdrawal of the land, could also be understood: The land had itself become a zone of idolatry and disobedience, and the possession of the land had therefore become a contradiction.

A new and positive understanding of the diaspora could also arise from this way of thinking: Israel was scattered across the world so that it might everywhere create space for God and thus fulfill the purpose of creation suggested by the first creation account (cf. Gen 1:1–2, 4): The Sabbath is the goal of creation, and it shows what creation is for. The world exists, in other words, because God wanted to create a zone of response to his love, a zone of obedience and freedom. Step by step, as Israel accepted and suffered all the vicissitudes of its history as God's people, the idea of the land grew in depth and breadth, shifting its focus increasingly away from national possession and increasingly toward the universality of God's claim to the earth.

Of course, there is a sense in which the interplay between "meekness" and the promise of the land can also be seen as a perfectly ordinary piece of historical wisdom: Conquerors come and go, but the ones who remain are the simple, the humble, who cultivate the land and continue sowing and harvesting in the midst of sorrows and joys. The humble, the simple, outlast the violent, even from a purely historical point of view. But there is more. The gradual universalization of the concept of the land on the basis of a theology of hope also reflects the universal horizon that we found in the promise of Zechariah: The land of the king of peace is not a nation-state—it stretches from "sea to sea" (Zech 9:10). Peace aims at the overcoming of boundaries and at the renewal of the earth through the peace that comes from God. The earth ultimately belongs to the meek, to the peaceful, the Lord tells us. It is meant to become the "land of the king of peace." The third Beatitude invites us to orient our lives toward this goal.

Every eucharistic assembly is for us Christians a place where the king of peace reigns in this sense. The universal communion of Christ's Church is thus a preliminary sketch of the world of tomorrow, which is destined to become a land of Jesus Christ's peace. In this respect, too, the third Beatitude harmonizes closely with the first: It goes some way toward explaining what "Kingdom of God" means, even though the claim behind this term extends beyond the promise of the land.

With the foregoing remarks, we have already anticipated the seventh Beatitude: "Blessed are the peacemakers, for they shall be called sons of God" (Mt 5:9). A few observations on the main points of this fundamentally important saying of Jesus may therefore suffice. First of all, we glimpse the events of secular history in the background. In his infancy narrative, Luke had already suggested the contrast between this child and the all-powerful Emperor Augustus, who was renowned as the "savior of the universal human race" and as the great peacemaker. Caesar had already claimed the title "bringer of world peace." The faithful in Israel would be reminded of Solomon, whose Hebrew name is rooted in the word for "peace" (*shalom*). The Lord had promised David: "I will give peace and quiet to Israel in his days. . . . He shall be my son, and I will be his father" (1 Chron 22:9f.). This brings to the fore a connection between divine Sonship and the kingship of peace: Jesus is the Son, and he is truly Son. He is therefore the true "Solomon"—the bringer of peace. Establishing peace is part of the very essence of Sonship. The seventh Beatitude thus invites us to be and do what the Son does, so that we ourselves may become "sons of God."

This applies first of all in the context of each person's life. It begins with the fundamental decision that Paul passionately begs us to make in the name of God: "We beseech you on behalf of Christ, be reconciled to God" (2 Cor 5:20). Enmity with God is the source of all that poisons man; overcoming this enmity is the basic condition for peace in the world. Only the man who is reconciled with God can also be reconciled and in harmony with himself, and only the man who is reconciled with God and with himself can establish peace around him and throughout the world. But the political context that emerges from Luke's infancy narrative as well as here in Matthew's Beatitudes indicates the full scope of these words. That there be peace on earth (cf. Lk 2:14) is the will of God and, for that reason, it is a task given to man as well. The Christian knows that lasting peace is connected with men abiding in God's *eudokia,* his "good pleasure." The struggle to abide in peace with God is an indispensable part of the struggle for "peace on earth"; the former is the source of the criteria and the energy for the latter. When men lose sight of God, peace disintegrates and violence proliferates to a formerly unimaginable degree of cruelty. This we see only too clearly today.

Let us go back to the second Beatitude: "Blessed are those who mourn, for they shall be comforted" (Mt 5:4). Is it good to mourn and to declare mourning blessed? There are two kinds of mourning. The first is the kind that has lost hope, that has become mistrustful of love and of truth, and that therefore eats away and destroys man from within. But there is also the mourning occasioned by the shattering encounter with truth, which leads man to undergo conversion and to resist evil. This mourning heals, because it teaches man to hope and to love again. Judas is an example of the first kind of mourning: Struck with horror at his own fall, he no longer dares to hope and hangs himself in despair. Peter is an example of the second kind: Struck by the Lord's gaze, he bursts into healing tears that plow up the soil of his soul. He begins anew and is himself renewed.

Ezekiel 9:4 offers us a striking testimony to how this positive kind of mourning can counteract the dominion of evil. Six men are charged with executing divine punishment on Jerusalem—on the land that is filled with bloodshed, on the city that is full of wickedness (cf. Ezek 9:9). Before they do, however, a man clothed in linen must trace the Hebrew letter *taw* (like the sign of the Cross) on the foreheads of all those "who sigh and groan over all the abominations that are committed in the city" (Ezek 9:4). Those who bear this mark are exempted from the punishment. They are people who do not run with the pack, who refuse to collude with the injustice that has become endemic, but who suffer under it instead. Even though it is not in their power to change the overall situation, they still counter the dominion of evil through the passive resistance of their suffering—through the mourning that sets bounds to the power of evil.

Tradition has yielded another image of mourning that brings salvation: Mary standing under the Cross with her sister, the wife of Clopas, with Mary Magdalene, and with John (Jn 19: 25ff.). Once again, as in the vision of Ezekiel, we encounter here the small band of people who remain true in a world full of cruelty and cynicism or else with fearful conformity. They cannot avert the disaster, but by "suffering with" the one condemned (by their com-passion in the etymological sense) they place themselves on his side, and by their "loving with" they are on the side of God, who is love. This "com-passion" reminds us of the magnificent saying in Saint Bernard of Clairvaux's commentary on the Song of Songs (sermon 26, no. 5): "Impassibilis est Deus, sed non incompassibilis"—God cannot suffer, but he can "suffer *with*." At the foot of Jesus' Cross we understand better than anywhere else what it means to say "blessed are those who mourn, for they shall be comforted." Those who do not harden their hearts to the pain and need of others, who do not give evil entry to their souls, but suffer under its power and so acknowledge the truth of God—they are the ones who open the windows of the world to let the light in. It is to those who mourn in this sense that great consolation is promised. The second Beatitude is thus intimately connected with the eighth: "Blessed are those who are persecuted for righteousness' sake, for theirs is the kingdom of heaven" (Mt 5:10).

The mourning of which the Lord speaks is nonconformity with evil; it is a way of resisting models of behavior that the individual is pressured to accept because "everyone does it." The world cannot tolerate this kind of resistance; it demands conformity. It considers this mourning to be an accusation directed against the numbing of consciences. And so it is. That is why those who mourn suffer persecution for the sake of righteousness. Those who mourn are promised comfort; those who are persecuted are promised the Kingdom of God—the same promise that is made to the poor in spirit. The two promises are closely related. The Kingdom of God—standing under the protection of God's power, secure in his love—that is true comfort.

The converse is also true. The sufferer is not truly comforted, his tears are not completely wiped away, until he and the powerless of this world are no longer threatened by murderous violence; comfort is not brought to completion until even past sufferings never previously understood are lifted up into the light of God and given the meaning of reconciliation by his goodness; true comfort only appears when the "last enemy," death (cf. 1 Cor 15:26), and all its accomplices have been stripped of their power. Christ's words about comforting thus help us to understand what he means by "Kingdom of God" (of the heavens), while "Kingdom of God" gives us in turn an idea of what consolation the Lord holds in store for all those who mourn and suffer in this world.

There is one further observation that we have to add here. Jesus' words concerning those persecuted for righteousness' sake had a prophetic significance for Matthew and his audience. For them this was the Lord foretelling the situation of the Church which they were living through. The Church had become a persecuted Church, persecuted "for righteousness' sake." *Righteousness* in the language of the Old Covenant is the term for fidelity to the Torah, to the word of God, as the Prophets were constantly reminding their hearers. It is the observance of the right path shown by God, with the Ten Commandments at its center. The term that in the New Testament corresponds to the Old Testament concept of righteousness is *faith*: The man of faith is the "righteous man" who walks in God's ways (cf. Ps 1; Jer 17:5–8). For faith is walking with Christ, in whom the whole Law is fulfilled; it unites us with the righteousness of Christ himself.

The people who are persecuted for righteousness' sake are those who live by God's righteousness—by faith. Because man constantly strives for emancipation from God's will in order to follow himself alone, faith will always appear as a contradiction to the "world"—to the ruling powers at any given time. For this reason, there will be persecution for the sake of righteousness in every period of history. This word of comfort is addressed to the persecuted Church of all times. In her powerlessness and in her sufferings, she knows that she stands in the place where God's Kingdom is coming.

If, then, we may once again identify an ecclesiological dimension, an interpretation of the nature of the Church, in the promise attached to this Beatitude, as we did in the case of earlier ones, so too we can identify a Christological basis to these words: The crucified Christ is the persecuted just man portrayed in the words of Old Covenant prophecy—particularly the Suffering Servant Songs—but also prefigured in Plato's writings (*The Republic*, II 361e–362a). And in this guise he himself is the advent of God's Kingdom. This Beatitude is an invitation to follow the crucified Christ—an invitation to the individual as well as to the Church as a whole.

The Beatitude concerning the persecuted contains, in the words that conclude the whole passage, a variant indicating something new. Jesus promises joy, exultation, and a great reward to those who for his sake are reviled, and persecuted, and have all manner of evil uttered falsely against them (cf. Mt 5:11). The "I" of Jesus himself, fidelity to his person, becomes the criterion of righteousness and salvation. In the other Beatitudes, Christology is present, so to speak, in veiled form; here, however, the message that he himself is the center of history emerges openly. Jesus ascribes to his "I" a normative status that no teacher of Israel—indeed, no teacher of the Church—has a right to claim for himself. Someone who speaks like this is no longer a prophet in the traditional sense, an ambassador and trustee of another; he himself is the reference point of the righteous life, its goal and center.

Later in the course of our meditations, we will come to see that this direct Christology is constitutive of the Sermon on the Mount as a whole. What is here only touched upon will be developed further as we proceed.

Let us turn now to one of the two Beatitudes still to be discussed: "Blessed are those who hunger and thirst for righteousness, for they shall be satisfied" (Mt 5:6). This saying is intrinsically related to Jesus' words concerning those who mourn and who will find comfort. In the earlier Beatitude, the ones who receive the promise are those who do not bow to the diktat of the prevailing opinions and customs, but resist it by suffering. Similarly, this Beatitude is concerned with those who are on the lookout, who are in search of something great, of true justice, of the true good. One of the textual strands of the Book of Daniel contains a statement that tradition has come to regard as a synthesis of the attitude that is under consideration here. Daniel is described there as a *vir desideriorum,* as a man of longings (Dan 9:23 in the Latin Vulgate). The people this Beatitude describes are those who are not content with things as they are and refuse to stifle the restlessness of heart that points man toward something greater and so sets him on the inward journey to reach it—rather like the wise men from the East seeking Jesus, the star that shows the way to truth, to love, to God. The people meant here are those whose interior sensitivity enables them to see and hear the subtle signs that God sends into the world to break the dictatorship of convention.

At this point, who can fail to be reminded of the humble saints in whom the Old Covenant opens itself to the New, and is transformed into it? Of Zachariah and Elizabeth, of Mary and Joseph, of Simeon and Anna, all of whom, in their different ways, await the salvation of Israel with inner watchfulness and who by their humble piety, their patient waiting and longing, "prepare the way" of the Lord? But do we also think of the twelve Apostles—of these men who, though coming (as we will see) from totally different intellectual and social backgrounds, had kept their hearts open amid their work and their everyday lives, ready to respond to the call of something greater? Or of the passion for righteousness of a man such as Paul, a misguided passion that nonetheless prepared him to be cast down by God, and so brought to a new clarity of vision? We could continue in this vein throughout the whole of history. Edith Stein once said that anyone who honestly and passionately searches for truth is on the way to Christ. It is of such people that the Beatitude speaks—of this thirst and hunger that is blessed because it leads men to God, to Christ, and therefore opens the world to the Kingdom of God.

It seems to me that this is the place to say something, based upon the New Testament, about the salvation of those who do not know Christ. The prevailing view today is that everyone should live by the religion—or perhaps by the atheism—in which he happens to find himself already. This, it is said, is the path of salvation for him. Such a view presupposes a strange picture of God and a strange idea of man and of the right way for man to live. Let us try to clarify this by asking a few practical questions. Does someone achieve blessedness and justification in God's eyes because he has conscientiously fulfilled the duties of blood vengeance? Because he has vigorously fought for and in "holy war"? Or because he has performed certain animal sacrifices? Or because he has practiced ritual ablutions and other observances? Because he has declared his opinions and wishes to be norms of conscience and so made himself the criterion? No, God demands the opposite: that we become inwardly attentive to his quiet exhortation, which is present in us and which tears us away from what is merely habitual and puts us on the road to truth. To "hunger and thirst for righteousness"—that is the path that lies open to everyone; that is the way that finds its destination in Jesus Christ.

There is one more Beatitude: "Blessed are the pure in heart, for they shall see God" (Mt 5:8). The organ for seeing God is the heart. The intellect alone is not enough. In order for man to become capable of perceiving God, the energies of his existence have to work in harmony. His will must be pure and so too must the underlying affective dimension of his soul, which gives intelligence and will their direction. Speaking of the *heart* in this way means precisely that man's perceptive powers play in concert, which also requires the proper interplay of body and soul, since this is essential for the totality of the creature we call "man." Man's fundamental affective disposition actually depends on just this unity of body and soul and on man's acceptance of being both body and spirit. This means he places his body under the discipline of the spirit, yet does not isolate intellect or will. Rather, he accepts himself as coming from God, and thereby also acknowledges and lives out the bodiliness of his existence as an enrichment for the spirit. The heart—the wholeness of man—must be pure, interiorly open and free, in order for man to be able to see God. Theophilus of Antioch (d. ca. 180) once put it like this in a debate with some disputants: "If you say, 'show me your God,' I should like to answer you, 'show me the man who is in you.' . . . For God is perceived by men who are capable of seeing him, who have the eyes of their spirit open. . . . Man's soul must be as pure as a shining mirror" (*Ad Autolycum,* I, 2, 7ff.).

This prompts the question: How is man's inner eye purified? How to remove the cataract that blurs his vision or even blinds it altogether? The mystical tradition that speaks of a "way of purification" ascending to final "union" was an attempt to answer this question. The Beatitudes have to be read first and foremost in the context of the Bible. There, we meet the motif of purity of heart above all in Psalm 24, which reflects an ancient gate liturgy: "Who shall ascend the hill of the LORD? And who shall stand in his holy place? He who has clean hands and a pure heart, who does not lift up his soul to what is false, and does not swear deceitfully" (Ps 24:3–4). Before the gate of the Temple, the question arises as to who may enter and stand in proximity to the living God. Clean hands and a pure heart are the condition.

The Psalm explains in many different ways the content of this condition for admission to God's dwelling place. One fundamental condition is that those who would enter into God's presence must inquire after him, must seek his face (Ps 24:6). The fundamental condition thus proves to be the same attitude that we saw earlier, described by the phrase "hunger and thirst for righteousness." Inquiring after God, seeking his face—that is the first and fundamental condition for the ascent that leads to the encounter with God. Even before that, however, the Psalm specifies that clean hands and a pure heart entail man's refusal to deceive or commit perjury; this requires honesty, truthfulness, and justice toward one's fellow men and toward the community—what we might call social ethics, although it actually reaches right down into the depths of the heart.

Psalm 15 elaborates further on this, and hence we can say that the condition for admission to God's presence is simply the content of the Decalogue—with an emphasis on the inward search for God, on journeying toward him (first tablet) and on love of neighbor, on justice toward the individual and the community (second tablet). No conditions specifically involving knowledge of Revelation are enumerated, only "inquiring after God" and the basic tenets of justice that a vigilant conscience—stirred into activity by the search for God—conveys to everyone. Our earlier reflection on the question of salvation finds further confirmation here.

On Jesus' lips, though, these words acquire new depth. For it belongs to his nature that he sees God, that he stands face-to-face with him, in permanent interior discourse—in a relation of Sonship. In other words, this Beatitude is profoundly Christological. We will see God when we enter into the "mind of Christ" (Phil 2:5). Purification of heart occurs as a consequence of following Christ, of becoming one with him. "It is no longer I who live, but Christ who lives in me" (Gal 2:20). And at this point something new comes to light: The ascent to God occurs precisely in the descent of humble service, in the descent of love, for love is God's essence, and is thus the power that truly purifies man and enables him to perceive God and to see him. In Jesus Christ, God has revealed himself in his descending: "Though he was in the form of God," he "did not count equality with God a thing to be grasped, but emptied himself, taking the form of a servant, being born in the likeness of men. . . . He humbled himself and became obedient unto death, even death on a cross. Therefore God has highly exalted him" (Phil 2:6–9).

These words mark a decisive turning point in the history of mysticism. They indicate what is new in Christian mysticism, which comes from what is new in the Revelation of Jesus Christ. God descends, to the point of death on the Cross. And precisely by doing so, he reveals himself in his true divinity. We ascend to God by accompanying him on this descending path. In this context, the "gate liturgy" in Psalm 24 receives a new significance: The pure heart is the loving heart that enters into communion of service and obedience with Jesus Christ. Love is the fire that purifies and unifies intellect, will, and emotion, thereby making man one with himself, inasmuch as it makes him one in God's eyes. Thus, man is able to serve the uniting of those who are divided. This is how man enters God's dwelling place and becomes able to see him. And that is just what it means for him to be "blessed."

After this attempt to penetrate somewhat more deeply into the interior vision of the Beatitudes (the theme of the "merciful" is addressed not in this chapter, but in connection with the parable of the Good Samaritan), we must still briefly ask ourselves two questions that pertain to the understanding of the whole. In Luke's Gospel, the four Beatitudes that he presents are followed by four proclamations of woe: "Woe to you who are rich. . . . Woe to you who are full now. . . . Woe to you who laugh now. . . . Woe to you when all men praise you" (Lk 6:24–26). These words terrify us. What are we to think of them?

Now, the first thing to say is that Jesus is here following the pattern that is also found in Jeremiah 17 and Psalm 1: After an account of the right path that leads man to salvation, there follows a warning sign to caution against the opposite path. This warning sign unmasks false promises and false offers; it is meant to save man from following a path that can only lead him fatally over the precipice. We will find the same thing again in the parable of the rich man and Lazarus.

If we have correctly understood the signposts of hope that we found in the Beatitudes, we recognize that here we are dealing simply with the opposite attitudes, which lock man into mere outward appearance, into provisionality, into the loss of his highest and deepest qualities and hence into the loss of God and neighbor—the path to ruin. Now we come to understand the real intention of this warning sign: The proclamations of woe are not condemnations; they are not an expression of hatred, or of envy, or of hostility. The point is not condemnation, but a warning that is intended to save.

But now the fundamental question arises: Is the direction the Lord shows us in the Beatitudes and in the corresponding warnings actually the right one? Is it really such a bad thing to be rich, to eat one's fill, to laugh, to be praised? Friedrich Nietzsche trained his angry critique precisely on this aspect of Christianity. It is not Christian doctrine that needs to be critiqued, he says, it is Christian morality that needs to be exposed as a "capital crime against life." And by "Christian morality," Nietzsche means precisely the direction indicated by the Sermon on the Mount.

"What has been the greatest sin on earth so far? Surely the words of the man who said 'Woe to those who laugh now'?" And, against Christ's promises, he says that we don't want the Kingdom of heaven. "We've become grown men, and so we want the kingdom of earth."

Nietzsche sees the vision of the Sermon on the Mount as a religion of resentment, as the envy of the cowardly and incompetent, who are unequal to life's demands and try to avenge themselves by blessing their failure and cursing the strong, the successful, and the happy. Jesus' wide perspective is countered with a narrow this-worldliness—with the will to get the most out of the world and what life has to offer now, to seek heaven here, and to be uninhibited by any scruples while doing so.

Much of this has found its way into the modern mindset and to a large extent shapes how our contemporaries feel about life. Thus, the Sermon on the Mount poses the question of the fundamental Christian option, and, as children of our time, we feel an inner resistance to it—even though we are still touched by Jesus' praise of the meek, the merciful, the peacemakers, the pure. Knowing now from experience how brutally totalitarian regimes have trampled upon human beings and despised, enslaved, and struck down the weak, we have also gained a new appreciation of those who hunger and thirst for righteousness; we have rediscovered the soul of those who mourn and their right to be comforted. As we witness the abuse of economic power, as we witness the cruelties of a capitalism that degrades man to the level of merchandise, we have also realized the perils of wealth, and we have gained a new appreciation of what Jesus meant when he warned of riches, of the man-destroying divinity Mammon, which grips large parts of the world in a cruel stranglehold. Yes indeed, the Beatitudes stand opposed to our spontaneous sense of existence, our hunger and thirst for life. They demand "conversion"—that we inwardly turn around to go in the opposite direction from the one we would spontaneously like to go in. But this U-turn brings what is pure and noble to the fore and gives a proper ordering to our lives.

The Greek world, whose zest for life is wonderfully portrayed in the Homeric epics, was nonetheless deeply aware that man's real sin, his deepest temptation, is hubris—the arrogant presumption of autonomy that leads man to put on the airs of divinity, to claim to be his own god, in order to possess life totally and to draw from it every last drop of what it has to offer. This awareness that man's true peril consists in the temptation to ostentatious self-sufficiency, which at first seems so plausible, is brought to its full depth in the Sermon on the Mount in light of the figure of Christ.

We have seen that the Sermon on the Mount is a hidden Christology. Behind the Sermon on the Mount stands the figure of Christ, the man who is God, but who, precisely because he is God, descends, empties himself, all the way to death on the Cross. The saints, from Paul through Francis of Assisi down to Mother Teresa, have lived out this option and have thereby shown us the correct image of man and his happiness. In a word, the true morality of Christianity is love. And love does admittedly run counter to self-seeking—it is an exodus out of oneself, and yet this is precisely the way in which man comes to himself. Compared with the tempting luster of Nietzsche's image of man, this way seems at first wretched, and thoroughly unreasonable. But it is the real high road of life; it is only on the way of love, whose paths are described in the Sermon on the Mount, that the richness of life and the greatness of man's calling are opened up.

The Torah of the Messiah

"You Have Heard That It Was Said . . . But I Say to You . . ."

The Messiah was expected to bring a renewed Torah—*his* Torah. Paul may be alluding to this in the Letter to the Galatians when he speaks of the "law of Christ" (Gal 6:2). His great, passionate defense of freedom from the Law culminates in the following statement in chapter 5: "For freedom Christ has set us free; stand fast therefore, and do not submit again to a yoke of slavery" (Gal 5:1). But when he goes on to repeat at 5:13 the claim that "you were called to freedom," he adds, "Only do not use your freedom as an opportunity for the flesh, but through love be servants of one another" (Gal 5:13). And now he explains what freedom is—namely, freedom in the service of good, freedom that allows itself to be led by the Spirit of God. It is precisely by letting oneself be led by God's Spirit, moreover, that one becomes free from the Law. Immediately after this Paul details what the freedom of the Spirit actually consists in and what is incompatible with it.

The "law of Christ" is freedom—that is the paradox of Paul's message in the Letter to the Galatians. This freedom has content, then, it has direction, and it therefore contradicts what only apparently liberates man, but in truth makes him a slave. The "Torah of the Messiah" is totally new and different—but it is precisely by being such that it fulfills the Torah of Moses.

The greater part of the Sermon on the Mount (cf. Mt 5: 17–7:27) is devoted to the same topic: After a programmatic introduction in the form of the Beatitudes, it goes on to present, so to speak, the Torah of the Messiah. Even in terms of the addressees and the actual intentions of the text, there is an analogy with the Letter to the Galatians: Paul writes there to Gentile Christians who had begun to wonder whether continued observance of the whole Torah as hitherto understood by Jewish Christians may in fact be necessary after all.

This uncertainty affected above all circumcision, the commandments concerning food, the whole area of prescriptions relating to purity, and how to keep the Sabbath. Paul sees these ideas as a return to the status quo before the messianic revolution, a relapse in which the essential content of this revolution is lost—namely, the universalization of the People of God, as a result of which Israel can now embrace all the peoples of the world; the God of Israel has truly been brought to the nations, in accordance with the promises, and has now shown that he is the God of them all, the one God.

The flesh—physical descent from Abraham—is no longer what matters; rather, it is the spirit: belonging to the heritage of Israel's faith and life through communion with Jesus Christ, who "spiritualizes" the Law and in so doing makes it the path to life for all. In the Sermon on the Mount Jesus speaks to his people, to Israel, as to the first bearer of the promise. But in giving them the new Torah, he opens them up, in order to bring to birth a great new family of God drawn from Israel and the Gentiles.

Matthew wrote his Gospel for Jewish Christians and, more widely, for the Jewish world, in order to renew this great impulse that Jesus had initiated. Through his Gospel, Jesus speaks to Israel in a new and ongoing manner. In the historical setting in which Matthew writes, he speaks in a very particular way to Jewish Christians, who thereby recognize both the novelty and the continuity of the history of God's dealings with mankind, beginning with Abraham and undergoing a revolution with Jesus. In this way they are to find the path of life.

But what does this Torah of the Messiah actually look like? At the very beginning there stands, as a sort of epigraph and interpretive key, a statement that never ceases to surprise us. It makes God's fidelity to himself and Jesus' fidelity to the faith of Israel unmistakably clear: "Think not that I have come to abolish the Law and the Prophets; I have come not to abolish them but to fulfill them. For truly, I say to you, till heaven and earth pass away, not an iota, not a dot, will pass from the Law until all is accomplished. Whoever then relaxes one of the least of these commandments and teaches men so, shall be called least in the kingdom of heaven; but he who does them and teaches them shall be called great in the kingdom of heaven" (Mt 5:17–19).

The intention is not to abolish, but to fulfill, and this fulfillment demands a surplus, not a deficit, of righteousness, as Jesus immediately goes on to say: "Unless your righteousness exceeds that of the scribes and Pharisees, you will never enter the kingdom of heaven" (Mt 5:20). Is the point, then, merely increased rigor in obeying the Law? What else is this greater righteousness if not that?

True, at the beginning of this "*relecture*"—this new reading of essential portions of the Torah—there is an emphasis on extreme fidelity and unbroken continuity. Yet as we listen further, we are struck by Jesus' presentation of the relationship of Moses' Torah to the Torah of the Messiah in a series of antitheses: "It was said to them of old . . . but I say to you . . ." Jesus' "I" is accorded a status that no teacher of the Law can legitimately allow himself. The crowd feels this—Matthew tells us explicitly that the people "were alarmed" at his way of teaching. He teaches not as the rabbis do, but as one who has "authority" (Mt 7:28; cf. Mk 1:22; Lk 4:32). Obviously this does not refer to the rhetorical quality of Jesus' discourses, but rather to the open claim that he himself is on the same exalted level as the Lawgiver—as God. The people's "alarm" (the RSV translation unfortunately tones this down to "astonishment") is precisely over the fact that a human being dares to speak with the authority of God. Either he is misappropriating God's majesty—which would be terrible—or else, and this seems almost inconceivable, he really does stand on the same exalted level as God.

How, then, are we to understand this Torah of the Messiah? Which path does it point toward? What does it tell us about Jesus, about Israel, about the Church? What does it say about us, and to us? In my search for answers, I have been greatly helped by the book I mentioned earlier by the Jewish scholar Jacob Neusner: *A Rabbi Talks with Jesus.*

Neusner, a believing Jew and rabbi, grew up with Catholic and Protestant friends, teaches with Christian theologians at the university, and is deeply respectful of the faith of his Christian colleagues. He remains, however, profoundly convinced of the validity of the Jewish interpretation of Holy Scripture. His reverence for the Christian faith and his fidelity to Judaism prompted him to seek a dialogue with Jesus.

In this book, he takes his place among the crowds of Jesus' disciples on the "mount" in Galilee. He listens to Jesus and compares his words with those of the Old Testament and with the rabbinic traditions as set down in the Mishnah and Talmud. He sees in these works an oral tradition going back to the beginnings, which gives him the key to interpreting the Torah. He listens, he compares, and he speaks with Jesus himself. He is touched by the greatness and the purity of what is said, and yet at the same time he is troubled by the ultimate incompatibility that he finds at the heart of the Sermon on the Mount. He then accompanies Jesus on his journey to Jerusalem and listens as Jesus' words return to the same ideas and develop them further. He constantly tries to understand; he is constantly moved by the greatness of Jesus; again and again he talks with him. But in the end he decides not to follow Jesus. He remains—as he himself puts it—with the "eternal Israel."

The rabbi's dialogue with Jesus shows that faith in the word of God in the Holy Scriptures creates a contemporaneous bond across the ages: Setting out from Scripture, the rabbi can enter into the "today" of Jesus, just as Jesus, setting out from Scripture, can enter into our "today." This dialogue is conducted with great honesty. It highlights the differences in all their sharpness, but it also takes place in great love. The rabbi accepts the otherness of Jesus' message, and takes his leave free of any rancor; this parting, accomplished in the rigor of truth, is ever mindful of the reconciling power of love.

Let us try to draw out the essential points of this conversation in order to know Jesus and to understand our Jewish brothers better. The central point, it seems to me, is wonderfully revealed in one of the most moving scenes that Neusner presents in his book. In his interior dialogue Neusner has just spent the whole day following Jesus, and now he retires for prayer and Torah study with the Jews of a certain town, in order to discuss with the rabbi of that place—once again he is thinking in terms of contemporaneity across the millennia—all that he has heard. The rabbi cites from the Babylonian Talmud: "Rabbi Simelai expounded: 'Six hundred and thirteen commandments were given to Moses, three hundred and sixty-five negative ones, corresponding to the number of the days of the solar year, and two hundred forty-eight positive commandments, corresponding to the parts of man's body.

"'David came and reduced them to eleven. . . .

"'Isaiah came and reduced them to six. . . .

"'Isaiah again came and reduced them to two. . . .

"'Habakkuk further came and based them on one, as it is said: "But the righteous shall live by his faith"' (Hab 2:4)."

Neusner then continues his book with the following dialogue: "'So,' the master says, 'is this what the sage, Jesus, had to say?'

"I: 'Not exactly, but close.'

"He: 'What did he leave out?'

"I: 'Nothing.'

"He: 'Then what did he add?'

"I: 'Himself'" (pp. 107–8). This is the central point where the believing Jew Neusner experiences alarm at Jesus' message, and this is the central reason why he does not wish to follow Jesus, but remains with the "eternal Israel": the centrality of Jesus' "I" in his message, which gives everything a new direction. At this point Neusner cites as evidence of this "addition" Jesus' words to the rich young man: "If you would be perfect, go, sell all you have and come, follow *me*" (cf. Mt 19:21; Neusner, p. 109 [emphasis added]). Perfection, the state of being holy as God is holy (cf. Lev 19:2, 11:44), as demanded by the Torah, now consists in following Jesus.

It is only with great respect and reverence that Neusner addresses this mysterious identification of Jesus and God that is found in the discourses of the Sermon on the Mount. Nonetheless, his analysis shows that this is the point where Jesus' message diverges fundamentally from the faith of the "eternal Israel." Neusner demonstrates this after investigating Jesus' attitude toward three fundamental commandments: the fourth commandment (the commandment to love one's parents), the third commandment (to keep holy the Sabbath), and, finally, the commandment to be holy as God is holy (which we touched upon just a moment ago). Neusner comes to the disturbing conclusion that Jesus is evidently trying to persuade him to cease following these three fundamental commandments of God and to adhere to Jesus instead.

The Dispute Concerning the Sabbath

Let us follow Rabbi Neusner's dialogue with Jesus, beginning with the Sabbath. For Israel, observing the Sabbath with scrupulous care is the central expression of life in Covenant with God. Even the superficial reader of the Gospels realizes that the dispute over what does and does not belong to the Sabbath is at the heart of Jesus' differences with the people of Israel of his time. The conventional interpretation is that Jesus broke open a narrow-minded, legalistic practice and replaced it with a more generous, more liberal view, and thereby opened the door for acting rationally in accord with the given situation. Jesus' statement that "the sabbath was made for man, not man for the sabbath" (Mk 2:27) is cited as evidence, the idea being that it represents an anthropocentric view of reality, from which a "liberal" interpretation of the commandments supposedly follows naturally. It was, in fact, the Sabbath disputes that became the basis for the image of the liberal Jesus. His critique of the Judaism of his time, so it is said, was a freedom-loving and rational man's critique of an ossified legalism—hypocritical to the core and guilty of dragging religion down to the level of a slavish system of utterly unreasonable obligations that hold man back from developing his work and his freedom. It goes without saying that this interpretation did not favor a particularly friendly image of Judaism. Of course, the modern critique—beginning with the Reformation—saw in Catholicism the return of this supposedly "Jewish" element.

At any rate, the question about Jesus—who he really was, and what he really wanted—as well as the whole question as to what Judaism and Christianity actually are: This is the point at issue. Was Jesus in reality a liberal rabbi—a forerunner of Christian liberalism? Is the Christ of faith, and therefore the whole faith of the Church, just one big mistake?

Neusner is surprisingly quick to brush this sort of interpretation aside—as well he might, because he lays bare the real bone of contention so convincingly. Commenting on the dispute over the disciples' right to pluck the ears of wheat, he simply writes: "What troubles me, therefore, is not that the disciples do not obey one of the rules of the Sabbath. That is trivial and beside the point" (p. 83). To be sure, when we read the dispute over the healings on the Sabbath and the accounts of Jesus' angry grief at the hard-heartedness of those who spoke for the dominant interpretation of the Sabbath, we see that these debates concern deeper questions about man and about the right way to honor God. This side of the conflict is therefore by no means simply "trivial." Neusner is nonetheless right to identify Jesus' answer in the dispute over the ears of wheat as the place where the heart of the conflict is laid bare.

Jesus begins his defense of the disciples' way of satisfying their hunger by pointing out that David and his companions entered the House of God and ate the holy bread, "which it was not lawful for him to eat nor for those who were with him, but only for the priests" (Mt 12:4). Jesus then continues: "Or have you not read in the law how on the sabbath the priests in the temple profane the sabbath, and are guiltless? I tell you, something greater than the temple is here. And if you had known what this means, 'I desire mercy, and not sacrifice' (cf. Hos 6:6; 1 Sam 15:22), you would not have condemned the guiltless. For the Son of man is lord of the sabbath" (Mt 12:5–8). Neusner comments: "He [Jesus] and his disciples may do on the Sabbath what they do because they stand in the place of the priests in the Temple; the holy place has shifted, now being formed by the circle made up of the master and his disciples" (pp. 83f.).

At this point we need to pause for a moment in order to see what the Sabbath meant for Israel. This will also help us to understand what is at stake in this dispute. God rested on the seventh day, as the creation account in Genesis tells us. Neusner rightly concludes that "on that day we . . . celebrate creation" (p. 74). He then adds: "Not working on the Sabbath stands for more than nitpicking ritual. It is a way of imitating God" (p. 75). The Sabbath is therefore not just a negative matter of not engaging in outward activities, but a positive matter of "resting," which must also be expressed in a spatial dimension: "So to keep the Sabbath, one remains at home. It is not enough merely not to work. One also has to rest. And resting means, re-forming one day a week the circle of family and household, everyone at home and in place" (p. 80). The Sabbath is not just a matter of personal piety; it is the core of the social order. This day "makes eternal Israel what it is, the people that, like God in creating the world, rest from creation on the Seventh Day" (p. 74).

We could easily stop here to consider how salutary it would also be for our society today if families set aside one day a week to stay together and make their home the dwelling place and the fulfillment of communion in God's rest. But let us forgo such reflections here and remain with the dialogue between Jesus and Israel, which is also inevitably a dialogue between Jesus and us and between us and the Jewish people of today.

For Neusner, the key word *rest,* understood as an integral element of the Sabbath, is the connecting link to Jesus' exclamation immediately prior to the story of the disciples plucking the ears of wheat in Matthew's Gospel. It is the so-called Messianic *Jubelruf* (joyful shout), which begins as follows: "I thank thee, Father, Lord of heaven and earth, that thou hast hidden these things from the wise and understanding and revealed them to babes" (Mt 11:25–30). We are accustomed to considering these as two totally distinct texts. The first one speaks of Jesus' divinity, the other of the dispute surrounding the Sabbath. When we read Neusner, we realize that the two texts are closely related, for in both cases the issue is the mystery of Jesus—the "Son of Man," the "Son" par excellence.

The verses immediately preceding the Sabbath narrative read as follows: "Come to me, all who labor and are heavy laden, and I will give you rest. Take my yoke upon you, and learn from me; for I am gentle and lowly in heart, and you will find rest for your souls. For my yoke is easy, and my burden is light" (Mt 11:28–30). This is usually interpreted in terms of the idea of the liberal Jesus, that is, moralistically. Jesus' liberal understanding of the Law makes for a less burdensome life than "Jewish legalism." This interpretation is not very convincing in practice, though, for following Christ is not comfortable—and Jesus never said it would be, either.

What follows from this? Neusner shows us that we are dealing not with some kind of moralism, but with a highly theological text, or, to put it more precisely, a Christological one. Because it features the motif of rest, and the connected motifs of labor and burden, it belongs thematically with the question of the Sabbath. The rest that is intended here has to do with Jesus. Jesus' teaching about the Sabbath now appears fully in harmony with his *Jubelruf* and his words about the Son of Man being Lord of the Sabbath. Neusner sums up the overall content as follows: "My yoke is easy, I give you rest, the son of man is lord of the Sabbath indeed, because the son of man is now Israel's Sabbath: how we act like God" (p. 86).

Neusner can now say even more clearly than before: "No wonder, then, that the son of man is lord of the Sabbath! The reason is not that he interprets the Sabbath restrictions in a liberal manner. . . . Jesus was not just another reforming rabbi, out to make life 'easier' for people. . . . No, the issue is not that the burden is light . . . . Jesus' claim to authority is at issue" (p. 85). "Christ now stands on the mountain, he now takes the place of the Torah" (p. 87). The conversation between the practicing Jew and Jesus comes to the decisive point here. His noble reserve leads him to put the question to Jesus' disciple, rather than to Jesus himself: "Is it really so that your master, the son of man, is lord of the Sabbath? . . . I ask again—is your master God?" (p. 88).

The issue that is really at the heart of the debate is thus finally laid bare. Jesus understands himself as the Torah—as the word of God in person. The tremendous prologue of John's Gospel—"in the beginning was the Word, and the Word was with God, and the Word was God" (Jn 1:1)—says nothing different from what the Jesus of the Sermon on the Mount and the Jesus of the Synoptic Gospels says. The Jesus of the Fourth Gospel and the Jesus of the Synoptics is one and the same: the true "historical" Jesus.

The heart of the Sabbath disputes is the question about the Son of Man—the question about Jesus Christ himself. Yet again we see how far Harnack and the liberal exegesis that followed him went wrong in thinking that the Son, Christ, is not really part of the Gospel about Jesus. The truth is that he is always at the center of it.

Now, though, we need to consider a further aspect of the question that arises more sharply in connection with the fourth commandment. What disturbs Rabbi Neusner about Jesus' message concerning the Sabbath is not just the centrality of Jesus himself. He throws this centrality into clear relief, but it is not the ultimate bone of contention for him. Rather, he is concerned with the consequence of Jesus' centrality for Israel's daily life: The Sabbath loses its great social function. The Sabbath is one of the essential elements that hold Israel together. Centering upon Jesus breaks open this sacred structure and imperils an essential element that cements the unity of the People of God.

Jesus' claim entails that the community of his disciples is the new Israel. How can this not unsettle someone who has the "eternal Israel" at heart? The issue of Jesus' claim to be Temple and Torah in person also has implications for the question of Israel—the issue of the living community of the people in whom God's word is actualized. Neusner devotes a fairly large portion of his book to underscoring just this second aspect, as we shall see in what follows.

At this point, the question arises for the Christian: Was it a good idea to jeopardize the great social function of the Sabbath, to break up Israel's sacred order for the sake of a community of disciples that is defined, as it were, solely in terms of the figure of Jesus? This question could and can be clarified only within the emerging community of disciples—the Church. We cannot enter into this discussion here. The Resurrection of Jesus "on the first day of the week" meant that for Christians this "first day"—the beginning of the creation—became the "Lord's day." The essential elements of the Old Testament Sabbath then naturally passed over to the Lord's day in the context of table fellowship with Jesus.

The Church thus recuperated the social function of the Sabbath as well, always in relation to the "Son of Man." An unmistakable signal of this was the fact that Constantine's Christian-inspired reform of the legal system granted slaves certain freedoms on Sundays; the Lord's day was thus introduced as a day of freedom and rest into a legal system now shaped on Christian principles. I find it extremely worrying that modern liturgists want to dismiss this social function of Sunday as a Constantinian aberration, despite the fact that it stands in continuity with the Torah of Israel. Of course, this brings up the whole question of the relationship between faith and social order, between faith and politics. We will need to focus on this point in the next section.

The Fourth Commandment: The Family, the People, and the Community of Jesus' Disciples

"Honor your father and your mother, that your days may be long in the land which the LORD your God gives you"

(Ex 20:12)—this is the version of the fourth commandment that is given in the Book of Exodus. The commandment is addressed to sons and it speaks of parents. It thus strengthens the relationship between generations and the community of the family as an order both willed and protected by God. It speaks of the land and of the stable continuance of life in the land. In other words, it connects the land, as the place for the people to live, with the basic order of the family. It binds the continued existence of people and land to the coexistence of the generations that is built up within the family structure.

Now, Rabbi Neusner rightly sees this commandment as anchoring the heart of the social order, the cohesion of the "eternal Israel"—this real, living, ever-present family of Abraham and Sarah, Isaac and Rebecca, Jacob, Leah, and Rachel (pp. 58, 70). According to Neusner, it is this family of Israel that is threatened by Jesus' message, and the foundations of Israel's social order are thrust aside by the primacy of his person. "We pray to the God we know, to begin with, through the testimony of our family, to the God of Abraham and Sarah, Isaac and Rebecca, Jacob and Leah and Rachel. So to explain who we are, eternal Israel, sages appeal to the metaphor of genealogy . . . . to the fleshly connection, the family, as the rationale for Israel's social existence" (p. 58).

But this is exactly the connection that Jesus calls into question. He is told that his mother and brothers are outside waiting to speak to him. His answer: "Who is my mother and who are my brothers?" And he stretches out his hand over his disciples and says: "Here are my mother and my brothers! For whoever does the will of my Father in heaven is my brother, and sister, and mother" (Mt 12:46–50).

Faced with this text, Neusner asks: "Does Jesus not teach me to violate one of the two great commandments . . . . that concern the social order?" (p. 59). The accusation here is a twofold one. The first problem is the seeming individualism of Jesus' message. While the Torah presents a very definite social order, giving the people a juridical and social framework for war and peace, for just politics and for daily life, there is nothing like that to be found in Jesus' teaching. Discipleship of Jesus offers no politically concrete program for structuring society. The Sermon on the Mount cannot serve as a foundation for a state and a social order, as is frequently and correctly observed. Its message seems to be located on another level. Israel's ordinances have guaranteed its continued existence through the millennia and through all the vicissitudes of history, yet here they are set aside. Jesus' new interpretation of the fourth commandment affects not only the parent-child relation, but the entire scope of the social structure of the people of Israel.

This restructuring of the social order finds its basis and its justification in Jesus' claim that he, with his community of disciples, forms the origin and center of a new Israel. Once again we stand before the "I" of Jesus, who speaks on the same level as the Torah itself, on the same level as God. The two spheres—on one hand the modification of the social structure, the opening up of the "eternal Israel" into a new community, and on the other hand Jesus' divine claim—are directly connected.

It should be pointed out that Neusner does not try to score any easy victories by critiquing a straw man. He reminds his reader that students of the Torah were also called by their teachers to leave home and family and had to turn their backs on wife and children for long periods in order to devote themselves totally to the study of the Torah (p. 60). "The Torah then takes the place of genealogy, and the master of Torah gains a new lineage" (p. 63). In this sense, it seems that Jesus' claim to be founding a new family does remain after all in the framework of what the school of the Torah—the "eternal Israel"—allows.

And yet there is a fundamental difference. In Jesus' case it is not the universally binding adherence to the Torah that forms the new family. Rather, it is adherence to Jesus himself, to his Torah. For the rabbis, everyone is tied by the same relationships to a permanent social order; everyone is subject to the Torah and so everyone is equal within the larger body of all Israel. Neusner thus concludes: "I now realize, only God can demand of me what Jesus is asking" (p. 68).

We come to the same conclusion as in our earlier analysis of the commandment to keep the Sabbath. The Christological (theological) argument and the social argument are inextricably entwined. If Jesus is God, then he is entitled and able to handle the Torah as he does. On that condition alone does he have the right to interpret the Mosaic order of divine commands in such a radically new way as only the Lawgiver—God himself—can claim to do.

But here the question arises: Was it right and proper to create a new community of disciples founded entirely on him? Was it good to set aside the social order of the "eternal Israel," founded on and subsisting through Abraham and Jacob according to the flesh? To declare it to be an "Israel according to the flesh," as Paul will put it? Is there any point that we can discover to all of this?

Now, when we read the Torah together with the entire Old Testament canon, the Prophets, the Psalms, and the Wisdom Literature, we realize very clearly a point that is already substantially present in the Torah itself. That is, Israel does not exist simply for itself, in order to live according to the "eternal" dispositions of the Law—it exists to be a light to the nations. In the Psalms and the prophetic books we hear more and more clearly the promise that God's salvation will come to all the nations. We hear more and more clearly that the God of Israel—being, as he is, the only God, the true God, the Creator of heaven and earth, the God of all peoples and all men, who holds their fate in his hands—does not wish to abandon the nations to themselves. We hear that all will come to know him, that Egypt and Babylon—the two secular powers opposed to Israel—will give Israel their hand and join together in worshiping the one God. We hear that the boundaries will fall and that the God of Israel will be acknowledged and revered by all the nations as their God, as the one God.

It is our Jewish interlocutors who, quite rightly, ask again and again: So what has your "Messiah" Jesus actually brought? He has not brought world peace, and he has not conquered the world's misery. So he can hardly be the true Messiah, who, after all, is supposed to do just that. Yes, what has Jesus brought? We have already encountered this question and we know the answer. He has brought the God of Israel to the nations, so that all the nations now pray to him and recognize Israel's Scriptures as his word, the word of the living God. He has brought the gift of universality, which was the one great definitive promise to Israel and the world. This universality, this faith in the one God of Abraham, Isaac, and

Jacob—extended now in Jesus' new family to all nations over and above the bonds of descent according to the flesh—is the fruit of Jesus' work. It is what proves him to be the Messiah. It signals a new interpretation of the messianic promise that is based on Moses and the Prophets, but also opens them up in a completely new way.

The vehicle of this universalization is the new family, whose only admission requirement is communion with Jesus, communion in God's will. For Jesus' "I" is by no means a self-willed ego revolving around itself alone. "Whoever does the will of my Father in heaven is my brother, and sister, and mother" (Mk 3:34f.): Jesus' "I" incarnates the Son's communion of will with the Father. It is an "I" that hears and obeys. Communion with him is filial communion with the Father—it is a yes to the fourth commandment on a new level, the highest level. It is entry into the family of those who call God Father and who can do so because they belong to a "we"—formed of those who are united with Jesus and, by listening to him, united with the will of the Father, thereby attaining to the heart of the obedience intended by the Torah.

This unity with the will of God the Father through communion with Jesus, whose "food" is to do the Father's will (cf. Jn 4:34), now gives us a new perspective on the individual regulations of the Torah as well. The Torah did indeed have the task of giving a concrete juridical and social order to this particular people, Israel. But while Israel is on one hand a definite nation, whose members are bound together by birth and the succession of generations, on the other hand it has been from the beginning and is by its very nature the bearer of a universal promise. In Jesus' new family, which will later be called "the Church," these individual juridical and social regulations no longer apply universally in their literal historical form. This was precisely the issue at the beginning of the "Church of the Gentiles," and it was the bone of contention between Paul and the so-called Judaizers. A literal application of Israel's social order to the people of all nations would have been tantamount to a denial of the universality of the growing community of God. Paul saw this with perfect clarity. The Torah of the Messiah could not be like that. Nor is it, as the Sermon on the Mount shows—and likewise the whole dialogue with Rabbi Neusner, a believing Jew and a truly attentive listener.

That said, what is happening here is an extremely important process whose full scope was not grasped until modern times, even though the moderns at first understood it in a one-sided and false way. Concrete juridical and social forms and political arrangements are no longer treated as a sacred law that is fixed *ad litteram* for all times and so for all peoples. The decisive thing is the underlying communion of will with God given by Jesus. It frees men and nations to discover what aspects of political and social order accord with this communion of will and so to work out their own juridical arrangements. The absence of the whole social dimension in Jesus' preaching, which Neusner discerningly critiques from a Jewish perspective, includes, but also conceals, an epoch-making event in world history that has not occurred as such in any other culture: The concrete political and social order is released from the directly sacred realm, from theocratic legislation, and is transferred to the freedom of man, whom Jesus has established in God's will and taught thereby to see the right and the good.

This brings us back to the Torah of the Messiah, to the Letter to the Galatians. "You were called to freedom" (Gal 5: 13)—not to a blind and arbitrary freedom, to a freedom "understood according to the flesh," as Paul would say, but to a "seeing" freedom, anchored in communion of will with Jesus and so with God himself. It is a freedom that, as a result of this new way of seeing, is able to build the very thing that is at the heart of the Torah—with Jesus, universalizing the essential content of the Torah and thus truly "fulfilling" it.

In our day, of course, this freedom has been totally wrenched away from any godly perspective or from communion with Jesus. Freedom for universality and so for the legitimate secularity of the state has been transformed into an absolute secularism, for which forgetfulness of God and exclusive concern with success seem to have become guiding principles. For the believing Christian, the commandments of the Torah remain a decisive point of reference, that he constantly keeps in view; for him the search for God's will in communion with Jesus is above all a signpost for his reason, without which it is always in danger of being dazzled and blinded.

There is another essential observation. This universalization of Israel's faith and hope, and the concomitant liberation from the letter of the Law for the new communion with Jesus, is tied to Jesus' authority and his claim to Sonship. It loses its historical weight and its whole foundation if Jesus is interpreted merely as a liberal reform rabbi. A liberal interpretation of the Torah would be nothing but the personal opinion of one teacher—it would have no power to shape history. It would also relativize both the Torah itself and its origin in God's will. For each statement there would be only human authority: the authority of one scholar. There can be no new faith community built upon that. The leap into universality, the new freedom that such a leap requires, is possible only on the basis of a greater obedience. Its power to shape history can come into play only if the authority of the new interpretation is no less than the authority of the original: It must be a divine authority. The new universal family is the purpose of Jesus' mission, but his divine authority—his Sonship in communion with the Father—is the prior condition that makes possible the irruption of a new and broader reality without betrayal or high-handedness.

We have heard that Neusner asks Jesus whether he is trying to tempt him into violating two or three of God's commandments. If Jesus does not speak with the full authority of the Son, if his interpretation is not the beginning of a new communion in a new, free obedience, then there is only one alternative: Jesus is enticing us to disobedience against God's commandment.

It is fundamentally important for the Christian world in every age to pay careful attention to the connection between transcendence and fulfillment. We have seen that Neusner, despite his reverence for Jesus, strongly criticizes the dissolution of the family that for him is implied by Jesus' invitation to "transgress" the fourth commandment. He mounts a similar critique against Jesus' threat to the Sabbath, which is a cardinal point of Israel's social order. Now, Jesus' intention is not to abolish either the family or the Sabbath-as-celebration-of-creation, but he has to create a new and broader context for both. It is true that his invitation to join him as a member of a new and universal family through sharing his obedience to the Father does at first break up the social order of Israel. But from her very inception, the Church that emerged, and continues to emerge, has attached fundamental importance to defending the family as the core of all social order, and to standing up for the fourth commandment in the whole breadth of its meaning. We see how hard the Church fights to protect these things today. Likewise it soon became clear that the essential content of the Sabbath had to be reinterpreted in terms of the Lord's day. The fight for Sunday is another of the Church's major concerns in the present day, when there is so much to upset the rhythm of time that sustains community.

The proper interplay of Old and New Testaments was and is constitutive for the Church. In his discourses after the Resurrection, Jesus insists that he can be understood only in the context of "the Law and the Prophets" and that his community can live only in this properly understood context. From the beginning, the Church has been, and always will be, exposed to two opposite dangers on this score: on one hand a false legalism of the sort Paul fought against, which throughout history has unfortunately been given the unhappy name of "Judaizing," and on the other hand a repudiation of Moses and the Prophets—of the Old Testament. This was first proposed by Marcion in the second century, and it is one of the great temptations of modernity. It is no accident that Harnack, leading exponent of liberal theology that he was, insisted that it was high time to fulfill the inheritance of Marcion and free Christianity from the burden of the Old Testament once and for all. Today's widespread temptation to give the New Testament a purely spiritual interpretation, in isolation from any social and political relevance, tends in the same direction.

Conversely, political theologies, of whatever sort, theologize one particular political formula in a way that contradicts the novelty and breadth of Jesus' message. It would, however, be false to characterize such tendencies as a "Judaizing" of Christianity, because Israel offers obedience to the concrete social ordinances of the Torah for the sake of the "eternal Israel's" ethnic community and does not hold up this obedience as a universal political recipe. All in all, it would be good for the Christian world to look respectfully at this obedience of Israel, and thus to appreciate better the great commandments of the Decalogue, which Christians have to transfer into the context of God's universal family and which Jesus, as the "new Moses," has given to us. In him we see the fulfillment of the promise made to Moses: "The LORD your God will raise up for you a prophet like me from among you, from your brethren" (Deut 18:15).

Compromise and Prophetic Radicalism

In following the dialogue of the Jewish rabbi with Jesus, adding our own thoughts and observations, we have already moved some distance beyond the Sermon on the Mount and have accompanied Jesus on his journey to Jerusalem. We must now go back once more to the antitheses of the Sermon on the Mount, where Jesus takes up questions associated with the second tablet of the Decalogue and brings a new radicalism to bear on the old commandments of the Torah in their understanding of justice before God. Not only are we not to kill, but we must offer reconciliation to our unreconciled brother. No more divorce. Not only are we to be even-handed in justice (eye for eye, tooth for tooth), but we must let ourselves be struck without striking back. We are to love not simply our neighbor, but also our enemy.

The lofty ethics that is expressed here will continue to astonish people of all backgrounds and to impress them as the height of moral greatness. We need only recall Mahatma Gandhi's interest in Jesus, which was based on these very texts. But is what Jesus says here actually realistic? Is it incumbent upon us—is it even legitimate—to act like this? Doesn't some of it, as Neusner objects, destroy all concrete social order? Is it possible to build up a community, a people, on such a basis?

Recent scholarly exegesis has gained important insights about this question through a precise investigation of the internal structure of the Torah and its legislation. Particularly important for our question is the analysis of the so-called Book of the Covenant (Ex 20:22–23:19). Two kinds of law [*Recht*] can be distinguished in this code: so-called casuistic law and apodictic law.

What is called casuistic law stipulates legal arrangements for very specific juridical issues: those pertaining to the ownership and emancipation of slaves, bodily injury by people or animals, recompense for theft, and so forth. No theological explanations are offered here, just specific sanctions that are proportionate to the wrong done. These juridical norms emerged from practice and they form a practically oriented legal corpus that serves to build up a realistic social order, corresponding to the concrete possibilities of a society in a particular historical and cultural situation.

In this respect, the body of law in question is also historically conditioned and entirely open to criticism, often—at least from our ethical perspective—actually in need of it. Even within the context of Old Testament legislation, it undergoes further development. Newer prescriptions contradict older ones regarding the same object. These casuistic provisions, while situated in the fundamental context of faith in the God of Revelation who spoke on Sinai, are nonetheless not directly divine law, but are developed from the underlying deposit of divine law, and are therefore subject to further development and correction.

And the fact of the matter is that social order has to be capable of development. It must address changing historical situations within the limits of the possible, but without ever losing sight of the ethical standard as such, which gives law its character as law. As Olivier Artus and others have shown, there is a sense in which the prophetic critique of Isaiah, Hosea, Amos, and Micah is also aimed at casuistic law that, although it is contained in the Torah, has in practice become a form of injustice. This happens when, in view of Israel's particular economic situation, the law no longer serves to protect the poor, widows, and orphans, though the Prophets would see such protection as the highest intention of the legislation given by God.

There are affinities to this critique of the Prophets, though, in parts of the book of the Covenant itself, the parts concerned with so-called apodictic law (Ex 22:20, 23:9–12). This apodictic law is pronounced in the name of God himself; there are no concrete sanctions indicated here. "You shall not wrong a stranger or oppress him, for you were strangers in the land of Egypt. You shall not afflict any widow or orphan" (Ex 22:21f.). It was these great norms that formed the basis of the Prophets' critique, serving as a constant touchstone for challenging concrete legal provisions, so that the essential divine nucleus of law could be vindicated as the standard and rule of every juridical development and every social order. F. Crüsemann, to whom we owe much of our essential knowledge on this subject, has termed the commandments of apodictic law "metanorms," which provide a platform for critiquing the rules of casuistic law. He explains the relationship between casuistic and apodictic law in terms of the distinction between "rules" and "principles."

Within the Torah itself, then, there are quite different levels of authority. As Artus puts it, the Torah contains an ongoing dialogue between historically conditioned norms and metanorms. The latter express the perennial requirements of the Covenant. Fundamentally, the metanorms reflect God's option to defend the poor, who are easily deprived of justice and cannot procure it for themselves.

This is connected with a further point. The fundamental norm in the Torah, on which everything depends, is insistence upon faith in the one God (YHWH): He alone may be worshiped. But now, as the Prophets develop the Torah, responsibility for the poor, widows, and orphans gradually ascends to the same level as the exclusive worship of the one God. It fuses with the image of God, defining it very specifically. The social commandments are theological commandments, and the theological commandments have a social character—love of God and love of neighbor are inseparable, and love of neighbor, understood in this context as recognition of God's immediate presence in the poor and the weak, receives a very practical definition here.

All of this is essential if we are to understand the Sermon on the Mount correctly. Within the Torah itself, and subsequently in the dialogue between the Law and the Prophets, we already see the contrast between changeable casuistic law, which shapes the social structure of a given time, and the essential principles of the divine law itself, in terms of which practical norms constantly have to be measured, developed, and corrected.

Jesus does nothing new or unprecedented when he contrasts the practical, casuistic norms developed in the Torah with the pure will of God, which he presents as the "greater righteousness" (Mt 5:20) expected of God's children. He takes up the intrinsic dynamism of the Torah itself, as further developed by the Prophets, and—in his capacity as the Chosen Prophet who sees God face-to-face (Deut 18:15)—he gives it its radical form. Obviously, then, these words do not formulate a social order, but they do provide social orderings with their fundamental criteria—even though these criteria can never be purely realized as such in any given social order. By giving actual juridical and social ordinances a new dynamism, by removing them from the immediate purview of the divine and transferring responsibility for them to enlightened reason, Jesus reflects the internal structure of the Torah itself.

In the antitheses of the Sermon on the Mount, Jesus stands before us neither as a rebel nor as a liberal, but as the prophetic interpreter of the Torah. He does not abolish it, but he fulfills it, and he does so precisely by assigning reason its sphere of responsibility for acting within history. Consequently, Christianity constantly has to reshape and reformulate social structures and "Christian social teaching." There will always be new developments to correct what has gone before. In the inner structure of the Torah, in its further development under the critique of the Prophets, and in Jesus' message, which takes up both elements, Christianity finds the wide scope for necessary historical evolution as well as the solid ground that guarantees the dignity of man by rooting it in the dignity of God.

CHAPTER FIVE

The Lord's Prayer

The Sermon on the Mount, as we have seen, draws a comprehensive portrait of the right way to live. It aims to show us how to be a human being. We could sum up its fundamental insights by saying that man can be understood only in light of God, and that his life is made righteous only when he lives it in relation to God. But God is not some distant stranger. He shows us his face in Jesus. In what Jesus does and wills, we come to know the mind and will of God himself.

If being human is essentially about relation to God, it is clear that speaking with, and listening to, God is an essential part of it. This is why the Sermon on the Mount also includes a teaching about prayer. The Lord tells us how we are to pray.

In Matthew's Gospel, the Lord's Prayer is preceded by a short catechesis on prayer. Its main purpose is to warn against false forms of prayer. Prayer must not be an occasion for showing off before others; it requires the discretion that is essential to a relation of love. God addresses every individual by a name that no one else knows, as Scripture tells us (cf. Rev 2:17). God's love for each individual is totally personal and includes this mystery of a uniqueness that cannot be divulged to other human beings.

This discretion, which is of the very essence of prayer, does not exclude prayer in common. The Our Father is itself a prayer uttered in the first person plural, and it is only by becoming part of the "we" of God's children that we can reach up to him beyond the limits of this world in the first place. And yet this "we" awakens the inmost core of the person; in the act of prayer the totally personal and the communal must always pervade each other, as we will see more closely in our exposition of the Our Father. Just as in the relationship between man and woman there is a totally personal dimension that requires a zone of discretion for its protection, though at the same time the relationship of the two in marriage and family by its very nature also includes public responsibility, so it is also in our relation to God: The "we" of the praying community and the utterly personal intimacy that can be shared only with God are closely interconnected.

The other false form of prayer the Lord warns us against is the chatter, the verbiage, that smothers the spirit. We are all familiar with the danger of reciting habitual formulas while our mind is somewhere else entirely. We are at our most attentive when we are driven by inmost need to ask God for something or are prompted by a joyful heart to thank him for good things that have happened to us. Most importantly, though, our relationship to God should not be confined to such momentary situations, but should be present as the bedrock of our soul. In order for that to happen, this relation has to be constantly revived and the affairs of our everyday lives have to be constantly related back to it. The more the depths of our souls are directed toward God, the better we will be able to pray. The more prayer is the foundation that upholds our entire existence, the more we will become men of peace. The more we can bear pain, the more we will be able to understand others and open ourselves to them. This orientation pervasively shaping our whole consciousness, this silent presence of God at the heart of our thinking, our meditating, and our being, is what we mean by "prayer without ceasing." This is ultimately what we mean by love of God, which is at the same time the condition and the driving force behind love of neighbor.

This is what prayer really is—being in silent inward communion with God. It requires nourishment, and that is why we need articulated prayer in words, images, or thoughts. The more God is present in us, the more we will really be able to be present to him when we utter the words of our prayers. But the converse is also true: Praying actualizes and deepens our communion of being with God. Our praying can and should arise above all from our heart, from our needs, our hopes, our joys, our sufferings, from our shame over sin, and from our gratitude for the good. It can and should be a wholly personal prayer. But we also constantly need to make use of those prayers that express in words the encounter with God experienced both by the Church as a whole and by individual members of the Church. For without these aids to prayer, our own praying and our image of God become subjective and end up reflecting ourselves more than the living God. In the formulaic prayers that arose first from the faith of Israel and then from the faith of praying members of the Church, we get to know God and ourselves as well. They are a "school of prayer" that transforms and opens up our life.

In his Rule, Saint Benedict coined the formula *Mens nostra concordet voci nostrae*—our mind must be in accord with our voice (Rule, 19, 7). Normally, thought precedes word; it seeks and formulates the word. But praying the Psalms and liturgical prayer in general is exactly the other way round: The word, the voice, goes ahead of us, and our mind must adapt to it. For on our own we human beings do not "know how to pray as we ought" (Rom 8:26)—we are too far removed from God, he is too mysterious and too great for us. And so God has come to our aid: He himself provides the words of our prayer and teaches us to pray. Through the prayers that come from him, he enables us to set out toward him; by praying together with the brothers and sisters he has given us, we gradually come to know him and draw closer to him.

In Saint Benedict's writings, the phrase cited just now refers directly to the Psalms, the great prayer book of the People of God of the Old and New Covenant. The Psalms are words that the Holy Spirit has given to men; they are God's Spirit become word. We thus pray "in the Spirit," with the Holy Spirit. This applies even more, of course, to the Our Father. When we pray the Our Father, we are praying to God with words given by God, as Saint Cyprian says. And he adds that when we pray the Our Father, Jesus' promise regarding the true worshipers, those who adore the Father "in spirit and in truth" (Jn 4:23), is fulfilled in us. Christ, who is the truth, has given us these words, and in them he gives us the Holy Spirit (*De dominica oratione* 2; *CSEL* III, 1, pp. 267f.). This also reveals something of the specificity of Christian mysticism. It is not in the first instance immersion in the depths of oneself, but encounter with the Spirit of God in the word that goes ahead of us. It is encounter with the Son and the Holy Spirit and thus a becoming-one with the living God who is always both in us and above us.

While Matthew introduces the Our Father with a short catechesis on prayer in general, we find it in a different context in Luke—namely, Jesus' journey to Jerusalem. Luke prefaces the Lord's Prayer with the following remark: Jesus "was praying in a certain place, and when he ceased, one of his disciples said to him, 'Lord, teach us to pray . . .'" (Lk 11:1).

The context, then, is that the disciples see Jesus praying and it awakens in them the wish to learn from him how to pray. This is typical for Luke, who assigns a very special place in his Gospel to Jesus' prayer. Jesus' entire ministry arises from his prayer, and is sustained by it. Essential events in the course of his journey, in which his mystery is gradually unveiled, appear in this light as prayer events. Peter's confession that Jesus is the Holy One of God is connected with encountering Jesus at prayer (cf. Lk 9:18ff.); the Transfiguration of Jesus is a prayer event (cf. Lk 9:28f.).

The fact that Luke places the Our Father in the context of Jesus' own praying is therefore significant. Jesus thereby involves us in his own prayer; he leads us into the interior dialogue of triune love; he draws our human hardships deep into God's heart, as it were. This also means, however, that the words of the Our Father are signposts to interior prayer, they provide a basic direction for our being, and they aim to configure us to the image of the Son. The meaning of the Our Father goes much further than the mere provision of a prayer text. It aims to form our being, to train us in the inner attitude of Jesus (cf. Phil 2:5).

This has two different implications for our interpretation of the Our Father. First of all, it is important to listen as accurately as possible to Jesus' words as transmitted to us in Scripture. We must strive to recognize the thoughts Jesus wished to pass on to us in these words. But we must also keep in mind that the Our Father originates from his own praying, from the Son's dialogue with the Father. This means that it reaches down into depths far beyond the words. It embraces the whole compass of man's being in all ages and can therefore never be fully fathomed by a purely historical exegesis, however important this may be.

The great men and women of prayer throughout the centuries were privileged to receive an interior union with the Lord that enabled them to descend into the depths beyond the word. They are therefore able to unlock for us the hidden treasures of prayer. And we may be sure that each of us, along with our totally personal relationship with God, is received into, and sheltered within, this prayer. Again and again, each one of us with his *mens,* his own spirit, must go out to meet, open himself to, and submit to the guidance of the *vox,* the word that comes to us from the Son. In this way his own heart will be opened, and each individual will learn the particular way in which the Lord wants to pray with him.

The Our Father has been transmitted to us in a shorter form in Luke, whereas it comes down to us in Matthew in the version that the Church has adopted for purposes of prayer. The discussion about which text is more original is not superfluous, but neither is it the main issue. In both versions we are praying with Jesus, and we are grateful that Matthew's version, with its seven petitions, explicitly unfolds things that Luke seems in part only to touch upon.

Before we enter into the detailed exposition, let us now very briefly look at the structure of the Our Father as Matthew transmits it. It comprises an initial salutation and seven petitions. Three are "thou-petitions," while four are "we-petitions." The first three petitions concern the cause of God himself in this world; the four following petitions concern our hopes, needs, and hardships. The relationship between the two kinds of petitions in the Our Father could be compared to the relationship between the two tablets of the Decalogue. Essentially they are explications of the two parts of the great commandment to love God and our neighbor—in other words, they are directions toward the path of love.

The Our Father, then, like the Ten Commandments, begins by establishing the primacy of God, which then leads naturally to a consideration of the right way of being human. Here, too, the primary concern is the path of love, which is at the same time a path of conversion. If man is to petition God in the right way, he must stand in the truth. And the truth is: first God, first his Kingdom (cf. Mt 6:33). The first thing we must do is step outside ourselves and open ourselves to God. Nothing can turn out right if our relation to God is not rightly ordered. For this reason, the Our Father begins with God and then, from that starting point, shows us the way toward being human. At the end we descend to the ultimate threat besetting man, for whom the Evil one lies in wait—we may recall the image of the apocalyptic dragon that wages war against those "who keep the commandments of God and bear testimony to Jesus" (Rev 12:17).

Yet the beginning remains present throughout: Our Father—we know that he is with us to hold us in his hand and save us. In his book of spiritual exercises, Father Peter-Hans Kolvenbach, the Superior General of the Jesuits, tells the story of a *staretz,* or spiritual advisor of the Eastern Church, who yearned "to begin the Our Father with the last verse, so that one might become worthy to finish the prayer with the initial words—'Our Father.'" In this way, the *staretz* explained, we would be following the path to Easter. "We begin in the desert with the temptation, we return to Egypt, then we travel the path of the Exodus, through the stations of forgiveness and God's manna, and by God's will we attain the promised land, the kingdom of God, where he communicates to us the mystery of his name: 'Our Father'" (*Der österliche Weg,* pp. 65f.).

Let both these ways, the way of ascent and the way of descent, be a reminder that the Our Father is always a prayer of Jesus and that communion with him is what opens it up for us. We pray to the Father in heaven, whom we know through his Son. And that means that Jesus is always in the background during the petitions, as we will see in the course of our detailed exposition of the prayer. A final point—because the Our Father is a prayer of Jesus, it is a Trinitarian prayer: We pray with Christ through the Holy Spirit to the Father.

Our Father Who Art in Heaven

We begin with the salutation "Father." Reinhold Schneider writes apropos of this in his exposition of the Our Father: "The Our Father begins with a great consolation: we are allowed to say 'Father.' This one word contains the whole history of redemption. We are allowed to say 'Father,' because the Son was our brother and has revealed the Father to us; because, thanks to what Christ has done, we have once more become children of God" (*Das Vaterunser*, p. 10). It is true, of course, that contemporary men and women have difficulty experiencing the great consolation of the word *father* immediately, since the experience of the father is in many cases either completely absent or is obscured by inadequate examples of fatherhood.

We must therefore let Jesus teach us what *father* really means. In Jesus' discourses, the Father appears as the source of all good, as the measure of the rectitude (perfection) of man. "But I say to you, love your enemies and pray for those who persecute you, so that you may be sons of your Father who is in heaven; for he makes his sun rise on the evil and on the good" (Mt 5:44–45). The love that endures "to the end" (Jn 13:1), which the Lord fulfilled on the Cross in praying for his enemies, shows us the essence of the Father. He is this love. Because Jesus brings it to completion, he is entirely "Son," and he invites us to become "sons" according to this criterion.

Let us consider a further text as well. The Lord reminds us that fathers do not give their children stones when they ask for bread. He then goes on to say: "If you then, who are evil, know how to give good gifts to your children, how much more will your Father who is in heaven give good things to those who ask him!" (Mt 7:9ff.). Luke specifies the "good gifts" that the Father gives; he says "how much more will the heavenly Father give the Holy Spirit to those who ask him!" (Lk 11:13). This means that the gift of God is God himself. The "good things" that he gives us are himself. This reveals in a surprising way what prayer is really all about: It is not about this or that, but about God's desire to offer us the gift of himself—that is the gift of all gifts, the "one thing necessary." Prayer is a way of gradually purifying and correcting our wishes and of slowly coming to realize what we really need: God and his Spirit.

When the Lord teaches us to recognize the essence of God the Father through love of enemies, and to find "perfection" in that love so as to become "sons" ourselves, the connection between Father and Son becomes fully evident. It then becomes plain that the figure of Jesus is the mirror in which we come to know who God is and what he is like: through the Son we find the Father. At the Last Supper, when Philip asks Jesus to "show us the Father," Jesus says, "He who sees me sees the Father" (Jn 14:8f.). "Lord, show us the Father," we say again and again to Jesus, and the answer again and again is the Son himself. Through him, and only through him, do we come to know the Father. And in this way the criterion of true fatherliness is made clear. The Our Father does not project a human image onto heaven, but shows us from heaven—from Jesus—what we as human beings can and should be like.

Now, however, we must look even more closely, because we need to realize that, according to Jesus' message, there are two sides of God's Fatherhood for us to see. First of all, God is our Father in the sense that he is our Creator. We belong to him because he has created us. "Being" as such comes from him and is consequently good; it derives from God. This is especially true of human beings. Psalm 33:15 says in the Latin translation, "He who has fashioned the hearts of all, considers all their works." The idea that God has created each individual human being is essential to the Bible's image of man. Every human being is unique, and willed as such by God. Every individual is known to him. In this sense, by virtue of creation itself man is the "child" of God in a special way, and God is his true Father. To describe man as God's image is another way of expressing this idea.

This brings us to the second dimension of God's Fatherhood. There is a unique sense in which Christ is the "image of God" (2 Cor 4:4; Col 1:15). The Fathers of the Church therefore say that when God created man "in his image," he looked toward the Christ who was to come, and created man according to the image of the "new Adam," the man who is the criterion of the human. Above all, though, Jesus is "the Son" in the strict sense—he is of one substance with the Father. He wants to draw all of us into his humanity and so into his Sonship, into his total belonging to God.

This gives the concept of being God's children a dynamic quality: We are not ready-made children of God from the start, but we are meant to become so increasingly by growing more and more deeply in communion with Jesus. Our sonship turns out to be identical with following Christ. To name God as Father thus becomes a summons to us: to live as a "child," as a son or daughter. "All that is mine is thine," Jesus says in his high-priestly prayer to the Father (Jn 17:10), and the father says the same thing to the elder brother of the Prodigal Son (Lk 15:31). The word *father* is an invitation to live from our awareness of this reality. Hence, too, the delusion of false emancipation, which marked the beginning of mankind's history of sin, is overcome. Adam, heeding the words of the serpent, wants to become God himself and to shed his need for God. We see that to be God's child is not a matter of dependency, but rather of standing in the relation of love that sustains man's existence and gives it meaning and grandeur.

One last question remains: Is God also mother? The Bible does compare God's love with the love of a mother: "As one whom his mother comforts, so I will comfort you" (Is 66:13). "Can a woman forget her suckling child, that she should have no compassion on the son of her womb? Even these may forget, yet I will not forget you" (Is 49:15). The mystery of God's maternal love is expressed with particular power in the Hebrew word *rahamim*. Etymologically, this word means "womb," but it was later used to mean divine compassion for man, God's mercy. The Old Testament constantly uses the names of organs of the human body to describe basic human attitudes or inner dispositions of God, just as today we use *heart* or *brain* when referring to some aspect of our own existence. In this way the Old Testament portrays the basic attitudes of our existence, not with abstract concepts, but in the image language of the body. The womb is the most concrete expression for the intimate interrelatedness of two lives and of loving concern for the dependent, helpless creature whose whole being, body and soul, nestles in the mother's womb. The image language of the body furnishes us, then, with a deeper understanding of God's dispositions toward man than any conceptual language could.

Although this use of language derived from man's bodiliness inscribes motherly love into the image of God, it is nonetheless also true that God is never named or addressed as mother, either in the Old or in the New Testament. "Mother" in the Bible is an image but not a title for God. Why not? We can only tentatively seek to understand. Of course, God is neither a man nor a woman, but simply God, the Creator of man and woman. The mother-deities that completely surrounded the people of Israel and the New Testament Church create a picture of the relation between God and the world that is completely opposed to the biblical image of God. These deities always, and probably inevitably, imply some form of pantheism in which the difference between Creator and creature disappears. Looked at in these terms, the being of things and of people cannot help looking like an emanation from the maternal womb of being, which, in entering time, takes shape in the multiplicity of existing things.

By contrast, the image of the Father was and is apt for expressing the otherness of Creator and creature and the sovereignty of his creative act. Only by excluding the mother-deities could the Old Testament bring its image of God, the pure transcendence of God, to maturity. But even if we cannot provide any absolutely compelling arguments, the prayer language of the entire Bible remains normative for us, in which, as we have seen, while there are some fine images of maternal love, "mother" is not used as a title or a form of address for God. We make our petitions in the way that Jesus, with Holy Scripture in the background, taught us to pray, and not as we happen to think or want. Only thus do we pray properly.

Finally, we need to consider the word *our*. Jesus alone was fully entitled to say "my Father," because he alone is truly God's only-begotten Son, of one substance with the Father. By contrast, the rest of us have to say "our Father." Only within the "we" of the disciples can we call God "Father," because only through communion with Jesus Christ do we truly become "children of God." In this sense, the word *our* is really rather demanding: It requires that we step out of the closed circle of our "I." It requires that we surrender ourselves to communion with the other children of God. It requires, then, that we strip ourselves of what is merely our own, of what divides. It requires that we accept the other, the others—that we open our ear and our heart to them. When we say the word *our,* we say Yes to the living Church in which the Lord wanted to gather his new family. In this sense, the Our Father is at once a fully personal and a thoroughly ecclesial prayer. In praying the Our Father, we pray totally with our own heart, but at the same time we pray in communion with the whole family of God, with the living and the dead, with men of all conditions, cultures, and races. The Our Father overcomes all boundaries and makes us one family.

This word *our* also gives us the key to understanding the words that come next: "Who art in heaven." With these words, we are not pushing God the Father away to some distant planet. Rather, we are testifying to the fact that, while we have different earthly fathers, we all come from one single Father, who is the measure and source of all fatherhood. As Saint Paul says: "I bow my knees before the Father, from whom every fatherhood in heaven and on earth is named" (Eph 3:14–15). In the background we hear the Lord himself speaking: "Call no man your father on earth, for you have one Father, who is in heaven" (Mt 23:9).

God's fatherhood is more real than human fatherhood, because he is the ultimate source of our being; because he has thought and willed us from all eternity; because he gives us our true paternal home, which is eternal. And if earthly fatherhood divides, heavenly fatherhood unites. Heaven, then, means that other divine summit from which we all come and to which we are all meant to return. The fatherhood that is "in heaven" points us toward the greater "we" that transcends all boundaries, breaks down all walls, and creates peace.

Hallowed Be Thy Name

The first petition of the Our Father reminds us of the second commandment of the Decalogue: Thou shalt not speak the name of the Lord thy God in vain. But what is this "name of God"? When we speak of God's name, we see in our mind's eye the picture of Moses in the desert beholding a thornbush that burns but is not consumed. At first it is curiosity that prompts him to go and take a closer look at this mysterious sight, but then a voice calls to him from out of the bush, and this voice says to him: "I am the God of your fathers, the God of Abraham, the God of Isaac, and the God of Jacob" (Ex 3:6). This God sends Moses back to Egypt with the task of leading the people of Israel out of that country into the Promised Land. Moses is charged with demanding in the name of God that Pharaoh let Israel go.

But in the world of Moses' time there were many gods. Moses therefore asks the name of this God that will prove his special authority vis-à-vis the gods. In this respect, the idea of the divine name belongs first of all to the polytheistic world, in which this God, too, has to give himself a name. But the God who calls Moses is truly God, and God in the strict and true sense is not plural. God is by essence one. For this reason he cannot enter into the world of the gods as one among many; he cannot have one name among others.

God's answer to Moses is thus at once a refusal and a pledge. He says of himself simply, "I am who I am"—he *is* without any qualification. This pledge is a name and a non-name at one and the same time. The Israelites were therefore perfectly right in refusing to utter this self-designation of God, expressed in the word YHWH, so as to avoid degrading it to the level of names of pagan deities. By the same token, recent Bible translations were wrong to write out this name—which Israel always regarded as mysterious and unutterable—as if it were just any old name. By doing so, they have dragged the mystery of God, which cannot be captured in images or in names lips can utter, down to the level of some familiar item within a common history of religions.

It remains true, of course, that God did not simply refuse Moses' request. If we want to understand this curious interplay between name and non-name, we have to be clear about what a name actually is. We could put it very simply by saying that the name creates the possibility of address or invocation. It establishes relationship. When Adam names the animals, what this means is not that he indicates their essential natures, but that he fits them into his human world, puts them within reach of his call. Having said this, we are now in a position to understand the positive meaning of the divine name: God establishes a relationship between himself and us. He puts himself within reach of our invocation. He enters into relationship with us and enables us to be in relationship with him. Yet this means that in some sense he hands himself over to our human world. He has made himself accessible and, therefore, vulnerable as well. He assumes the risk of relationship, of communion, with us.

The process that was brought to completion in the Incarnation had begun with the giving of the divine name. When we come to consider Jesus' high-priestly prayer, in fact, we will see that he presents himself there as the new Moses: "I have manifested thy name to . . . men" (Jn 17:6). What began at the burning bush in the Sinai desert comes to fulfillment at the burning bush of the Cross. God has now truly made himself accessible in his incarnate Son. He has become a part of our world; he has, as it were, put himself into our hands.

This enables us to understand what the petition for the sanctification of the divine name means. The name of God can now be misused and so God himself can be sullied. The name of God can be co-opted for our purposes and so the image of God can also be distorted. The more he gives himself into our hands, the more we can obscure his light; the closer he is, the more our misuse can disfigure him. Martin Buber once said that when we consider all the ways in which God's name has been so shamefully misused, we almost despair of uttering it ourselves. But to keep it silent would be an outright refusal of the love with which God comes to us. Buber says that our only recourse is to try as reverently as possible to pick up and purify the polluted fragments of the divine name. But there is no way we can do that alone. All we can do is plead with him not to allow the light of his name to be destroyed in this world.

Moreover, this plea—that he himself take charge of the sanctification of his name, protect the wonderful mystery of his accessibility to us, and constantly assert his true identity as opposed to our distortion of it—this plea, of course, is always an occasion for us to examine our consciences seriously. How do I treat God's holy name? Do I stand in reverence before the mystery of the burning bush, before his incomprehensible closeness, even to the point of his presence in the Eucharist, where he truly gives himself entirely into our hands? Do I take care that God's holy companionship with us will draw us up into his purity and sanctity, instead of dragging him down into the filth?

Thy Kingdom Come

In connection with the petition for God's Kingdom, we recall all our earlier considerations concerning the term "Kingdom of God." With this petition, we are acknowledging first and foremost the primacy of God. Where God is absent, nothing can be good. Where God is not seen, man and the world fall to ruin. This is what the Lord means when he says to "seek first his Kingdom and his righteousness, and all these things shall be yours as well" (Mt 6:33). These words establish an order of priorities for human action, for how we approach everyday life.

This is not a promise that we will enter the Land of Plenty on condition that we are devout or that we are somehow attracted to the Kingdom of God. This is not an automatic formula for a well-functioning world, not a utopian vision of a classless society in which everything works out well of its own accord, simply because there is no private property. Jesus does not give us such simple recipes. What he does do, though—as we saw earlier—is to establish an absolutely decisive priority. For "Kingdom of God" means "dominion of God," and this means that his will is accepted as the true criterion. His will establishes justice, and part of justice is that we give God his just due and, in so doing, discover the criterion for what is justly due among men.

The order of priorities that Jesus indicates for us here may remind us of the Old Testament account of Solomon's first prayer after his accession to office. The story goes that the Lord appeared to the young king in a dream at night and gave him leave to make a request that the Lord promised to grant. A classic dream motif of mankind! What does Solomon ask for? "Give thy servant therefore a listening heart to govern thy people, that I may discern between good and evil" (1 Kings 3:9). God praises him because instead of asking for wealth, fortune, honor, or the death of his enemies, or even long life (2 Chron 1:11), tempting as that would have been, he asked for the truly essential thing: a listening heart, the ability to discern between good and evil. And for this reason Solomon receives those other things as well.

With the petition "thy Kingdom come" (not "our kingdom"), the Lord wants to show us how to pray and order our action in just this way. The first and essential thing is a listening heart, so that God, not we, may reign. The Kingdom of God comes by way of a listening heart. That is its path. And that is what we must pray for again and again.

The encounter with Christ makes this petition even deeper and more concrete. We have seen that Jesus is the Kingdom of God in person. The Kingdom of God is present wherever he is present. By the same token, the request for a listening heart becomes a request for communion with Jesus

Christ, the petition that we increasingly become "one" with him (Gal 3:28). What is requested in this petition is the true following of Christ, which becomes communion with him and makes us one body with him. Reinhold Schneider has expressed this powerfully: "The life of this Kingdom is Christ's continuing life in those who are his own. In the heart that is no longer nourished by the vital power of Christ, the Kingdom ends; in the heart that is touched and transformed by it, the Kingdom begins. . . . The roots of the indestructible tree seek to penetrate into each heart. The Kingdom is one. It exists solely through the Lord who is its life, its strength, and its center" (*Das Vaterunser*, pp. 31f.). To pray for the Kingdom of God is to say to Jesus: Let us be yours, Lord! Pervade us, live in us; gather scattered humanity in your body, so that in you everything may be subordinated to God and you can then hand over the universe to the Father, in order that "God may be all in all" (1 Cor 15:28).

Thy Will Be Done on Earth as It Is in Heaven

Two things are immediately clear from the words of this petition: God has a will with and for us and it must become the measure of our willing and being; and the essence of "heaven" is that it is where God's will is unswervingly done. Or, to put it in somewhat different terms, where God's will is done is heaven. The essence of heaven is oneness with God's will, the oneness of will and truth. Earth becomes "heaven" when and insofar as God's will is done there; and it is merely "earth," the opposite of heaven, when and insofar as it withdraws from the will of God. This is why we pray that it may be on earth as it is in heaven—that earth may become "heaven."

But what is "God's will"? How do we recognize it? How can we do it? The Holy Scriptures work on the premise that man has knowledge of God's will in his inmost heart, that anchored deeply within us there is a participation in God's knowing, which we call conscience (cf., for example, Rom 2:15). But the Scriptures also know that this participation in the Creator's knowledge, which he gave us in the context of our creation "according to his likeness," became buried in the course of history. It can never be completely extinguished, but it has been covered over in many ways, like a barely flickering flame, all too often at risk of being smothered under the ash of all the prejudices that have piled up within us. And that is why God has spoken to us anew, uttering words in history that come to us from outside and complete the interior knowledge that has become all too hidden.

The heart of this historically situated "complementary teaching" contained in biblical Revelation is the Decalogue given on Mount Sinai. As we have seen, this is by no means abolished by the Sermon on the Mount, nor is it reduced to an "old law," but it is simply developed further in a way that allows its full depth and grandeur to shine forth in all its purity. The Decalogue is not, as we have seen, some burden imposed upon man from the outside. It is a revelation of the essence of God himself—to the extent that we are capable of receiving it—and hence it is an exegesis of the truth of our being. The notes of our existence are deciphered for us so that we can read them and translate them into life. God's will flows from his being and therefore guides us into the truth of our being, liberating us from self-destruction through falsehood.

Because our being comes from God, we are able, despite all of the defilement that holds us back, to set out on the way to God's will. The Old Testament concept of the "just man" meant exactly that: to live from the word of God, and so from his will, and to find the path that leads into harmony with this will.

Now, when Jesus speaks to us of God's will and of heaven, the place where God's will is fulfilled, the core of what he says is again connected with his mission. At Jacob's well, he says to the disciples who bring him food: "My food is to do the will of him who sent me, and to accomplish his work" (Jn 4:34). What he means is that his oneness with the Father's will is the foundation of his life. The unity of his will with the Father's will is the core of his very being. Above all, though, what we hear in this petition of the Our Father is an echo of Jesus' own passionate struggle in dialogue with his Father on the Mount of Olives: "My Father, if it be possible, let this cup pass from me; nevertheless, not as I will, but as thou wilt"—"My Father, if this cannot pass unless I drink it, thy will be done" (Mt 26:39, 42). When we come to consider Jesus' Passion, we will need to focus explicitly on this prayer, in which Jesus gives us a glimpse into his human soul and its "becoming-one" with the will of God.

The author of the Letter to the Hebrews finds the key to the heart of the mystery of Jesus in the agony on the Mount of Olives (cf. Heb 5:7). Basing himself on this glimpse into Jesus' soul, he uses Psalm 40 to interpret the mystery. He reads the Psalm thus: "Sacrifices and offerings thou hast not desired, but a body hast thou prepared for me. . . . Then I said, 'Yes, I have come to do thy will, O God,' as it is written of me in the roll of the book" (Heb 10:5ff.; cf. Ps 40:7–9). Jesus' whole existence is summed up in the words "Yes, I have come to do thy will." It is only against this background that we fully understand what he means when he says, "My food is to do the will of him who sent me" (Jn 4:34).

And in this light, we now understand that Jesus himself is "heaven" in the deepest and truest sense of the word—he in whom and through whom God's will is wholly done. Looking at him, we realize that left to ourselves we can never be completely just: The gravitational pull of our own will constantly draws us away from God's will and turns us into mere "earth." But he accepts us, he draws us up to himself, into himself, and in communion with him we too learn God's will. Thus, what we are ultimately praying for in this third petition of the Our Father is that we come closer and closer to him, so that God's will can conquer the downward pull of our selfishness and make us capable of the lofty height to which we are called.

Give Us This Day Our Daily Bread

The fourth petition of the Our Father appears to us as the most "human" of all of the petitions: Though the Lord directs our eyes to the essential, to the "one thing necessary," he also knows about and acknowledges our earthly needs. While he says to his disciples, "Do not be anxious about your life, what you shall eat" (Mt 6:25), he nevertheless invites us to pray for our food and thus to turn our care over to God.

Bread is "the fruit of the earth and the work of human hands," but the earth bears no fruit unless it receives sunlight and rain from above. This coming together of cosmic powers, outside our control, stands opposed to the temptation that comes to us through our pride to give ourselves life purely through our own power. Such pride makes man violent and cold. It ends up destroying the earth. It cannot be otherwise, because it is contrary to the truth that we human beings are oriented toward self-transcendence and that we become great and free and truly ourselves only when we open up to God. We have the right and the duty to ask for what we need. We know that if even earthly fathers give their children good things when they ask for them, God will not refuse us the good things that he alone can give (cf. Lk 11:9–13).

In his exposition of the Lord's Prayer, Saint Cyprian draws our attention to two important aspects of the fourth petition. He has already underscored the far-reaching significance of the word *our* in his discussion of the phrase "our Father," and here likewise he points out that the reference is to "our" bread. Here, too, we pray in the communion of the disciples, in the communion of the children of God, and for this reason no one may think only of himself. A further step follows: we pray for *our* bread—and that means we also pray for bread for others. Those who have an abundance of bread are called to share. In his exposition of the First Letter to the Corinthians—of the scandal Christians were causing in Corinth—Saint John Chrysostom emphasizes that "every bite of bread in one way or another is a bite of the bread that belongs to everyone, of the bread of the world." Father Kolvenbach adds: "If we invoke our Father over the Lord's

Table and at the celebration of the Lord's Supper, how can we exempt ourselves from declaring our unshakable resolve to help all men, our brothers, to obtain their daily bread?" (*Der österliche Weg*, p. 98). By expressing this petition in the first person plural, the Lord is telling us: "Give them something to eat yourselves" (Mk 6:37).

Cyprian makes a second important observation: Anyone who asks for bread for today is poor. This prayer presupposes the poverty of the disciples. It presupposes that there are people who have renounced the world, its riches, and its splendor for the sake of faith and who no longer ask for anything beyond what they need to live. "It is right for the disciple to pray for the necessities of life only for today, since he is forbidden to worry about tomorrow. Indeed, he would be contradicting himself if he wanted to live long in this world, since we pray instead that God's Kingdom will come quickly" (*De dominica oratione* 19; *CSEL* III, 1, p. 281). There must always be people in the Church who leave everything in order to follow the Lord, people who depend radically on God, on his bounty by which we are fed—people, then, who in this way present a sign of faith that shakes us out of our heedlessness and the weakness of our faith.

We cannot ignore the people who trust so totally in God that they seek no security other than him. They encourage us to trust God—to count on him amid life's great challenges. At the same time, this poverty, motivated entirely by commitment to God and his Kingdom, is also an act of solidarity with the world's poor, an act that historically has created new standards of value and a new willingness for service and for commitment on behalf of others.

Moreover, the prayer for bread just for today also evokes

Israel's forty years of wandering in the desert, when the people lived on manna—on the bread that God sent from heaven. Each Israelite was to gather only as much as was needed for that particular day; only on the sixth day was it permissible to gather enough of the gift for two days, so as to be able to keep the Sabbath (Ex 16:16–22). The community of the disciples, which draws new life from God's goodness every day, relives in a new way the experience of the wandering People of God, whom God fed even in the desert.

The petition for bread just for today thus opens up vistas that reach beyond the horizon of the nourishment that is needed day by day. It presupposes that the community of his closest disciples followed the Lord in a radical way, renouncing worldly possessions and adhering to the way of those who "considered abuse suffered for the Christ greater wealth than the treasures of Egypt" (Heb 11:26). The eschatological horizon comes into view here—pointing to a future that is weightier and more real than the present.

With that we touch upon one of the words of this petition that sounds quite innocuous in our usual translations: Give us this day our *daily* bread. "Daily" renders the Greek word *epiousios.* Referring to this word, one of the great masters of the Greek language—the theologian Origen (d. ca. 254)—says that it does not occur anywhere else in Greek, but that it was coined by the Evangelists. Since Origen's time, it is true, an instance of this word has been found in a papyrus dating from the fifth century after Christ. But this one example alone is insufficient to give us any certainty about the meaning of this word, which is at any rate very unusual and rare. We have to depend on etymologies and the study of the context.

Today there are two principal interpretations. One maintains that the word means "what is necessary for existence." On this reading, the petition would run as follows: Give us today the bread that we need in order to live. The other interpretation maintains that the correct translation is "bread for the future," for the following day. But the petition to receive tomorrow's bread today does not seem to make sense when looked at in the light of the disciple's existence. The reference to the future would make more sense if the object of the petition were the bread that really does belong to the future: the true manna of God. In that case, it would be an eschatological petition, the petition for an anticipation of the world to come, asking the Lord to give already "today" the future bread, the bread of the new world—himself. On such a reading, the petition would acquire an eschatological meaning. Some ancient translations hint in this direction. An example is Saint Jerome's Vulgate, which translates the mysterious word *epiousios* as *supersubstantialis* (i.e., super-substantial), thereby pointing to the new, higher "substance" that the Lord gives us in the Holy Sacrament as the true bread of our life.

The fact is that the Fathers of the Church were practically unanimous in understanding the fourth petition of the Our Father as a eucharistic petition; in this sense the Our Father figures in the Mass liturgy as a eucharistic table-prayer (i.e., "grace"). This does not remove the straightforward earthly sense of the disciples' petition that we have just shown to be the text's immediate meaning. The Fathers consider different dimensions of the saying that begins as a petition for today's bread for the poor, but insofar as it directs our gaze to the Father in heaven who feeds us, it recalls the wandering People of God, who were fed by God himself. Read in the light of Jesus' great discourse on the bread of life, the miracle of the manna naturally points beyond itself to the new world in which the Logos—the eternal Word of God—will be our bread, the food of the eternal wedding banquet.

Is it legitimate to think in such dimensions, or is that a false "theologizing" of a word intended only in a straightforwardly earthly sense? There is a fear of such theologizing today, which is not totally unfounded, but neither should it be overstated. I think that in interpreting the petition for bread, it is necessary to keep in mind the larger context of Jesus' words and deeds, a context in which essential elements of human life play a major role: water, bread, and, as a sign of the festive character and beauty of the world, the vine and wine. The theme of bread has an important place in Jesus' message—from the temptation in the desert and the multiplication of the loaves right up to the Last Supper.

The great discourse on the bread of life in John 6 discloses the full spectrum of meaning of this theme. It begins with the hunger of the people who have been listening to Jesus and whom he does not send away without food, that is to say, the "necessary bread" that we require in order to live. But Jesus does not allow us to stop there and reduce man's needs to bread, to biological and material necessities. "Man shall not live by bread alone, but by every word that proceeds from the mouth of God" (Mt 4:4; Deut 8:3). The miraculously multiplied bread harks back to the miracle of manna in the desert and at the same time points beyond itself: to the fact that man's real food is the Logos, the eternal Word, the eternal meaning, from which we come and toward which our life is directed. If this initial transcendence of the physical realm prima facie tells us no more than what philosophy has found and is still capable of discovering, there is nevertheless a further transcendence to consider: The eternal Logos does not concretely become bread for man until he has "taken flesh" and speaks to us in human words.

This is followed by the third, absolutely essential, transcendence, which nevertheless proves scandalous to the people of Capernaum: The incarnate Lord gives himself to us in the Sacrament, and in that way the eternal Word for the first time becomes fully manna, the gift of the bread of the future given to us already today. Then, however, the Lord brings everything together once more: This extreme "becoming-corporeal" is actually the real "becoming-spiritual": "It is the spirit that gives life, the flesh is of no avail" (Jn 6:63). Are we to suppose that Jesus excluded from the petition for bread everything that he tells us about bread and everything that he wants to give us as bread? When we consider Jesus' message in its entirety, then it is impossible to expunge the eucharistic dimension from the fourth petition of the Our Father. True, the earthly nitty-gritty of the petition for daily bread for everyone is essential. But this petition also helps us to transcend the purely material and to request already now what is to come "tomorrow," the new bread. And when we pray for "tomorrow's" bread today, we are reminded to live already today from tomorrow, from the love of God, which calls us all to be responsible for one another.

At this point I would like to quote Cyprian once again. He emphasizes both dimensions. But he also specifically relates the word *our*, which we spoke of earlier, to the Eucharist, which in a special sense is "our" bread, the bread of Jesus' disciples. He says: We who are privileged to receive the Eucharist as our bread must nevertheless always pray that none of us be permanently cut off and severed from the body of Christ. "On this account we pray that 'our' bread, Christ, be given to us every day, that we, who remain and live in Christ, may not depart from his healing power and from his body" (*De dominica oratione* 18; *CSEL* III, 1, pp. 280f.).

And Forgive Us Our Trespasses, as We Forgive Those Who Trespass Against Us

The fifth petition of the Our Father presupposes a world in which there is trespass—trespass of men in relation to other men, trespass in relation to God. Every instance of trespass among men involves some kind of injury to truth and to love and is thus opposed to God, who is truth and love. How to overcome guilt is a central question for every human life; the history of religions revolves around this question. Guilt calls forth retaliation. The result is a chain of trespasses in which the evil of guilt grows ceaselessly and becomes more and more inescapable. With this petition, the Lord is telling us that guilt can be overcome only by forgiveness, not by retaliation. God is a God who forgives, because he loves his creatures; but forgiveness can only penetrate and become effective in one who is himself forgiving.

"Forgiveness" is a theme that pervades the entire Gospel. We meet it at the very beginning of the Sermon on the Mount in the new interpretation of the fifth commandment, when the Lord says to us: "So if you are offering your gift at the altar, and there remember that your brother has something against you, leave your gift there before the altar and go; first be reconciled to your brother, and then come and offer your gift" (Mt 5:23f.). You cannot come into God's presence unreconciled with your brother; anticipating him in the gesture of reconciliation, going out to meet him, is the prerequisite for true worship of God. In so doing, we should keep in mind that God himself—knowing that we human beings stood against him, unreconciled—stepped out of his divinity in order to come toward us, to reconcile us. We should recall that, before giving us the Eucharist, he knelt down before his disciples and washed their dirty feet, cleansing them with his humble love. In the middle of Matthew's Gospel we find the parable of the unforgiving servant (cf. Mt 18:23–35). He, a highly placed satrap of the king, has just been released from an unimaginably large debt of ten thousand talents. Yet he himself is unwilling to cancel a debt of a hundred denarii—in comparison a laughable sum. Whatever we have to forgive one another is trivial in comparison with the goodness of God, who forgives us. And ultimately we hear Jesus' petition from the Cross: "Father, forgive them; for they know not what they do" (Lk 23:34).

If we want to understand the petition fully and make it our own, we must go one step further and ask: What is forgiveness, really? What happens when forgiveness takes place? Guilt is a reality, an objective force; it has caused destruction that must be repaired. For this reason, forgiveness must be more than a matter of ignoring, of merely trying to forget. Guilt must be worked through, healed, and thus overcome. Forgiveness exacts a price—first of all from the person who forgives. He must overcome within himself the evil done to him; he must, as it were, burn it interiorly and in so doing renew himself. As a result, he also involves the other, the trespasser, in this process of transformation, of inner purification, and both parties, suffering all the way through and overcoming evil, are made new. At this point, we encounter the mystery of Christ's Cross. But the very first thing we encounter is the limit of our power to heal and to overcome evil. We encounter the superior power of evil, which we cannot master with our unaided powers. Reinhold Schneider says apropos of this that "evil lives in a thousand forms; it occupies the pinnacles of power . . . it bubbles up from the abyss. Love has just one form—your Son" (*Das Vaterunser*, p. 68).

The idea that God allowed the forgiveness of guilt, the healing of man from within, to cost him the death of his Son has come to seem quite alien to us today. That the Lord "has borne our diseases and taken upon himself sorrows," that "he was pierced for our transgressions, he was crushed for our iniquities," and that "with his wounds we are healed" (Is 53:4–6) no longer seems plausible to us today. Militating against this, on one side, is the trivialization of evil in which we take refuge, despite the fact that at the very same time we treat the horrors of human history, especially of the most recent human history, as an irrefutable pretext for denying the existence of a good God and slandering his creature man. But the understanding of the great mystery of expiation is also blocked by our individualistic image of man. We can no longer grasp substitution because we think that every man is ensconced in himself alone. The fact that all individual beings are deeply interwoven and that all are encompassed in turn by the being of the One, the Incarnate Son, is something we are no longer capable of seeing. When we come to speak of Christ's Crucifixion, we will have to take up these issues again.

In the meantime, an idea of Cardinal John Henry Newman may suffice. Newman once said that while God could create the whole world out of nothing with just one word, he could overcome men's guilt and suffering only by bringing himself into play, by becoming in his Son a sufferer who carried this burden and overcame it through his self-surrender. The overcoming of guilt has a price: We must put our heart—or, better, our whole existence—on the line. And even this act is insufficient; it can become effective only through communion with the One who bore the burdens of us all.

The petition for forgiveness is more than a moral exhortation—though it is that as well, and as such it challenges us anew every day. But, at its deepest core, it is—like the other petitions—a Christological prayer. It reminds us of he who allowed forgiveness to cost him descent into the hardship of human existence and death on the Cross. It calls us first and foremost to thankfulness for that, and then, with him, to work through and suffer through evil by means of love. And while we must acknowledge day by day how little our capacities suffice for that task, and how often we ourselves keep falling into guilt, this petition gives us the great consolation that our prayer is held safe within the power of his love—with which, through which, and in which it can still become a power of healing.

And Lead Us Not into Temptation

The way this petition is phrased is shocking for many people: God certainly does not lead us into temptation. In fact, as Saint James tells us: "Let no one say when he is tempted, 'I am tempted by God'; for God cannot be tempted with evil and he himself tempts no one" (Jas 1:13).

We are helped a further step along when we recall the words of the Gospel: "Then Jesus was led up by the Spirit into the wilderness to be tempted by the devil" (Mt 4:1). Temptation comes from the devil, but part of Jesus' messianic task is to withstand the great temptations that have led man away from God and continue to do so. As we have seen, Jesus must suffer through these temptations to the point of dying on the Cross, which is how he opens the way of redemption for us. Thus, it is not only after his death, but already by his death and during his whole life, that Jesus "descends into hell," as it were, into the domain of our temptations and defeats, in order to take us by the hand and carry us upward. The Letter to the Hebrews places special emphasis on this aspect, which it presents as an essential component of Jesus' path: "For because he himself has suffered and been tempted, he is able to help those who are tempted" (Heb 2:18). "For we have not a high priest who is unable to sympathize with our weaknesses, but one who in every respect has been tempted as we are, yet without sin" (Heb 4:15).

A brief look at the Book of Job, which in so many respects prefigures the mystery of Christ, can help us clarify things further. Satan derides man in order to deride God: God's creature, whom he has formed in his own image, is a pitiful creature. Everything that seems good about him is actually just a façade. The reality is that the only thing man—each man—ever cares about is his own well-being. This is the judgment of Satan, whom the Book of Revelation calls "the accuser of our brethren . . . who accuses them day and night before our God" (Rev 12:10). The calumniation of man and creation is in the final instance a calumniation of God, an excuse for renouncing him.

Satan wants to prove his case through the righteous man Job: Just let everything be taken away from him, Satan says, and he will quickly drop his piety, too. God gives Satan the freedom to test Job, though within precisely defined boundaries: God does not abandon man, but he does allow him to be tried. This is a very subtle, still implicit, yet real glimpse of the mystery of substitution that takes on a major profile in Isaiah 53: Job's sufferings serve to justify man. By his faith, proved through suffering, he restores man's honor. Job's sufferings are thus by anticipation sufferings in communion with Christ, who restores the honor of us all before God and shows us the way never to lose faith in God even amid the deepest darkness.

The Book of Job can also help us to understand the difference between trial and temptation. In order to mature, in order to make real progress on the path leading from a superficial piety into profound oneness with God's will, man needs to be tried. Just as the juice of the grape has to ferment in order to become a fine wine, so too man needs purifications and transformations; they are dangerous for him, because they present an opportunity for him to fall, and yet they are indispensable as paths on which he comes to himself and to God. Love is always a process involving purifications, renunciations, and painful transformations of ourselves—and that is how it is a journey to maturity. If Francis Xavier was able to pray to God, saying, "I love you, not because you have the power to give heaven or hell, but simply because you are you—my king and my God," then surely he had needed a long path of inner purifications to reach such ultimate freedom—a path through stages of maturity, a path beset with temptation and the danger of falling, but a necessary path nonetheless.

Now we are in a position to interpret the sixth petition of the Our Father in a more practical way. When we pray it, we are saying to God: "I know that I need trials so that my nature can be purified. When you decide to send me these trials, when you give evil some room to maneuver, as you did with Job, then please remember that my strength goes only so far. Don't overestimate my capacity. Don't set too wide the boundaries within which I may be tempted, and be close to me with your protecting hand when it becomes too much for me." It was in this sense that Saint Cyprian interpreted the sixth petition. He says that when we pray, "And lead us not into temptation," we are expressing our awareness "that the enemy can do nothing against us unless God has allowed it beforehand, so that our fear, our devotion and our worship may be directed to God—because the Evil One is not permitted to do anything unless he is given authorization" (*De dominica oratione* 25; *CSEL* III, 25, p. 285f.).

And then, pondering the psychological pattern of temptation, he explains that there can be two different reasons why God grants the Evil One a limited power. It can be as a penance for us, in order to dampen our pride, so that we may reexperience the paltriness of our faith, hope, and love and avoid forming too high an opinion of ourselves. Let us think of the Pharisee who recounts his own works to God and imagines that he is not in need of grace. Cyprian unfortunately does not go on to explain in more detail what the other sort of trial is about—the temptation that God lays upon us *ad gloriam,* for his glory. But should it not put us in mind of the fact that God has placed a particularly heavy burden of temptation on the shoulders of those individuals who were especially close to him, the great saints, from Anthony in his desert to Thérèse of Lisieux in the pious world of her Carmelite monastery? They follow in the footsteps of Job, so to speak; they offer an apologia for man that is at the same time a defense of God. Even more, they enjoy a very special communion with Jesus Christ, who suffered our temptations to the bitter end. They are called to withstand the temptations of a particular time in their own skin, as it were, in their own souls. They are called to bear them through to the end for us ordinary souls and to help us persist on our way to the One who took upon himself the burden of us all.

When we pray the sixth petition of the Our Father, we must therefore, on one hand, be ready to take upon ourselves the burden of trials that is meted out to us. On the other hand, the object of the petition is to ask God not to mete out more than we can bear, not to let us slip from his hands. We make this prayer in the trustful certainty that Saint Paul has articulated for us: "God is faithful, and he will not let you be tempted beyond your strength, but with the temptation will also provide the way of escape, that you may be able to endure it" (1 Cor 10:13).

But Deliver Us from Evil

The last petition of the Our Father takes up the previous one again and gives it a positive twist. The two petitions are therefore closely connected. In the next-to-last petition the *not* set the dominant note (do not give the Evil One more room to maneuver than we can bear). In the last petition we come before the Father with the hope that is at the center of our faith: "Rescue, redeem, free us!" In the final analysis, it is a plea for redemption. What do we want to be redeemed from? The new German translation of the Our Father says "*vom Bösen,*" thus leaving it open whether "evil" or "the Evil One" is meant. The two are ultimately inseparable. Indeed, we see before us the dragon of which the Book of Revelation speaks (cf. chapters 12 and 13). John portrays the "beast rising out of the sea," out of the dark depths of evil, with the symbols of Roman imperial power, and he thus puts a very concrete face on the threat facing the Christians of his day: the total claim placed upon man by the emperor cult and the resulting elevation of political-military economic might to the peak of absolute power—to the personification of the evil that threatens to devour us. This is coupled with the erosion of ethical principles by a cynical form of skepticism and enlightenment. Thus imperiled, the Christian in time of persecution calls upon the Lord as the only power that can save him: "Deliver us, free us from evil."

Notwithstanding the dissolution of the Roman Empire and its ideologies, this remains very contemporary! Today there are on one hand the forces of the market, of traffic in weapons, in drugs, and in human beings, all forces that weigh upon the world and ensnare humanity irresistibly. Today, on the other hand, there is also the ideology of success, of well-being, that tells us, "God is just a fiction, he only robs us of our time and our enjoyment of life. Don't bother with him!

Just try to squeeze as much out of life as you can." These temptations seem irresistible as well. The Our Father in general and this petition in particular are trying to tell us that it is only when you have lost God that you have lost yourself; then you are nothing more than a random product of evolution. Then the "dragon" really has won. So long as the dragon cannot wrest God from you, your deepest being remains unharmed, even in the midst of all the evils that threaten you. Our translation is thus correct to say: "Deliver us from evil," with *evil* in the singular. Evils (plural) can be necessary for our purification, but evil (singular) destroys. This, then, is why we pray from the depths of our soul not to be robbed of our faith, which enables us to see God, which binds us with Christ. This is why we pray that, in our concern for goods, we may not lose the Good itself; that even faced with the loss of goods, we may not also lose the Good, which is God; that we ourselves may not be lost: Deliver us from evil!

Cyprian, the martyr bishop who personally had to endure the situation described in the Book of Revelation, once again finds a marvelous way of putting all of this: "When we say 'deliver us from evil,' then there is nothing further left for us to ask for. Once we have asked for and obtained protection against evil, we are safely sheltered against everything the devil and the world can contrive. What could the world make you fear if you are protected in the world by God himself?" (*De dominica oratione* 19; *CSEL* III, 27, p. 287). This certainty sustained the martyrs, it made them joyful and confident in a world full of affliction, and it "delivered" them at the core of their being, freeing them for true freedom.

This same confidence was wonderfully put into words by Saint Paul: "If God is for us, who is against us? . . . Who shall separate us from the love of Christ? Shall tribulation, or distress, or persecution, or famine, or nakedness, or peril, or sword? . . . No, in all these things we are more than conquerors through him who loved us. For I am sure that neither death, nor life, nor angels, nor principalities, nor things present, nor things to come, nor powers, nor height, nor depth, nor anything else in all creation, will be able to separate us from the love of God in Christ Jesus our Lord" (Rom 8:31–39).

In this sense, the last petition brings us back to the first three: In asking to be liberated from the power of evil, we are ultimately asking for God's Kingdom, for union with his will, and for the sanctification of his name. Throughout the ages, though, men and women of prayer have interpreted this petition in a broader sense. In the midst of the world's tribulations, they have also begged God to set a limit to the evils that ravage the world and our lives.

This very human way of interpreting the petition has entered into the liturgy: In every liturgy, with the sole exception of the Byzantine, the final petition of the Our Father is extended into a separate prayer. In the old Roman liturgy it ran thus: "Free us, Lord, from all evils, past, present, and future. By the intercession . . . of all the saints, give peace in our day. Come to our aid with your mercy that we may be ever free from sins and protected from confusion." We sense the hardships of times of war, we hear the cry for total redemption. This "embolism," with which the liturgy enhances the last petition of the Our Father, shows the humanity of the Church. Yes, we may and we should ask the Lord also to free the world, ourselves, and the many individuals and peoples who suffer from the tribulations that make life almost unbearable.

We may and we should understand this extension of the final petition of the Our Father also as an examination of conscience directed at ourselves—as an appeal to collaborate in breaking the predominance of "evils." But for all that, we must not lose sight of the proper order of goods and of the connection of evils with "evil." Our petition must not sink into superficiality; even on this interpretation of the Our Father petition, the central point is still "that we be freed from sins," that we recognize "evil" as the quintessence of "evils," and that our gaze may never be diverted from the living God.

CHAPTER SIX

The Disciples

In all the stages of Jesus' activity that we have considered so far, it has become evident that Jesus is closely connected with the "we" of the new family that he gathers by his proclamation and his action. It has become evident that this "we" is in principle intended to be universal: It no longer rests on birth, but on communion with Jesus, who is himself God's living Torah. This "we" of the new family is not amorphous. Jesus calls an inner core of people specially chosen by him, who are to carry on his mission and give this family order and shape. That was why Jesus formed the group of the Twelve. The title "apostle" originally extended beyond this group, but was later restricted more and more to the Twelve. In Luke, for example, who always speaks of the twelve Apostles, this word is practically synonymous with the Twelve. There is no need here to inquire into the widely discussed issues concerning the development of the use of the word *apostle;* let us simply listen to the most important texts that show the formation of the community of Jesus' closest disciples.

The central text for this is Mark 3:13–19. It begins by saying that Jesus "went up on the mountain, and called to him those whom he desired; and they came to him" (Mk 3:13). The events leading up to this had taken place by the lake, and now Jesus ascends "the mountain," which signifies the place of his communion with God—the place on the heights, above the works and deeds of everyday life. Luke underscores this point even more vigorously in his parallel account: "In these days he went out to the mountain to pray; and all night he continued in prayer to God. And when it was day, he called his disciples, and chose from them twelve, whom he named apostles"(Lk 6:12f.).

The calling of the disciples is a prayer event; it is as if they were begotten in prayer, in intimacy with the Father. The calling of the Twelve, far from being purely functional, takes on a deeply theological meaning: Their calling emerges from the Son's dialogue with the Father and is anchored there. This is also the necessary starting point for understanding Jesus' words, "Pray therefore the Lord of the harvest to send out laborers into his harvest" (Mt 9:38): We cannot simply pick the laborers in God's harvest in the same way that an employer seeks his employees. God must always be asked for them and he himself must choose them for this service. This theological character is reinforced in Mark's phrase: "Jesus called to him those whom he desired." You cannot make yourself a disciple—it is an event of election, a free decision of the Lord's will, which in its turn is anchored in his communion of will with the Father.

The text then continues: "And he appointed [literally: "made"] twelve, whom he also called apostles, to be with him, and to be sent out to preach" (Mk 3:14). The first thing to ponder is the expression "he made twelve," which sounds strange to us. In reality, these words of the Evangelist take up the Old Testament terminology for appointment to the priesthood (cf. 1 Kings 12:31; 13:33) and thus characterize the apostolic office as a priestly ministry. Moreover, the fact that the ones chosen are then individually named links them with the Prophets of Israel, whom God calls by name. Mark thus presents the apostolic ministry as a fusion of the priestly and prophetic missions (Feuillet, *Études*, p. 178). "He made twelve": Twelve was the symbolic number of Israel—the number of the sons of Jacob. From them the twelve tribes of Israel were descended, though of these practically only the tribe of Judah remained after the Exile. In this sense, the number twelve is a return to the origins of Israel, and yet at the same time it is a symbol of hope: The whole of Israel is restored and the twelve tribes are newly assembled.

Twelve—the number of the tribes—is at the same time a cosmic number that expresses the comprehensiveness of the newly reborn People of God. The Twelve stand as the patriarchs of this universal people founded on the Apostles. In the vision of the New Jerusalem found in the Apocalypse, the symbolism of the Twelve is elaborated into an image of splendor (cf. Rev 21:9–14) that helps the pilgrim People of God understand its present in the light of its future and illumines it with the spirit of hope: Past, present, and future intermingle when viewed in terms of the Twelve.

This is also the right context for the prophecy in which Jesus gives Nathanael a glimpse of his true nature: "You will see heaven opened, and the angels of God ascending and descending upon the Son of Man" (Jn 1:51). Jesus reveals himself here as the new Jacob. The patriarch dreamed that he saw a ladder set up beside his head, which reached up to heaven and on which God's angels were ascending and descending. This dream has become a reality with Jesus. He himself is the "gate of heaven" (Gen 28:10–22); he is the true Jacob, the "Son of Man," the patriarch of the definitive Israel.

Let us return to our text from Mark. Jesus appoints the Twelve with a double assignment: "to be with him, and to be sent out to preach." They must be with him in order to get to know him; in order to attain that intimate acquaintance with him that could not be given to the "people"—who saw him only from the outside and took him for a prophet, a great figure in the history of religions, but were unable to perceive his uniqueness (cf. Mt 16:13ff.). The Twelve must be with him so as to be able to recognize his oneness with the Father and thus become witnesses to his mystery. As Peter will say before the election of Matthias, they had to be present during the time that "the Lord Jesus went in and out among us" (cf. Acts 1:8, 21). One might say that they have to pass from outward to inward communion with Jesus. At the same time, however, they are there in order to become Jesus' envoys—"apostles," no less—who bring his message to the world, first to the lost sheep of the House of Israel, but then "to the ends of the earth." Being with Jesus and being sent by him seem at first sight mutually exclusive, but they clearly belong together. The Apostles have to learn to be with him in a way that enables them, even when they go to the ends of the earth, to be with him still. Being with him includes the missionary dynamic by its very nature, since Jesus' whole being is mission.

What does the text say they are sent to do? "To preach and have authority to cast out demons" (Mk 3:14f.). Matthew gives a somewhat more detailed description of the content of this mission: "And he gave them authority over unclean spirits, to cast them out, and to heal every disease and every infirmity" (Mt 10:1). The first task is preaching: to give people the light of the word, the message of Jesus. The Apostles are first and foremost Evangelists—like Jesus, they preach the Kingdom of God and thereby gather people into God's new family. But the preaching of God's Kingdom is never just words, never just instruction. It is an event, just as Jesus himself is an event, God's Word in person. By announcing him, the Apostles lead their listeners to encounter him.

Because the world is ruled by the powers of evil, this preaching is at the same time a struggle with those powers. "In following Jesus, his herald has to exorcise the world, to establish a new form of life in the Holy Spirit that brings release to those who are possessed" (Pesch, *Markusevangelium*, I, p. 205). And, as Henri de Lubac in particular has shown, the ancient world did in fact experience the birth of Christianity as a liberation from the fear of demons that, in spite of skepticism and enlightenment, was all-pervasive at the time. The same thing also happens today wherever Christianity replaces old tribal religions, transforming and integrating their positive elements into itself. We feel the full impact of this leap forward when Paul says: "'There is no God but one.' For although there may be so-called gods in heaven or on earth—as indeed there are many 'gods' and many 'lords'—yet for us there is one God, the Father, from whom are all things and for whom we exist, and one Lord, Jesus Christ, through whom are all things and through whom we exist" (1 Cor 8:4f.). These words imply a great liberating power—the great exorcism that purifies the world. No matter how many gods may have been at large in the world, God is only one, and only one is Lord. If we belong to him, everything else loses its power; it loses the allure of divinity.

The world is now seen as something rational: It emerges from eternal reason, and this creative reason is the only true power over the world and in the world. Faith in the one God is the only thing that truly liberates the world and makes it "rational." When faith is absent, the world only *appears* to be more rational. In reality the indeterminable powers of chance now claim their due; "chaos theory" takes its place alongside insight into the rational structure of the universe, confronting man with obscurities that he cannot resolve and that set limits to the world's rationality. To "exorcise" the world—to establish it in the light of the *ratio* (reason) that comes from eternal creative reason and its saving goodness and refers back to it—that is a permanent, central task of the messengers of Jesus Christ.

In the Letter to the Ephesians, Saint Paul once described this "exorcistic" character of Christianity from another perspective: "Finally, be strong in the Lord and in the strength of his might. Put on the whole armor of God, that you may be able to stand against the wiles of the devil. For we are not contending against flesh and blood, but against the principalities, against the powers, against the world rulers of this present darkness, against the spiritual hosts of wickedness in the heavenly places" (Eph 6:10–12). This portrayal of the Christian struggle, which we today find surprising, or even disturbing, Heinrich Schlier has explained as follows: "The enemies are not this or that person, not even myself. They are not flesh and blood. . . . The conflict goes deeper. It is a fight against a host of opponents that never stop coming; they cannot really be pinned down and have no proper name, only collective denominations. They also start out with superior advantage over man, and that is because of their superior position, their position 'in the heavens' of existence. They are also superior because their position is impenetrable and unassailable—their position, after all, is the 'atmosphere' of existence, which they themselves tilt in their favor and propagate around themselves. These enemies are, finally, all full of essential, deadly malice" (*Brief an die Epheser*, p. 291).

Who could fail to see here a description of our world as well, in which the Christian is threatened by an anonymous atmosphere, by "something in the air" that wants to make the faith seem ludicrous and absurd to him? And who could fail to see the poisoning of the spiritual climate all over the world that threatens the dignity of man, indeed his very existence? The individual human being, and even communities of human beings, seem to be hopelessly at the mercy of such powers. The Christian knows that he cannot master this threat by his own resources alone. But in faith, in communion with the only true Lord of the world, he is given the "armor of God." It enables him—in the communion of the whole body of Christ—to oppose these powers, knowing that the Lord's gift of faith restores the pure breath of life: the breath of the Creator, the breath of the Holy Spirit, which alone can give health to the world.

Alongside the commission to exorcise, Matthew adds the mission to heal. The Twelve are sent "to heal every disease and every infirmity" (Mt 10:1). Healing is an essential dimension of the apostolic mission and of Christian faith in general. Eugen Biser even goes so far as to call Christianity a "therapeutic religion"—a religion of healing (*Einweisung*). When understood at a sufficiently deep level, this expresses the entire content of "redemption." The authority to cast out demons and to free the world from their dark threat, for the sake of the one true God, is the same authority that rules out any magical understanding of healing through attempts to manipulate these mysterious powers. Magical healing is always tied to the art of turning the evil onto someone else and setting the "demons" against him. God's dominion, God's Kingdom, means precisely the disempowerment of these forces by the intervention of the one God, who is good, who is the Good itself. The healing power of the messengers of Jesus Christ is opposed to the spirits of magic; it exorcises the world in medical terms as well. In the miracles of healing performed by the Lord and by the Twelve, God displays his gracious power over the world. They are essentially "signs" that point to God himself and serve to set man in motion toward God. Only becoming-one with God can be the true process of man's healing.

For Jesus himself and for his followers, miracles of healing are thus a subordinate element within the overall range of his activity, which is concerned with something deeper, with nothing less than the "Kingdom of God": his becoming-Lord in us and in the world. Just as exorcism drives out the fear of demons and commits the world—which comes from God's reason—to our human reason, so, too, healing by God's power is both a summons to faith in God and a summons to use the powers of reason in the service of healing. The "reason" meant here, of course, is wide open—it is the kind of reason that perceives God and therefore also recognizes man as a unity of body and soul. Whoever truly wishes to heal man must see him in his wholeness and must know that his ultimate healing can only be God's love.

Let us return to our text from Mark's Gospel. After specifying the mission of the Twelve, Mark lists them by name. We have already seen that this is an intimation of the prophetic dimension of their mission. God knows us by name and he calls us by name. This is not the place to portray the individual figures who form the group of the Twelve in light of the Bible and tradition. The important thing for us is the composition of the whole group, and it is quite heterogeneous.

Two members of the group came from the Zealot party: Simon, who in Luke 6:15 is called "the Zealot" and in Matthew and Mark "the Cananaean"—which according to recent scholarship means the same thing—and Judas. The word *Iscariot* can simply mean "the man from Karioth," but it may also designate him as a Sicarian, a radical variant of the Zealots. The zeal (*zelos*) for the Law that gave this movement its name looked to the great "zealots" of Israel's history for its models: from Phinehas, who killed an idolatrous Israelite before the whole community (Num 25:6–13), and Elijah, who had the priests of Baal killed on Mount Carmel (1 Kings 18), to Mattathias, the patriarch of the Maccabees, who initiated the uprising against the Hellenistic king Antiochus' attempt to extinguish Israel's faith by killing a conformist who was about to sacrifice publicly to the gods in accordance with the king's decree (1 Mac 2:17–28). The Zealots regarded this historical chain of great "zealots" as a heritage that committed them to fight against the Roman occupiers in their own day.

At the other extreme within the group of the Twelve we find Levi-Matthew, who, as a tax collector, worked hand in glove with the reigning power and had to be classed as a public sinner on account of his social position. The main group within the Twelve is composed of the fishermen from Lake Genesareth. Simon, whom the Lord would name Cephas (Peter), "rock," was apparently the head of a fishing cooperative (cf. Lk 5:10), in which he worked alongside his older brother Andrew and the sons of Zebedee, John and James, whom the Lord nicknamed "Boanerges"—sons of thunder. Some scholars argue that this name, too, indicates an association with the Zealot movement, but this is probably incorrect. It is the Lord's way of referring to their stormy temperament, which also emerges very clearly in the Gospel of John. Finally, there are two men with Greek names, Philip and Andrew, to whom Greek-speaking Jews address themselves on Palm Sunday at the time of the Passover festival, in order to make contact with Jesus (cf. Jn 12:21ff.).

We may presume that all of the Twelve were believing and observant Jews who awaited the salvation of Israel. But in terms of their actual opinions, of their thinking about the way Israel was to be saved, they were an extremely varied group. This helps us to understand how difficult it was to initiate them gradually into Jesus' mysterious new way, of the kinds of tension that had to be overcome. For example, how much purification must the zeal of the Zealots have needed before it could be united with Jesus' "zeal," about which John's Gospel tells us (cf. Jn 2:17)? His zeal reaches its completion on the Cross. Precisely in this wide range of backgrounds, temperaments, and approaches, the Twelve personify the Church of all ages and its difficult task of purifying and unifying these men in the zeal of Jesus Christ.

Only Luke tells us that Jesus formed a second group of disciples, which was composed of seventy (or seventy-two) and was sent out with a mission similar to that of the Twelve (cf. Lk 10:1–12). Like the number twelve, the number seventy (or seventy-two—the manuscripts variously report one or the other) is symbolic. Based on a combination of Deuteronomy 32:8 and Exodus 1:5, seventy was considered to be the number of the nations of the world. According to Exodus 1:5, seventy was the number of people who accompanied Jacob into Egypt; "they were all Jacob's offspring." A recent variant of Deuteronomy 32:8, which has become the generally received version, runs as follows: "When the Most High gave to the nations their inheritance, when he separated the sons of men, he fixed the bounds of the peoples according to the number of the sons of Israel"—this is a reference to the seventy members of the house of Jacob at the time of the emigration to Egypt. Alongside the twelve sons, who prefigure Israel, stand the seventy, who represent the whole world and are thus considered also to have some connection with Jacob, with Israel.

This tradition also forms the background of the legend transmitted in the so-called Letter of Aristeas, according to which the Greek translation of the Old Testament made in the third century before Christ was produced by seventy scholars (or seventy-two, with six representing each of the twelve tribes of Israel) under a special inspiration of the Holy Spirit. The legend is a way of interpreting this translation as the opening of Israel's faith to the nations.

And in fact the Septuagint did play a decisive role in directing many searching souls in late antiquity toward the God of Israel. The earlier myths had lost their credibility; philosophical monotheism was not enough to bring people to a living relationship with God. Many cultured men thus found a new access to God in Israel's monotheism, which was not philosophically conceived, but had been given from above within a history of faith. Many cities saw the formation of a circle of the "God-fearing," of pious "pagans," who neither could nor wanted to become full-fledged Jews, but participated in the synagogue liturgy and thus in Israel's faith. It was in this circle that the earliest Christian missionary preaching found its first foothold and began to spread. Now at last, these men could belong wholly to the God of Israel, because this God—according to Paul's preaching about him—had in Jesus truly become the God of all men. Now at last, by believing in Jesus as the Son of God, they could become full members in the People of God. When Luke speaks of a group of seventy alongside the Twelve, the meaning is clear: They are an intimation of the universal character of the Gospel, which is meant for all the peoples of the earth.

At this point it may be appropriate to mention another item peculiar to Luke. In the opening verses of chapter 8, he recounts to us that Jesus, as he was making his way with the Twelve and preaching, was also accompanied by women. He mentions three names and then adds: "and many others, who provided for them out of their means" (Lk 8:3). The difference between the discipleship of the Twelve and the discipleship of the women is obvious; the tasks assigned to each group are quite different. Yet Luke makes clear—and the other Gospels also show this in all sorts of ways—that "many" women belonged to the more intimate community of believers and that their faith-filled following of Jesus was an essential element of that community, as would be vividly illustrated at the foot of the Cross and at the Resurrection.

Perhaps it is a good idea at this point to draw attention to a few other details specific to the Evangelist Luke. Just as he was especially sensitive to the significance of women, he is also the Evangelist of the poor, and his "preferential option for the poor" is unmistakable.

Again, he shows a particular understanding for the Jews; the passions that were stirred up by the incipient separation between the Synagogue and the nascent Church—which left their traces in both Matthew and John—are nowhere to be found in him. I find particularly significant the way he concludes the story of the new wine and the old or new wineskins. In Mark we find, "And no one puts new wine into old wineskins; if he does, the wine will burst the skins, and the wine is lost, and so are the skins; but new wine is for fresh skins" (Mk 2:22). The text reads similarly in Matthew 9:17. Luke transmits to us the same saying, but at the end he adds: "And no one after drinking old wine desires new; for he says, 'The old is good'" (Lk 5:39). There do seem to be good grounds for interpreting this as a word of understanding for those who wished to remain with the "old wine."

Finally—on the subject of specifically Lukan features—we have already seen several times that this Evangelist devotes special attention to Jesus' prayer as the source of his preaching and action. He shows us that all of Jesus' words and deeds issue from his inner oneness with the Father, from the dialogue between Father and Son. If we have good reason to be convinced that the Holy Scriptures are "inspired," that they matured in a special sense under the guidance of the Holy Spirit, then we also have good reason to be convinced that precisely these specific aspects of the Lukan tradition preserve essential features of the original figure of Jesus for us.

CHAPTER SEVEN

The Message of the Parables

The Nature and Purpose of the Parables

There is no doubt that the parables constitute the heart of Jesus' preaching. While civilizations have come and gone, these stories continue to touch us anew with their freshness and their humanity. Joachim Jeremias, who wrote a fundamental book about Jesus' parables, has rightly pointed out that comparison of Jesus' parables with Pauline similitudes or rabbinical parables reveals "a definite personal character, a unique clarity and simplicity, a matchless mastery of construction" (*The Parables of Jesus,* p. 12). Here we have a very immediate sense—partly because of the originality of the language, in which the Aramaic text shines through—of closeness to Jesus as he lived and taught. At the same time, though, we find ourselves in the same situation as Jesus' contemporaries and even his disciples: We need to ask him again and again what he wants to say to us in each of the parables (cf. Mk 4:10). The struggle to understand the parables correctly is ever present throughout the history of the Church. Even historical-critical exegesis has repeatedly had to correct itself and cannot give us any definitive information.

One of the great masters of critical exegesis, Adolf Jülicher, published a two-volume work on Jesus' parables (*Die Gleichnisreden Jesu*, 1899; 2nd ed. 1910) that inaugurated a new phase in their interpretation, in which it seemed as if the definitive formula had been found for explaining them. Jülicher begins by emphasizing the radical difference between allegory and parable: Allegory had evolved in Hellenistic culture as a method for interpreting ancient authoritative religious texts that were no longer acceptable as they stood. Their statements were now explained as figures intended to veil a mysterious content hidden behind the literal meaning. This made it possible to understand the language of the texts as metaphorical discourse; when explained passage by passage and step by step, they were meant to be seen as figurative representations of the philosophical opinion that now emerged as the real content of the text. In Jesus' environment, allegory was the most common way of using textual images; it therefore seemed obvious to interpret the parables as allegories on this pattern. The Gospels themselves repeatedly place allegorical interpretations of parables on Jesus' lips, for example, concerning the parable of the sower, whose seed falls by the wayside, on rocky ground, among the thorns, or else on fruitful soil (Mk 4:1–20). Jülicher, for his part, sharply distinguished Jesus' parables from allegory; rather than allegory, he said, they are a piece of real life intended to communicate *one* idea, understood in the broadest possible sense—a single "salient point." The allegorical interpretations placed on Jesus' lips are regarded as later additions that already reflect a degree of misunderstanding.

In itself, Jülicher's basic idea of the distinction between parable and allegory is correct, and it was immediately adopted by scholars everywhere. Yet gradually the limitations of his theories began to emerge. Although the contrast between the parables and allegory is legitimate as such, the radical separation of them cannot be justified on either historical or textual grounds. Judaism, too, made use of allegorical discourse, especially in apocalyptic literature; it is perfectly possible for parable and allegory to blend into each other. Jeremias has shown that the Hebrew word *mashal* (parable, riddle) comprises a wide variety of genres: parable, similitude, allegory, fable, proverb, apocalyptic revelation, riddle, symbol, pseudonym, fictitious person, example (model), theme, argument, apology, refutation, jest (p. 20). Form criticism had already tried to make progress by dividing the parables into categories: "A distinction was drawn between metaphor, simile, parable, similitude, allegory, illustration" (ibid.).

If it was already a mistake to try to pin down the genre of the parable to a single literary type, the method by which Jülicher thought to define the "salient point"—supposedly the parable's sole concern—is even more dated. Two examples should suffice. According to Jülicher, the parable of the rich fool (Lk 12:16–21) is intended to convey the message that "even the richest of men is at every moment wholly dependent upon the power and mercy of God." The salient point in the parable of the unjust householder (Lk 16:1–8) is said to be this: "wise use of the present as the condition of a happy future." Jeremias rightly comments as follows: "We are told that the parables announce a genuine religious humanity; they are stripped of their eschatological import. Imperceptibly Jesus is transformed into an 'apostle of progress' [Jülicher, II 483], a teacher of wisdom who inculcates moral precepts and a simplified theology by means of striking metaphors and stories. But nothing could be less like him" (p. 19). C. W. F. Smith expresses himself even more bluntly: "No one would crucify a teacher who told pleasant stories to enforce prudential morality" (*The Jesus of the Parables,* p. 17; cited in Jeremias, p. 21).

I recount this in such detail here because it enables us to glimpse the limits of liberal exegesis, which in its day was viewed as the *ne plus ultra* of scientific rigor and reliable historiography and was regarded even by Catholic exegetes with envy and admiration. We have already seen in connection with the Sermon on the Mount that the type of interpretation that makes Jesus a moralist, a teacher of an enlightened and individualistic morality, for all of its significant historical insights, remains theologically impoverished, and does not even come close to the real figure of Jesus.

While Jülicher had in effect conceived the "salient point" in completely humanistic terms in keeping with the spirit of his time, it was later identified with imminent eschatology: The parables all ultimately amounted to a proclamation of the proximity of the inbreaking *éschaton*—of the "Kingdom of God." But that, too, does violence to the variety of the texts; with many of the parables, an interpretation in terms of imminent eschatology can only be imposed artificially. By contrast, Jeremias has rightly underlined the fact that each parable has its own context and thus its own specific message. With this in mind, he divides the parables into nine thematic groups, while continuing nevertheless to seek a common thread, the heart of Jesus' message. Jeremias acknowledges his debt here to the English exegete C. H. Dodd, while at the same time distancing himself from Dodd on one crucial point.

Dodd made the thematic orientation of the parables toward the Kingdom or dominion of God the core of his exegesis, but he rejected the German exegetes' imminent eschatological approach and linked eschatology with Christology: The Kingdom arrives in the person of Christ. In pointing to the Kingdom, the parables thus point to him as the Kingdom's true form. Jeremias felt that he could not accept this thesis of a "realized eschatology," as Dodd called it, and he spoke instead of an "eschatology that is in process of realization" (p. 230). He thus does end up retaining, though in a somewhat attenuated form, the fundamental idea of German exegesis, namely, that Jesus preached the (temporal) proximity of the coming of God's Kingdom and that he presented it to his hearers in a variety of ways through the parables. The link between Christology and eschatology is thereby further weakened. The question remains as to what the listener two thousand years later is supposed to think of all this. At any rate, he has to regard the horizon of imminent eschatology then current as a mistake, since the Kingdom of God in the sense of a radical transformation of the world by God did not come; nor can he appropriate this idea for today. All of our reflections up to this point have led us to acknowledge that the immediate expectation of the end of the world was an aspect of the early reception of Jesus' message. At the same time, it has become evident that this idea cannot simply be superimposed onto all Jesus' words, and that to treat it as the central theme of Jesus' message would be blowing it out of proportion. In that respect, Dodd was much more on the right track in terms of the real dynamic of the texts.

From our study of the Sermon on the Mount, but also from our interpretation of the Our Father, we have seen that the deepest theme of Jesus' preaching was his own mystery, the mystery of the Son in whom God is among us and keeps his word; he announces the Kingdom of God as coming and as having come in his person. In this sense, we have to grant that Dodd was basically right. Yes, Jesus' Sermon on the Mount is "eschatological," if you will, but eschatological in the sense that the Kingdom of God is "realized" in his coming. It is thus perfectly possible to speak of an "eschatology in process of realization": Jesus, as the One who has come, is nonetheless the One who comes throughout the whole of history, and ultimately he speaks to us of this "coming." In this sense, we can thoroughly agree with the final words of Jeremias' book: "God's acceptable year has come. For he has been manifested whose veiled kingliness shines through every word and through every parable: the Savior" (p. 230).

We have, then, good grounds for interpreting all the parables as hidden and multilayered invitations to faith in Jesus as the "Kingdom of God in person." But there is one vexed saying of Jesus concerning the parables that stands in the way. All three Synoptics relate to us that Jesus first responded to the disciples' question about the meaning of the parable of the sower with a general answer about the reason for preaching in parables. At the heart of Jesus' answer is a citation from Isaiah 6:9f., which the Synoptics transmit in different versions. Mark's text reads as follows in Jeremias' painstakingly argued translation: "To you [that is, to the circle of disciples] has God given the secret of the Kingdom of God: but to those who are without, everything is obscure, in order that they (as it is written) may 'see and yet not see, may hear and yet not understand, unless they turn and God will forgive them'" (Mk 4:12; Jeremias, p. 17). What does this mean? Is the point of the Lord's parables to make his message inaccessible and to reserve it only for a small circle of elect souls for whom he interprets them himself? Is it that the parables are intended not to open doors, but to lock them? Is God partisan—does he want only an elite few, and not everyone?

If we want to understand the Lord's mysterious words, we must read them in light of Isaiah, whom he cites, and we must read them in light of his own path, the outcome of which he already knows. In saying these words, Jesus places himself in the line of the Prophets—his destiny is a prophet's destiny. Isaiah's words taken overall are much more severe and terrifying than the extract that Jesus cites. In the Book of Isaiah it says: "Make the heart of this people fat, and their ears heavy, and shut their eyes; lest they see with their eyes, and hear with their ears, and understand with their hearts, and turn and be healed"(Is 6:10). Prophets fail: Their message goes too much against general opinion and the comfortable habits of life. It is only through failure that their word becomes efficacious. This failure of the Prophets is an obscure question mark hanging over the whole history of Israel, and in a certain way it constantly recurs in the history of humanity. Above all, it is also again and again the destiny of Jesus Christ: He ends up on the Cross. But that very Cross is the source of great fruitfulness.

And here, unexpectedly, we see a connection with the parable of the sower, which is the context where the Synoptics report these words of Jesus. It is striking what a significant role the image of the seed plays in the whole of Jesus' message. The time of Jesus, the time of the disciples, is the time of sowing and of the seed. The "Kingdom of God" is present in seed form. Observed from the outside, the seed is something minuscule. It is easy to overlook. The mustard seed—an image of the Kingdom of God—is the smallest of seeds, yet it bears a whole tree within it. The seed is the presence of what is to come in the future. In the seed, that which is to come is already here in a hidden way. It is the presence of a promise. On Palm Sunday, the Lord summarized the manifold seed parables and unveiled their full meaning: "Truly, truly, I say to you, unless a grain of wheat falls into the earth and dies, it remains alone; but if it dies, it bears much fruit" (Jn 12:24). He himself is the grain of wheat. His "failure" on the Cross is exactly the way leading from the few to the many, to all: "And I, when I am lifted up from the earth, will draw all men to myself" (Jn 12:32).

The failure of the Prophets, his failure, appears now in another light. It is precisely the way to reach the point where "they turn and God will forgive them." It is precisely the method for opening the eyes and ears of all. It is on the Cross that the parables are unlocked. In his Farewell Discourses, the Lord says, apropos of this: "I have said this to you in parables [i.e., veiled discourse]; the hour is coming when I shall no longer speak to you in parables but tell you plainly of the Father" (Jn 16:25). The parables speak in a hidden way, then, of the mystery of the Cross; they do not only speak of it—they are part of it themselves. For precisely because they allow the mystery of Jesus' divinity to be seen, they lead to contradiction. It is just when they emerge into a final clarity, as in the parable of the unjust vintners (cf. Mk 12:1–12), that they become stations on the way to the Cross. In the parables Jesus is not only the sower who scatters the seed of God's word, but also the seed that falls into the earth in order to die and so to bear fruit.

Jesus' disturbing explanation of the point of his parables, then, is the very thing that leads us to their deepest meaning, provided—true to the nature of God's written word—we read the Bible, and especially the Gospels, as an overall unity expressing an intrinsically coherent message, notwithstanding their multiple historical layers. It may be worthwhile, though, to follow up this thoroughly theological explanation gleaned from the heart of the Bible with a consideration of the parables from the specifically human point of view as well. What is a parable exactly? And what is the narrator of the parable trying to convey?

Now, every educator, every teacher who wants to communicate new knowledge to his listeners naturally makes constant use of example or parable. By using an example, he draws to their attention a reality that until now has lain outside their field of vision. He wants to show how something they have hitherto not perceived can be glimpsed via a reality that does fall within their range of experience. By means of parable he brings something distant within their reach so that, using the parable as a bridge, they can arrive at what was previously unknown. A twofold movement is involved here. On one hand, the parable brings distant realities close to the listeners as they reflect upon it. On the other hand, the listeners themselves are led onto a journey. The inner dynamic of the parable, the intrinsic self-transcendence of the chosen image, invites them to entrust themselves to this dynamic and to go beyond their existing horizons, to come to know and understand things previously unknown. This means, however, that the parable demands the collaboration of the learner, for not only is something brought close to him, but he himself must enter into the movement of the parable and journey along with it. At this point we begin to see why parables can cause problems: people are sometimes unable to discover the dynamic and let themselves be guided by it. Especially in the case of parables that affect and transform their personal lives, people can be unwilling to be drawn into the required movement.

This brings us back to the Lord's words about seeing and not seeing, hearing and not understanding. For Jesus is not trying to convey to us some sort of abstract knowledge that does not concern us profoundly. He has to lead us to the mystery of God—to the light that our eyes cannot bear and that we therefore try to escape. In order to make it accessible to us, he shows how the divine light shines through in the things of this world and in the realities of our everyday life. Through everyday events, he wants to show us the real ground of all things and thus the true direction we have to take in our day-to-day lives if we want to go the right way. He shows us God: not an abstract God, but the God who acts, who intervenes in our lives, and wants to take us by the hand. He shows us through everyday things who we are and what we must therefore do. He conveys knowledge that makes demands upon us; it not only or even primarily adds to what we know, but it changes our lives. It is a knowledge that enriches us with a gift: "God is on the way to you." But equally it is an exacting knowledge: "Have faith, and let faith be your guide." The possibility of refusal is very real, for the parable lacks the necessary proof.

There can be a thousand rational objections—not only in Jesus' generation, but throughout all generations, and today maybe more than ever. For we have developed a concept of reality that excludes reality's translucence to God. The only thing that counts as real is what can be experimentally proven. God cannot be constrained into experimentation. That is exactly the reproach he made to the Israelites in the desert: "There your fathers tested me [tried to constrain me into experimentation], and put me to the proof, though they had seen my work" (Ps 95:9). God cannot be seen through the world—that is what the modern concept of reality says. And so there is even less reason to accept the demand he places on us: To believe in him as God and to live accordingly seems like a totally unreasonable requirement. In this situation, the parables really do lead to non-seeing and non-understanding, to "hardening of heart."

This means, though, that the parables are ultimately an expression of God's hiddenness in this world and of the fact that knowledge of God always lays claim to the whole person—that such knowledge is one with life itself, and that it cannot exist without "repentance." For in this world, marked by sin, the gravitational pull of our lives is weighted by the chains of the "I" and the "self." These chains must be broken to free us for a new love that places us in another gravitational field where we can enter new life. In this sense, knowledge of God is possible only through the gift of God's love becoming visible, but this gift too has to be accepted. In this sense, the parables manifest the essence of Jesus' message. In this sense, the mystery of the Cross is inscribed right at the heart of the parables.

Three Major Parables from the Gospel of Luke

To attempt an exposition of even a significant portion of Jesus' parables would far exceed the scope of this book. I would therefore like to limit myself to the three major parable narratives in Luke's Gospel, whose beauty and depth spontaneously touch believer and nonbeliever alike again and again: the story of the Good Samaritan, the parable of the Prodigal Son, and the tale of the rich man and Lazarus.

The Good Samaritan (Luke 10:25–37)

The story of the Good Samaritan concerns the fundamental human question. A lawyer—a master of exegesis, in other words—poses this question to the Lord: "Teacher, what shall I do to inherit eternal life?" (Lk 10:25). Luke comments that the scholar addresses this question to Jesus in order to put him to the test. Being a Scripture scholar himself, he knows how the Bible answers his question, but he wants to see what this prophet without formal biblical studies has to say about it. The Lord very simply refers him to the

Scripture, which of course he knows, and gets him to give the answer himself. The scholar does so by combining Deuteronomy 6:5 and Leviticus 19:18, and he is right on target: "You shall love the Lord your God with all your heart, and with all your soul, and with all your strength, and with all your mind; and your neighbor as yourself" (Lk 10:27). Jesus' teaching on this question is no different from that of the Torah, the entire meaning of which is contained in this double commandment. But now the learned man, who knew the answer to his own question perfectly well, has to justify himself. What the Scripture says is uncontroversial, but how it is to be applied in practice in daily life raises questions that really were controversial among scholars (and in everyday life).

The concrete question is who is meant by "neighbor." The conventional answer, for which scriptural support could be adduced, was that "neighbor" meant a fellow member of one's people. A people is a community of solidarity in which everyone bears responsibility for everyone else. In this community, each member is sustained by the whole, and so each member is expected to look on every other member "as himself," as a part of the same whole that gives him the space in which to live his life. Does this mean, then, that foreigners, men belonging to another people, are not neighbors? This would go against Scripture, which insisted upon love for foreigners also, mindful of the fact that Israel itself had lived the life of a foreigner in Egypt. It remained a matter of controversy, though, where the boundaries were to be drawn. Generally speaking, only the "sojourner" living among the people was reckoned as a member of the community of solidarity and so as a "neighbor." Other qualifications of the term enjoyed wide currency as well. One rabbinic saying ruled that there was no need to regard heretics, informers, and apostates as neighbors (Jeremias, pp. 202f.). It was also taken for granted that the Samaritans, who not long before (between the years A.D. 6 and 9) had defiled the Temple precincts in Jerusalem by "strewing dead men's bones" during the Passover festival itself (Jeremias, p. 204), were not neighbors.

Now that the question has been focused in this way, Jesus answers it with the parable of the man on the way from Jerusalem to Jericho who falls among robbers, is stripped of everything, and then is left lying half dead on the roadside. That was a perfectly realistic story, because such assaults were a regular occurrence on the Jericho road. A priest and a Levite—experts in the Law who know about salvation and are its professional servants—come along, but they pass by without stopping. There is no need to suppose that they were especially cold-hearted people; perhaps they were afraid themselves and were hurrying to get to the city as quickly as possible, or perhaps they were inexpert and did not know how to go about helping the man—especially since it looked as though he was quite beyond help anyway. At this point a Samaritan comes along, presumably a merchant who often has occasion to traverse this stretch of road and is evidently acquainted with the proprietor of the nearest inn; a Samaritan—someone, in other words, who does not belong to Israel's community of solidarity and is not obliged to see the assault victim as his "neighbor."

In this connection we need to recall that in the previous chapter the Evangelist has recounted that on the way to Jerusalem Jesus sent messengers ahead of him and that they entered a Samaritan village in order to procure him lodging:

"But the people would not receive him, because his face was set toward Jerusalem." The Sons of Thunder—James and John—became enraged and said to Jesus: "Lord, do you want us to bid fire come down from heaven and consume them?" (Lk 9:52f.). The Lord forbade them to do so. Lodging was found in another village.

And now the Samaritan enters the stage. What will he do? He does not ask how far his obligations of solidarity extend. Nor does he ask about the merits required for eternal life. Something else happens: His heart is wrenched open. The Gospel uses the word that in Hebrew had originally referred to the mother's womb and maternal care. Seeing this man in such a state is a blow that strikes him "viscerally," touching his soul. "He had compassion"—that is how we translate the text today, diminishing its original vitality. Struck in his soul by the lightning flash of mercy, he himself now becomes a neighbor, heedless of any question or danger. The burden of the question thus shifts here. The issue is no longer which other person is a neighbor to me or not. The question is about me. I have to become the neighbor, and when I do, the other person counts for me "as myself."

If the question had been "Is the Samaritan my neighbor, too?" the answer would have been a pretty clear-cut no given the situation at the time. But Jesus now turns the whole matter on its head: The Samaritan, the foreigner, makes himself the neighbor and shows me that I have to learn to be a neighbor deep within and that I already have the answer in myself. I have to become like someone in love, someone whose heart is open to being shaken up by another's need. Then I find my neighbor, or—better—then I am found by him.

Helmut Kuhn offers an exposition of this parable that, while certainly going beyond the literal sense of the text, nonetheless succeeds in conveying its radical message. He writes: "The love of friendship in political terms rests upon the equality of the partners. The symbolic parable of the Good Samaritan, by contrast, emphasizes their radical inequality: The Samaritan, a stranger to the people, is confronted with the anonymous other; the helper finds himself before the helpless victim of a violent holdup. *Agape,* the parable suggests, cuts right through all political alignments, governed as they are by the principle of *do ut des* ('If you give, I'll give'), and thereby displays its supernatural character. By the logic of its principle it is not only beyond these alignments, but is meant to overturn them: The last shall be first (cf. Mt 19:30) and the meek shall inherit the earth (cf. Mt 5:5)" (*"Liebe,"* pp. 88f.). One thing is clear: A new universality is entering the scene, and it rests on the fact that deep within I am already becoming a brother to all those I meet who are in need of my help.

The topical relevance of the parable is evident. When we transpose it into the dimensions of world society, we see how the peoples of Africa, lying robbed and plundered, matter to us. Then we see how deeply they are our neighbors; that our lifestyle, the history in which we are involved, has plundered them and continues to do so. This is true above all in the sense that we have wounded their souls. Instead of giving them God, the God who has come close to us in Christ, which would have integrated and brought to completion all that is precious and great in their own traditions, we have given them the cynicism of a world without God in which all that counts is power and profit, a world that destroys moral standards so that corruption and unscrupulous will to power are taken for granted. And that applies not only to Africa.

We do of course have material assistance to offer and we have to examine our own way of life. But we always give too little when we just give material things. And aren't we surrounded by people who have been robbed and battered? The victims of drugs, of human trafficking, of sex tourism, inwardly devastated people who sit empty in the midst of material abundance. All this is of concern to us, it calls us to have the eye and the heart of a neighbor, and to have the courage to love our neighbor, too. For—as we have said—the priest and the Levite may have passed by more out of fear than out of indifference. The risk of goodness is something we must relearn from within, but we can do that only if we ourselves become good from within, if we ourselves are "neighbors" from within, and if we then have an eye for the sort of service that is asked of us, that is possible for us, and is therefore also expected of us, in our environment and within the wider ambit of our lives.

The Church Fathers understood the parable Christologically. That is an allegorical reading, one might say—an interpretation that bypasses the text. But when we consider that in all the parables, each in a different way, the Lord really does want to invite us to faith in the Kingdom of God, which he himself is, then a Christological exposition is never a totally false reading. In some sense it reflects an inner potentiality in the text and can be a fruit growing out of it as from a seed. The Fathers see the parable in terms of world history: Is not the man who lies half dead and stripped on the roadside an image of "Adam," of man in general, who truly "fell among robbers"? Is it not true that man, this creature man, has been alienated, battered, and misused throughout his entire history? The great mass of humanity has almost always lived under oppression; conversely, are the oppressors the true image of man, or is it they who are really the distorted caricatures, a disgrace to man? Karl Marx painted a graphic picture of the "alienation" of man; even though he did not arrive at the real essence of alienation, because he thought only in material terms, he did leave us with a vivid image of man fallen among robbers.

Medieval theology read the two indications given in the parable concerning the battered man's condition as fundamental anthropological statements. The text says, first, that the victim of the assault was stripped (*spoliatus*) and, second, that he was beaten half dead (*vulneratus;* cf. Lk 10:30). The Scholastics took this as referring to the two dimensions of man's alienation. Man is, they said, *spoliatus supernaturalibus* and *vulneratus in naturalibus:* bereft of the splendor of the supernatural grace he had received and wounded in his nature. Now, that is an instance of allegory, and it certainly goes far beyond the literal sense. For all that, though, it is an attempt to identify precisely the two kinds of injury that weigh down human history.

The road from Jerusalem to Jericho thus turns out to be an image of human history; the half-dead man lying by the side of it is an image of humanity. Priest and Levite pass by; from earthly history alone, from its cultures and religions alone, no healing comes. If the assault victim is the image of Everyman, the Samaritan can only be the image of Jesus Christ. God himself, who for us is foreign and distant, has set out to take care of his wounded creature. God, though so remote from us, has made himself our neighbor in Jesus Christ. He pours oil and wine into our wounds, a gesture seen as an image of the healing gift of the sacraments, and he brings us to the inn, the Church, in which he arranges our care and also pays a deposit for the cost of that care.

We can safely ignore the individual details of the allegory, which change from Church Father to Church Father. But the great vision that sees man lying alienated and helpless by the roadside of history and God himself becoming man's neighbor in Jesus Christ is one that we can happily retain, as a deeper dimension of the parable that is of concern to us. For the mighty imperative expressed in the parable is not thereby weakened, but only now emerges in its full grandeur. The great theme of love, which is the real thrust of the text, is only now given its full breadth. For now we realize that we are all "alienated," in need of redemption. Now we realize that we are all in need of the gift of God's redeeming love ourselves, so that we too can become "lovers" in our turn. Now we realize that we always need God, who makes himself our neighbor so that we can become neighbors.

The two characters in this story are relevant to every single human being. Everyone is "alienated," especially from love (which, after all, is the essence of the "supernatural splendor" of which we have been despoiled); everyone must first be healed and filled with God's gifts. But then everyone is also called to become a Samaritan—to follow Christ and become like him. When we do that, we live rightly. We love rightly when we become like him, who loved all of us first (cf. 1 Jn 4:19).

The Parable of the Two Brothers (the Prodigal Son and the Son Who Remained at Home) and the Good Father (Luke 15:11–32)

Perhaps the most beautiful of Jesus' parables, this story is also known as the parable of the prodigal son. It is true that the figure of the prodigal son is so vividly drawn and his destiny, both in good and in evil, is so heart-rending that he inevitably appears to be the real center of the story. In reality, though, the parable has three protagonists. Jeremias and others have suggested that it would actually be better to call it the parable of the good father—that he is the true center of the text.

Pierre Grelot, on the other hand, has pointed out that the figure of the second brother is quite crucial, and he is therefore of the opinion—rightly, in my judgment—that the most accurate designation would be the parable of the two brothers. This relates directly to the situation which prompted the parable, which Luke 15:1f. presents as follows: "Now the tax collectors and sinners were all drawing near to hear him. And the Pharisees and the scribes murmured, saying, 'This man receives sinners and eats with them.'" Here we meet two groups, two "brothers": tax collectors and sinners on one hand, Pharisees and scribes on the other. Jesus responds with three parables: the parable of the lost sheep and the ninety-nine who remained at home; the parable of the lost drachma; and finally he begins anew, saying: "A man had two sons" (15:11). The story is about both sons.

In recounting this parable, the Lord is invoking a tradition that reaches way back into the past, for the motif of the two brothers runs through the entire Old Testament. Beginning with Cain and Abel, it continues down through Ishmael and Isaac to Esau and Jacob, only to be reflected once more in a modified form in the behavior of the eleven sons of Jacob toward Joseph. The history of those chosen by God is governed by a remarkable dialectic between pairs of brothers, and it remains as an unresolved question in the Old Testament. In a new hour of God's dealings in history, Jesus took up this motif again and gave it a new twist. In Matthew there is a text about two brothers that is related to our parable: one brother says he wants to do the father's will, but does not actually carry it out; the second says no to the father's will, but afterward he repents and carries out the task he had been given to do (cf. Mt 21:28–32). Here too it is the relationship between sinners and Pharisees that is at issue; here too the text is ultimately an appeal to say Yes once more to the God who calls us.

Let us now attempt to follow the parable step by step. The first figure we meet is that of the prodigal son, but right at the beginning we also see the magnanimity of the father. He complies with the younger son's wish for his share of the property and divides up the inheritance. He gives freedom. He can imagine what the younger son is going to do, but he lets him go his way.

The son journeys "into a far country." The Church Fathers read this above all as interior estrangement from the world of the father—the world of God—as interior rupture of relation, as the great abandonment of all that is authentically one's own. The son squanders his inheritance. He just wants to enjoy himself. He wants to scoop life out till there is nothing left. He wants to have "life in abundance" as he understands it. He no longer wants to be subject to any commandment, any authority. He seeks radical freedom. He wants to live only for himself, free of any other claim. He enjoys life; he feels that he is completely autonomous.

Is it difficult for us to see clearly reflected here the spirit of the modern rebellion against God and God's law? The leaving behind of everything we once depended on and the will to a freedom without limits? The Greek word used in the parable for the property that the son dissipates means "essence" in the vocabulary of Greek philosophy. The prodigal dissipates "his essence," himself.

At the end it is all gone. He who was once completely free is now truly a slave—a swineherd, who would be happy to be given pig feed to eat. Those who understand freedom as the radically arbitrary license to do just what they want and to have their own way are living in a lie, for by his very nature man is part of a shared existence and his freedom is shared freedom. His very nature contains direction and norm, and becoming inwardly one with this direction and norm is what freedom is all about. A false autonomy thus leads to slavery: In the meantime history has taught us this all too clearly. For Jews the pig is an unclean animal, which means that the swineherd is the expression of man's most extreme alienation and destitution. The totally free man has become a wretched slave.

At this point the "conversion" takes place. The prodigal son realizes that he is lost—that at home he was free and that his father's servants are freer than he now is, who had once considered himself completely free. "He went into himself," the Gospel says (Lk 15:17). As with the passage about the "far country," these words set the Church Fathers thinking philosophically: Living far away from home, from his origin, this man had also strayed far away from himself. He lived away from the truth of his existence.

His change of heart, his "conversion," consists in his recognition of this, his realization that he has become alienated and wandered into truly "alien lands," and his return to himself. What he finds in himself, though, is the compass pointing toward the father, toward the true freedom of a "son." The speech he prepares for his homecoming reveals to us the full extent of the inner pilgrimage he is now making. His words show that his whole life is now a steady progress leading "home"—through so many deserts—to himself and to the father. He is on a pilgrimage toward the truth of his existence, and that means "homeward." When the Church Fathers offer us this "existential" exposition of the son's journey home, they are also explaining to us what "conversion" is, what sort of sufferings and inner purifications it involves, and we may safely say that they have understood the essence of the parable correctly and help us to realize its relevance for today.

The father "sees the son from far off" and goes out to meet him. He listens to the son's confession and perceives in it the interior journey that he has made; he perceives that the son has found the way to true freedom. So he does not even let him finish, but embraces and kisses him and orders a great feast of joy to be prepared. The cause of this joy is that the son, who was already "dead" when he departed with his share of the property, is now alive again, has risen from the dead; "he was lost, and is found" (Lk 15:32).

The Church Fathers put all their love into their exposition of this scene. The lost son they take as an image of man as such, of "Adam," who all of us are—of Adam whom God has gone out to meet and whom he has received anew into his house. In the parable, the father orders the servants to bring quickly "the first robe." For the Fathers, this "first robe" is a reference to the lost robe of grace with which man had been originally clothed, but which he forfeited by sin. But now this "first robe" is given back to him—the robe of the son. The feast that is now made ready they read as an image of the feast of faith, the festive Eucharist, in which the eternal festal banquet is anticipated. To cite the Greek text literally, what the first brother hears when he comes home is "symphony and choirs"—again for the Fathers an image for the symphony of the faith, which makes being a Christian a joy and a feast.

But the kernel of the text surely does not lie in these details; the kernel is now unmistakably the figure of the father. Can we understand him? Can a father, may a father act like this? Pierre Grelot has drawn attention to the fact that Jesus is speaking here on a solidly Old Testament basis: The archetype of this vision of God the Father is found in Hosea 11:1–9. First the text speaks of Israel's election and subsequent infidelity: "My people abides in infidelity; they call upon Baal, but he does not help them" (Hos 11:2). But God also sees that this people is broken and that the sword rages in its cities (cf. Hos 11:6). And now the very thing that is described in our parable happens to the people: "How can I give you up, O Ephraim! How can I hand you over, O Israel! . . . My heart turns itself against me, my compassion grows warm and tender. I will not execute my fierce anger, I will not again destroy Ephraim; for I am God and not man, the Holy One in your midst" (Hos 11:8f.). Because God is God, the Holy

One, he acts as no man could act. God has a heart, and this heart turns, so to speak, against God himself: Here in Hosea, as in the Gospel, we encounter once again the word *compassion,* which is expressed by means of the image of the maternal womb. God's heart transforms wrath and turns punishment into forgiveness.

For the Christian, the question now arises: Where does Jesus Christ fit into all this? Only the Father figures in the parable. Is there no Christology in it? Augustine tried to work Christology in where the text says that the father embraced the son (cf. Lk 15:20). "The arm of the Father is the Son," he writes. He could have appealed here to Irenaeus, who referred to the Son and the Spirit as the two hands of the Father. "The arm of the Father is the Son." When he lays this arm on our shoulders as "his light yoke," then that is precisely not a burden he is loading onto us, but rather the gesture of receiving us in love. The "yoke" of this arm is not a burden that we must carry, but a gift of love that carries us and makes us sons. This is a very evocative exposition, but it is still an "allegory" that clearly goes beyond the text.

Pierre Grelot has discovered an interpretation that accords with the text and goes even deeper. He draws attention to the fact that Jesus uses this parable, along with the two preceding ones, to justify his own goodness toward sinners; he uses the behavior of the father in the parable to justify the fact that he too welcomes sinners. By the way he acts, then, Jesus himself becomes "the revelation of the one he called his Father." Attention to the historical context of the parable thus yields by itself an "implicit Christology." "His Passion and his Resurrection reinforce this point still further: How did God show his merciful love for sinners? In that 'while we were yet sinners Christ died for us' (Rom 5:8)." "Jesus cannot enter into the narrative framework of the parable because he lives in identification with the heavenly Father and bases his conduct on the Father's. The risen Christ remains today, in this point, in the same situation as Jesus of Nazareth during the time of his earthly ministry" (pp. 228f.). Indeed: In this parable, Jesus justifies his own conduct by relating it to, and identifying it with, the Father's. It is in the figure of the father, then, that Christ—the concrete realization of the father's action—is placed right at the heart of the parable.

The older brother now makes his appearance. He comes home from working in the fields, hears feasting at home, finds out why, and becomes angry. He finds it simply unfair that this good-for-nothing, who has squandered his entire fortune—the father's property—with prostitutes, should now be given a splendid feast straightaway without any period of probation, without any time of penance. That contradicts his sense of justice: The life he has spent working is made to look of no account in comparison to the dissolute past of the other. Bitterness arises in him: "Lo, these many years I have served you, and I never disobeyed one of your commands," he says to his father, "yet you never gave me a kid, that I might make merry with my friends" (Lk 15:29). The father goes out to meet the older brother, too, and now he speaks kindly to his son. The older brother knows nothing of the inner transformations and wanderings experienced by the younger brother, of his journey into distant parts, of his fall and his new self-discovery. He sees only injustice. And this betrays the fact that he too had secretly dreamed of a freedom without limits, that his obedience has made him inwardly bitter, and that he has no awareness of the grace of being at home, of the true freedom that he enjoys as a son. "Son, you are always with me, and all that is mine is yours" (Lk 15:31). The father explains to him the great value of sonship with these words—the same words that Jesus uses in his high-priestly prayer to describe his relationship to the Father: "All that is mine is thine, and all that is thine is mine" (Jn 17:10).

The parable breaks off here; it tells us nothing about the older brother's reaction. Nor can it, because at this point the parable immediately passes over into reality. Jesus is using these words of the father to speak to the heart of the murmuring Pharisees and scribes who have grown indignant at his goodness to sinners (cf. Lk 15:2). It now becomes fully clear that Jesus identifies his goodness to sinners with the goodness of the father in the parable and that all the words attributed to the father are the words that he himself addresses to the righteous. The parable does not tell the story of some distant affair, but is about what is happening here and now through him. He is wooing the heart of his adversaries. He begs them to come in and to share his joy at this hour of homecoming and reconciliation. These words remain in the Gospel as a pleading invitation. Paul takes up this pleading invitation when he writes: "We beseech you on behalf of Christ, be reconciled to God" (2 Cor 5:20).

On one hand, then, the parable is located quite realistically at the moment in history when Christ recounted it. At the same time, however, it points beyond the historical moment, for God's wooing and pleading continues. But to whom is the parable now addressed? The Church Fathers generally applied the two-brothers motif to the relation between Jews and Gentiles. It was not hard for them to recognize in the dissolute son who had strayed far from God and from himself an image of the pagan world, to which Jesus had now opened the door for communion with God in grace and for which he now celebrates the feast of his love. By the same token, neither was it hard for them to recognize in the brother who remained at home an image of the people of Israel, who could legitimately say: "Lo, these many years I have served you, and I never disobeyed one of your commands." Israel's fidelity and image of God are clearly revealed in such fidelity to the Torah.

This application to the Jews is not illegitimate so long as we respect the form in which we have found it in the text: as God's delicate attempt to talk Israel around, which remains entirely God's initiative. We should note that the father in the parable not only does not dispute the older brother's fidelity, but explicitly confirms his sonship: "Son, you are always with me, and all that is mine is yours." It would be a false interpretation to read this as a condemnation of the Jews, for which there is no support in the text.

While we may regard this application of the parable of the two brothers to Israel and the Gentiles as one dimension of the text, there are other dimensions as well. After all, what Jesus says about the older brother is aimed not simply at Israel (the sinners who came to him were Jews, too), but at the specific temptation of the righteous, of those who are "*en règle,*" at rights with God, as Grelot puts it (p. 229). In this connection, Grelot places emphasis on the sentence "I never disobeyed one of your commandments." For them, more than anything else God is Law; they see themselves in a juridical relationship with God and in that relationship they are at rights with him. But God is greater: They need to convert from the Law-God to the greater God, the God of love. This will not mean giving up their obedience, but rather that this obedience will flow from deeper wellsprings and will therefore be bigger, more open, and purer, but above all more humble.

Let us add a further aspect that has already been touched upon: Their bitterness toward God's goodness reveals an inward bitterness regarding their own obedience, a bitterness that indicates the limitations of this obedience. In their heart of hearts, they would have gladly journeyed out into that great "freedom" as well. There is an unspoken envy of what others have been able to get away with. They have not gone through the pilgrimage that purified the younger brother and made him realize what it means to be free and what it means to be a son. They actually carry their freedom as if it were slavery and they have not matured to real sonship. They, too, are still in need of a path; they can find it if they simply admit that God is right and accept his feast as their own. In this parable, then, the Father through Christ is addressing us, the ones who never left home, encouraging us too to convert truly and to find joy in our faith.

The Parable of the Rich Man and Lazarus (Luke 16:19–31)

This story once again presents us with two contrasting figures: the rich man, who carouses in his life of luxury, and the poor man, who cannot even catch the crumbs that the rich bon vivants drop from the table—according to the custom of the time, pieces of bread they used to wash their hands and then threw away. Some of the Church Fathers also classed this parable as an example of the two-brother pattern and applied it to the relationship between Israel (the rich man) and the Church (the poor man, Lazarus), but in so doing they mistook the very different typology that is involved here. This is evident already in the very different ending. Whereas the two-brother texts remain open, ending as a question and an invitation, this story already describes the definitive end of both protagonists.

For some background that will enable us to understand this narrative, we need to look at the series of Psalms in which the cry of the poor rises before God—the poor who live out their faith in God in obedience to his commandments, but experience only unhappiness, whereas the cynics who despise God go from success to success and enjoy every worldly happiness. Lazarus belongs to the poor whose voice we hear, for example, in Psalm 44: "Thou hast made us the taunt of our neighbors, the derision and scorn of those about us. . . . Nay, for thy sake we are slain all the day long, and accounted as sheep for the slaughter" (Ps 44:15–23; cf. Rom 8:36). The early wisdom of Israel had operated on the premise that God rewards the righteous and punishes the sinner, so that misfortune matches sin and happiness matches righteousness. This wisdom had been thrown into crisis at least since the time of the Exile. It was not just that the people of Israel as a whole suffered more than the surrounding peoples who led them into exile and oppression—in private life, too, it was becoming increasingly apparent that cynicism pays and that the righteous man is doomed to suffer in this world. In the Psalms and the later Wisdom Literature we witness the struggle to come to grips with this contradiction; we see a new effort to become "wise"—to understand life rightly, to find and understand anew the God who seems unjust or altogether absent.

One of the most penetrating texts concerning this struggle is Psalm 73, which we may regard as in some sense the intellectual backdrop of our parable. There we see the figure of the rich glutton before our very eyes and we hear the complaint of the praying Psalmist—Lazarus: "For I was envious of the arrogant, when I saw the prosperity of the wicked. For they have no pangs; their bodies are sound and sleek. They are not in trouble as other men are; they are not stricken like other men. Therefore pride is their necklace. . . . Their eyes swell out with fatness. . . . They set their mouths against the heavens. . . . Therefore the people turn and praise them; and find no fault in them. And they say, 'How can God know? Is there knowledge in the Most High?'" (Ps 73:3–11).

The suffering just man who sees all this is in danger of doubting his faith. Does God really not see? Does he not hear? Does he not care about men's fate? "All in vain have I kept my heart clean and washed my hands in innocence. For all the day long I have been stricken, and chastened every morning. My heart was embittered" (Ps 73:13ff.). The turning point comes when the suffering just man in the Sanctuary looks toward God and, as he does so, his perspective becomes broader. Now he sees that the seeming cleverness of the successful cynics is stupidity when viewed against the light. To be wise in that way is to be "stupid and ignorant . . . like a beast" (Ps 73:22). They remain within the perspective of animals and have lost the human perspective that transcends the material realm—toward God and toward eternal life.

We may be reminded here of another Psalm in which a persecuted man says at the end: "May their belly be filled with good things; may their children have more than enough. . . . As for me, I shall behold thy face in righteousness; when I awake, I shall be satisfied with beholding thy form" (Ps 77:14f.). Two sorts of satisfaction are contrasted here: being satiated with material goods, and satisfaction with beholding "thy form"—the heart becoming sated by the encounter with infinite love. The words "when I awake" are at the deepest level a reference to the awakening into new and eternal life, but they also speak of a deeper "awakening" here in this world: Man wakes up to the truth in a way that gives him a new satisfaction here and now.

It is of this awakening in prayer that Psalm 73 speaks. For now the psalmist sees that the happiness of the cynics that he had envied so much is only "like a dream that fades when one awakes, on awaking one forgets their phantoms" (Ps 73:20). And now he recognizes real happiness: "Nevertheless I am continually with thee; thou dost hold my right hand. . . . Whom have I in heaven but thee? And there is nothing upon earth that I desire besides thee. . . . But for me it is good to be near God" (Ps 73:23, 25, 28). This is not an encouragement to place our hope in the afterlife, but rather an awakening to the true stature of man's being—which does, of course, include the call to eternal life.

This has been only an apparent digression from our parable. In reality, the Lord is using this story in order to initiate us into the very process of "awakening" that is reflected in the Psalms. This has nothing to do with a cheap condemnation of riches and of the rich begotten of envy. In the Psalms that we have briefly considered all envy is left behind. The psalmist has come to see just how foolish it is to envy this sort of wealth because he has recognized what is truly good. After Jesus' Crucifixion two wealthy men make their appearance, Nicodemus and Joseph of Arimathea, who had discovered the Lord and were in the process of "awakening." The Lord wants to lead us from foolish cleverness toward true wisdom; he wants to teach us to discern the real good. And so we have good grounds, even though it is not there in the text, to say that, from the perspective of the Psalms, the rich glutton was already an empty-hearted man in this world, and that his carousing was only an attempt to smother this interior emptiness of his. The next life only brings to light the truth already present in this life. Of course, this parable, by awakening us, at the same time summons us to the love and responsibility that we owe now to our poor brothers and sisters—both on the large scale of world society and on the small scale of our everyday life.

In the description of the next life that now follows in the parable, Jesus uses ideas that were current in the Judaism of his time. Hence we must not force our interpretation of this part of the text. Jesus adopts existing images, without formally incorporating them into his teaching about the next life. Nevertheless, he does unequivocally affirm the substance of the images. In this sense, it is important to note that Jesus invokes here the idea of the intermediate state between death and the resurrection, which by then had become part of the universal patrimony of Jewish faith. The rich man is in Hades, conceived here as a temporary place, and not in "Gehenna" (hell), which is the name of the final state (Jeremias, p. 185). Jesus says nothing about a "resurrection in death" here. But as we saw earlier, this is not the principal message that the Lord wants to convey in this parable. Rather, as Jeremias has convincingly shown, the main point—which comes in the second part of the parable—is the rich man's request for a sign.

The rich man, looking up to Abraham from Hades, says what so many people, both then and now, say or would like to say to God: "If you really want us to believe in you and organize our lives in accord with the revealed word of the Bible, you'll have to make yourself clearer. Send us someone from the next world who can tell us that it is really so." The demand for signs, the demand for more evidence of Revelation, is an issue that runs through the entire Gospel. Abraham's answer—like Jesus' answer to his contemporaries' demand for signs in other contexts—is clear: If people do not believe the word of Scripture, then they will not believe someone coming from the next world either. The highest truths cannot be forced into the type of empirical evidence that only applies to material reality.

Abraham cannot send Lazarus to the rich man's father's house. But at this point something strikes us. We are reminded of the resurrection of Lazarus of Bethany, recounted to us in John's Gospel. What happens there? The Evangelist tells us, "Many of the Jews . . . believed in him" (Jn 11:45). They go to the Pharisees and report on what has happened, whereupon the Sanhedrin gathers to take counsel. They see the affair in a political light: If this leads to a popular movement, it might force the Romans to intervene, leading to a dangerous situation. So they decide to kill Jesus. The miracle leads not to faith, but to hardening of hearts (Jn 11:45–53).

But our thoughts go even further. Do we not recognize in the figure of Lazarus—lying at the rich man's door covered in sores—the mystery of Jesus, who "suffered outside the city walls" (Heb 13:12) and, stretched naked on the Cross, was delivered over to the mockery and contempt of the mob, his body "full of blood and wounds"? "But I am a worm, and no man; scorned by men, and despised by the people" (Ps 22:7).

He, the true Lazarus, *has* risen from the dead—and he has come to tell us so. If we see in the story of Lazarus Jesus' answer to his generation's demand for a sign, we find ourselves in harmony with the principal answer that Jesus gave to that demand. In Matthew, it reads thus: "An evil and adulterous generation seeks for a sign; but no sign shall be given to it except the sign of the Prophet Jonah. For as Jonah was three days and three nights in the belly of the whale, so will the Son of man be three days and three nights in the heart of the earth" (Mt 12:39f.). In Luke we read: "This generation is an evil generation; it seeks a sign, but no sign shall be given to it except the sign of Jonah. For as Jonah became a sign to the men of Nineveh, so will the Son of man be to this generation" (Lk 11:29f.).

We do not need to analyze here the differences between these two versions. One thing is clear: God's sign for men is the Son of Man; it is Jesus himself. And at the deepest level, he is this sign in his Paschal Mystery, in the mystery of his death and Resurrection. He himself is "the sign of Jonah." He, crucified and risen, is the true Lazarus. The parable is inviting us to believe and follow him, God's great sign. But it is more than a parable. It speaks of reality, of the most decisive reality in all history.

CHAPTER EIGHT

The Principal Images of John's Gospel

Introduction: The Johannine Question

Thus far, in our attempt to listen to Jesus and thereby to get to know him, we have limited ourselves for the most part to the witness of the Synoptic Gospels (Matthew, Mark, and Luke), while only occasionally glancing at John. It is therefore time to turn our attention to the image of Jesus presented by the Fourth Evangelist, an image that in many respects seems quite different from that of the other Gospels.

Listening to the Synoptics, we have realized that the mystery of Jesus' oneness with the Father is ever present and determines everything, even though it remains hidden beneath his humanity. On one hand, it was perceived by his sharp-eyed opponents. On the other hand, the disciples, who experienced Jesus at prayer and were privileged to know him intimately from the inside, were beginning—step by step, at key moments with great immediacy, and despite all their misunderstandings—to recognize this absolutely new reality. In John, Jesus' divinity appears unveiled. His disputes with the Jewish Temple authorities, taken together, could be said to anticipate his trial before the Sanhedrin, which John, unlike the Synoptics, does not mention specifically.

John's Gospel is different: Instead of parables, we hear extended discourses built around images, and the main theater of Jesus' activity shifts from Galilee to Jerusalem. These differences caused modern critical scholarship to deny the historicity of the text—with the exception of the Passion narrative and a few details—and to regard it as a later theological reconstruction. It was said to express a highly developed Christology, but not to constitute a reliable source for knowledge of the historical Jesus. The radically late datings of John's Gospel to which this view gave rise have had to be abandoned because papyri from Egypt dating back to the beginning of the second century have been discovered; this made it clear that the Gospel must have been written in the first century, if only during the closing years. Denial of the Gospel's historical character, however, continued unabated.

Interpretation of John's Gospel in the second half of the twentieth century was largely shaped by Rudolf Bultmann's commentary on John, the first edition of which appeared in 1941. Bultmann is convinced that the main influences on the Gospel of John are to be sought not in the Old Testament and the Judaism of the time, but in Gnosticism. This sentence typifies Bultmann's approach: "That is not to say that the idea of the incarnation of the redeemer has in some way penetrated Gnosticism from Christianity; it is itself originally Gnostic, and was taken over at a very early stage by Christianity, and made fruitful for Christology" (*The Gospel of John,* p. 26). Here is another in the same vein: "Gnosticism is the only possible source of the idea of absolute Logos" (*RGG,* 3rd ed., III, p. 846).

The reader asks: How does Bultmann know that? Bultmann's answer is breathtaking: "Even if the reconstruction of this kind of thinking has to be carried out in the main from sources which are later than John, nevertheless its *greater age* remains firmly established" (*The Gospel of John,* p. 27). On this decisive point Bultmann is wrong. In his inaugural lecture as professor at Tübingen, published in expanded form as *The Son of God* in 1975 (English translation 1976), Martin Hengel characterized "the hypothetical Gnostic myth of the sending of the Son of God into the world" as a "pseudo-scientific development of a myth." He then went on to remark: "In reality there is no Gnostic redeemer myth in the sources which can be demonstrated chronologically to be pre-Christian" (p. 33). "Gnosticism itself is first visible as a spiritual movement at the end of the first century A.D. at the earliest, and only develops fully in the second century" (p. 34).

Johannine scholarship in the generation after Bultmann took a radically different direction; the results have been thoroughly explored and discussed in Martin Hengel's book *The Johannine Question* (1989). If we look back from the vantage point of current scholarship to Bultmann's interpretation of John, we see how little protection the highly scientific approach can offer against fundamental mistakes. But what does today's scholarship tell us?

It has definitively confirmed and elaborated something that even Bultmann basically already knew: The Fourth Gospel rests on extraordinarily precise knowledge of times and places, and so can only have been produced by someone who had an excellent firsthand knowledge of Palestine at the time of Jesus. A further point that has become clear is that the Gospel thinks and argues entirely in terms of the Old Testament—of the Torah (Rudolf Pesch)—and that its whole way of arguing is deeply rooted in the Judaism of Jesus' time. The language of the Gospel, which Bultmann regarded as "Gnostic," actually bears unmistakable signs of the book's intimate association with this milieu. "The work was written in simple unliterary *koine* Greek, steeped in the language of Jewish piety. This Greek was also spoken by the upper classes in Jerusalem . . . [where] Scripture was read in Hebrew and Greek, and prayer and discussion went on in both languages" (Hengel, *The Johannine Question,* p. 113).

Hengel also points out that "in Herodian times a special Hellenized Jewish upper class with its own culture developed in Jerusalem" (ibid., p. 114) and he accordingly locates the origin of the Gospel in the priestly aristocracy of Jerusalem (ibid., pp. 124–35). We can perhaps regard a brief reference in John 18:15f. as corroboration for this thesis. There it is recounted that after his arrest Jesus is brought to the high priests for interrogation and that in the meantime Simon Peter and "another disciple" follow Jesus in order to find out what is going to happen next. Regarding this "other disciple," it is then said that "as this disciple was known to the high priest, he entered the court of the high priest along with Jesus." His connections with the household of the high priest were such that he was able to secure Peter's entry, thereby engineering the situation that led to Peter's denial. The circle of the disciples, then, extended as far as the high-priestly aristocracy, in whose language the Gospel is largely written.

This brings, us, however, to two decisive questions that are ultimately at stake in the "Johannine" question: Who is the author of this Gospel? How reliable is it historically? Let us try to approach the first question. The Gospel itself makes a clear statement about it in the context of the Passion story. It is reported that one of the soldiers pierced Jesus' side with a lance "and at once there came out blood and water" (Jn 19:34). These weighty words immediately follow: "He who saw it has borne witness—his testimony is true, and he knows that he tells the truth—that you also may believe" (Jn 19:35). The Gospel traces its origins to an eyewitness, and it is clear that this eyewitness is none other than the disciple who, as we have just been told, was standing under the Cross and was the disciple whom Jesus loved (cf. Jn 19:26). This disciple is once again named as the author of the Gospel in John 21:24. In addition, we meet this figure in John 13:23, 20:2–10, and 21:7, and probably in Jn 1:35, 40 and 18:15–16 as well.

These statements concerning the external origin of the Gospel take on a deeper dimension in the story of the washing of the feet, which points to its inward source. Here it is said that this disciple reclined at Jesus' side during the meal and that, when he asked who the betrayer was, he "leaned back on Jesus' breast" (Jn 13:25). These words are intended to parallel the end of the prologue of John's Gospel, where it is said apropos of Jesus: "No one has ever seen God; it is the only Son, who is nearest to the Father's heart, who has made him known" (Jn 1:18). Just as Jesus, the Son, knows about the mystery of the Father from resting in his heart, so too the

Evangelist has gained his intimate knowledge from his inward repose in Jesus' heart.

But who is this disciple? The Gospel never directly identifies him by name. In connection with the calling of Peter, as well as of other disciples, it points toward John, the son of Zebedee, but it never explicitly identifies the two figures. The intention is evidently to leave the matter shrouded in mystery. The Book of Revelation does, admittedly, specify John as its author (cf. Rev 1:1, 4), but despite the close connection between this book and the Gospel and Letters of John, it remains an open question whether the author is one and the same person.

The Lutheran exegete Ulrich Wilckens, in his extensive *Theologie des Neuen Testaments,* has recently presented new arguments for the thesis that the "beloved disciple" should be thought of not as a historical figure, but as a symbol for a basic structure of the faith: "*Scriptura sola* is impossible without the 'living voice' of the Gospel and that is impossible without the personal witness of a Christian in the function and authority of the 'beloved disciple,' in whom office and spirit unite and support each other" (*Theologie,* I, 4, p. 158). However correct this may be as a structural claim, it remains insufficient. If the favorite disciple in the Gospel expressly assumes the function of a witness to the truth of the events he recounts, he is presenting himself as a living person. He intends to vouch for historical events as a witness and he thus claims for himself the status of a historical figure. Otherwise the statements we have examined, which are decisive for the intention and the quality of the entire Gospel, would be emptied of meaning.

Since the time of Irenaeus of Lyon (d. ca. 202), Church tradition has unanimously regarded John, the son of Zebedee, as the beloved disciple and the author of the Gospel. This fits with the identification markers provided by the Gospel, which in any case point toward the hand of an Apostle and companion of Jesus from the time of the Baptism in the Jordan to the Last Supper, Cross, and Resurrection.

In modern times, it is true, increasingly strong doubts have been voiced concerning this identification. Can the fisherman from the Lake of Genesareth have written this sublime Gospel full of visions that peer into the deepest depths of God's mystery? Can he, the Galilean fisherman, have been as closely connected with the priestly aristocracy of Jerusalem, its language, and its mentality as the Evangelist evidently is? Can he have been related to the family of the high priest, as the text hints (cf. Jn 18:15)?

Now, the French exegete Henri Cazelles, drawing on studies by J. Colson, J. Winandy, and M.-E. Boismard, has shown in a sociological study of the Temple priesthood before its destruction ("Johannes") that such an identification is actually quite possible. The priests discharged their ministry on a rotating basis twice a year. The ministry itself lasted a week each time. After the completion of the ministry, the priest returned to his home, and it was not at all unusual for him also to exercise a profession to earn his livelihood. Furthermore, the Gospel makes clear that Zebedee was no simple fisherman, but employed several day laborers, which also explains why it was possible for his sons to leave him. "It is thus quite possible that Zebedee is a priest, but that at the same time he has his property in Galilee, while the fishing business on the lake helps him makes ends meet. He probably has a kind of pied-à-terre in or near the Jerusalem neighborhood where the Essenes lived" ("Johannes," p. 481). "The very meal during which this disciple rested on Jesus' breast took place in a room that in all probability was located in the Essene neighborhood of the city"—in the "pied-à-terre" of the priest Zebedee, who "lent the upper room to Jesus and the Twelve" (ibid., pp. 480, 481). Another observation Cazelles makes in his article is interesting in this connection: According to the Jewish custom, the host or, in his absence, as would have been the case here, "his firstborn son sat to the right of the guest, his head leaning on the latter's chest" (ibid., p. 480).

If in light of current scholarship, then, it is quite possible to see Zebedee's son John as the bystander who solemnly asserts his claim to be an eyewitness (cf. Jn 19:35) and thereby identifies himself as the true author of the Gospel, nevertheless, the complexity of the Gospel's redaction raises further questions.

The Church historian Eusebius of Caesarea (d. ca. 338) gives us a piece of information that is important in this context. Eusebius tells us about a five-volume work of the bishop of Hierapolis, Papias, who died around 120. Papias mentions there that he had not known or seen the holy Apostles himself, but that he had received the teaching of the faith from people who had been close to the Apostles. He also speaks of others who were likewise disciples of the Lord, and he mentions the names Aristion and "Presbyter John." Now, the important point is that he distinguishes between the Apostle and Evangelist John, on one hand, and "Presbyter John," on the other. Although he had not personally known the former, he had met the latter (Eusebius, *Historia Ecclesiastica,* III, 39).

This information is very remarkable indeed: When combined with related pieces of evidence, it suggests that in Ephesus there was something like a Johannine school, which traced its origins to Jesus' favorite disciple himself, but in which a certain "Presbyter John" presided as the ultimate authority. This "presbyter" John appears as the sender and author of the Second and Third Letters of John (in each case in the first verse of the first chapter) simply under the title "the presbyter" (without reference to the name John). He is evidently not the same as the Apostle, which means that here in the canonical text we encounter expressly the mysterious figure of the presbyter. He must have been closely connected with the Apostle; perhaps he had even been acquainted with Jesus himself. After the death of the Apostle, he was identified wholly as the bearer of the latter's heritage, and in the collective memory, the two figures were increasingly fused. At any rate, there seem to be grounds for ascribing to "Presbyter John" an essential role in the definitive shaping of the Gospel, though he must always have regarded himself as the trustee of the tradition he had received from the son of Zebedee.

I entirely concur with the conclusion that Peter Stuhlmacher has drawn from the above data. He holds "that the contents of the Gospel go back to the disciple whom Jesus (especially) loved. The presbyter understood himself as his transmitter and mouthpiece" (*Biblische Theologie,* II, p. 206). In a similar vein Stuhlmacher cites E. Ruckstuhl and P. Dschulnigg to the effect that "the author of the Gospel of John is, as it were, the literary executor of the favorite disciple" (ibid., p. 207).

With these observations, we have already taken a decisive step toward answering the question of the historical credibility of the Fourth Gospel. This Gospel ultimately goes back to an eyewitness, and even the actual redaction of the text was substantially the work of one of his closest followers within the living circle of his disciples.

Thinking along similar lines, Peter Stuhlmacher writes that there are grounds for the conjecture "that the Johannine school carried on the style of thinking and teaching that before Easter set the tone of Jesus' internal didactic discourses with Peter, James, and John (as well as with the whole group of the Twelve) . . . While the Synoptic tradition reflects the way in which the apostles and their disciples spoke about Jesus as they were teaching on Church missions or in Church communities, the Johannine circle took this instruction as the basis and premise for further thinking about, and discussion of, the mystery of revelation, of God's self-disclosure in 'the Son'" (*Biblische Theologie*, II, p. 207). Against this, though, it could be argued that according to the text of the Gospel itself, what we find are not so much internal didactic discourses but rather Jesus' dispute with the Temple aristocracy, in which we are given a kind of preview of his trial. In this context, the question "Are you the Christ, the Son of the Blessed?" (Mk 14:61), in its different forms, increasingly adopts center stage in the whole dispute, so that Jesus' claim to Sonship inevitably takes on more and more dramatic forms.

It is surprising that Martin Hengel, from whom we have learned so much about the historical rooting of the Gospel in the priestly aristocracy of Jerusalem—and so in the real context of Jesus' life—nonetheless offers an astonishingly negative, or (to put it more gently) extremely cautious, judgment of the historical character of the text. He says: "The Fourth Gospel is not a completely free 'Jesus poem' . . . Here we must distinguish between those traits which are historically plausible and others which remain chiefly suppositions. An inability to prove the historicity of something does not mean that it is pure unhistorical fiction. Certainly the evangelist is not narrating historical, banal recollections of the past but the rigorously interpretative spirit-paraclete leading into truth, which has the last word throughout the work" (p. 132). This raises an objection: What does this contrast mean? What makes historical recollection banal? Is the truth of what is recollected important or not? And what sort of truth can the Paraclete guide into if he leaves behind the historical because it is too banal?

The diagnosis of the exegete Ingo Broer reveals even more sharply the problem with these sorts of contrasts: "The Gospel of John thus stands before us as a *literary* work that bears witness to faith and is intended to strengthen faith, and not as a historical account" (*Einleitung*, p. 197). What faith does it "testify" to if, so to speak, it has left history behind? How does it strengthen faith if it presents itself as a historical testimony—and does so quite emphatically—but then does not report history? I think that we are dealing here with a false concept of the historical, as well as with a false concept of faith and of the Paraclete. A faith that discards history in this manner really turns into "Gnosticism." It leaves flesh, incarnation—just what true history is—behind.

If "historical" is understood to mean that the discourses of Jesus transmitted to us have to be something like a recorded transcript in order to be acknowledged as "historically" authentic, then the discourses of John's Gospel are not "historical." But the fact that they make no claim to literal accuracy of this sort by no means implies that they are merely "Jesus poems" that the members of the Johannine school gradually put together, claiming to be acting under the guidance of the Paraclete. What the Gospel is really claiming is that it has correctly rendered the substance of the discourses, of Jesus' self-attestation in the great Jerusalem disputes, so that the readers really do encounter the decisive content of this message and, therein, the authentic figure of Jesus.

We can take a further step toward defining more precisely the particular sort of historicity that is present in the Fourth Gospel if we attend to the mutual ordering of the various elements that Hengel regards as decisive for the composition of the text. Hengel begins by naming four of the essential elements of this Gospel: "the theological concern of the author . . . his personal recollections . . . church tradition and with them historical reality." Astonishingly, Hengel says that the Evangelist "altered, indeed we might even say violated" this history. Finally, as we have just seen, it is not "the recollections of the past but the rigorously interpretative spirit-paraclete leading into truth which has the last word" (*The Johannine Question,* p. 132).

Given the way that Hengel juxtaposes, and in a certain respect contraposes, these five elements, they cannot be brought into any meaningful synthesis. For how is the Paraclete supposed to have the last word if the Evangelist has already violated the actual history? What sort of relation is there between the redactional concern of the Evangelist, his personal message, and Church tradition? Is redactional concern more decisive than recollection, so that in its name reality may be violated? What, then, establishes the legitimacy of this redactional concern? How does it interact with the Paraclete?

I think that the five elements listed by Hengel are indeed the essential forces that shaped the composition of the Gospel, but they have to be seen in a different mutual relation, and the individual elements have to be differently understood.

First of all, the second and fourth elements—personal recollection and historical reality—form a pair. Together they constitute what the Fathers of the Church call the *factum historicum* that determines the literal sense of the text: the exterior side of the event, which the Evangelist knows partly from personal recollection and partly from Church tradition (no doubt he was familiar with the Synoptic Gospels in one or another version). His intention is to act as a "witness" reporting the things that happened. No one has emphasized this particular dimension of what actually happened—the "flesh" of history—to such an extent as John. "That which was from the beginning, which we have heard, which we have seen with our eyes, which we have looked upon and touched with our hands, concerning the word of life—the life was made manifest, and we saw it, and testify to it, and proclaim to you the eternal life which was with the Father and was made manifest to us" (1 Jn 1:1f.).

These two factors—historical reality and recollection—lead by their inner dynamic, however, to the third and fifth elements that Hengel lists: Church tradition and the guidance of the Holy Spirit. For, on one hand, the author of the Fourth Gospel gives a very personal accent to his own remembrance, as we see from his observation at the end of the Crucifixion scene (cf. Jn 19:35); on the other hand, it is never a merely private remembering, but a remembering in and with the "we" of the Church: "that which . . . *we* have heard, which we have seen with our eyes, which we have looked upon and touched with our hands." With John, the subject who remembers is always the "we"—he remembers in and with the community of the disciples, in and with the Church. However much the author stands out as an individual witness, the remembering subject that speaks here is always the "we" of the community of disciples, the "we" of the Church. Because the personal recollection that provides the foundation of the Gospel is purified and deepened by being inserted into the memory of the Church, it does indeed transcend the banal recollection of facts.

There are three important passages in his Gospel where John uses the word *remember* and so gives us the key to understanding what he means by "memory." In John's account of the cleansing of the Temple, we read: "His disciples remembered that it was written, 'Zeal for thy house will consume me' [Ps 69:10]" (Jn 2:17). The event that is taking place calls to mind a passage of Scripture and so the event becomes intelligible at a level beyond the merely factual. Memory sheds light on the sense of the act, which then acquires a deeper meaning. It appears as an act in which Logos is present, an act that comes from the Logos and leads into it. The link connecting Jesus' acting and suffering with God's word comes into view, and so the mystery of Jesus himself becomes intelligible.

In the account of the cleansing of the Temple there then

follows Jesus' prophecy that he will raise up the destroyed Temple again in three days. The Evangelist then comments: "When therefore he was raised from the dead, his disciples remembered that he had said this; and they believed the scripture and the word which Jesus had spoken" (Jn 2:22). The Resurrection evokes remembrance, and remembrance in light of the Resurrection brings out the sense of this hitherto puzzling saying and reconnects it to the overall context of Scripture. The unity of Logos and act is the goal at which the Gospel is aiming.

The word *remember* occurs once again, this time in the description of the events of Palm Sunday. John recounts that Jesus found a young ass and sat down on it: "As it is written, 'Fear not, daughter of Zion; behold, your king is coming, sitting on an ass's colt!'" (Jn 12:14–15; cf. Zach 9:9). The Evangelist then observes: "His disciples did not understand this at first; but when Jesus was glorified, then they remembered that this had been written of him and had been done to him" (Jn 12:16). Once again an event is reported that at first seems simply factual. And once again the Evangelist tells us that after the Resurrection the disciples' eyes were opened and they were able to understand what had happened. Now they "remember." A scriptural text that had previously meant nothing to them now becomes intelligible, in the sense foreseen by God, which gives the external action its meaning.

The Resurrection teaches us a new way of seeing; it uncovers the connection between the words of the Prophets and the destiny of Jesus. It evokes "remembrance," that is, it makes it possible to enter into the interiority of the events, into the intrinsic coherence of God's speaking and acting.

By means of these texts the Evangelist himself gives us the decisive indications as to how his Gospel is composed and what sort of vision lies behind it. It rests upon the remembering of the disciple, which, however, is a co-remembering in the "we" of the Church. This remembering is an understanding under the guidance of the Holy Spirit; by remembering, the believer enters into the depth of the event and sees what could not be seen on an immediate and merely superficial level. But in so doing he does not move away from the reality; rather, he comes to know it more deeply and thus sees the truth concealed in the outward act. The remembering of the Church is the context where what the Lord prophesied to his followers at the Last Supper actually happens: "When the Spirit of truth comes, he will guide you into all the truth; for he will not speak on his own authority, but whatever he hears he will speak, and he will declare to you the things that are to come" (Jn 16:13).

What John says in his Gospel about how remembering becomes understanding and the path "into all the truth" comes very close to what Luke recounts about remembering on the part of Jesus' mother. In three passages of the infancy narrative Luke depicts this process of "remembering" for us. The first passage occurs in the account of the annunciation of Jesus' conception by the Archangel Gabriel. There Luke tells us that Mary took fright at the angel's greeting and entered into an interior "dialogue" about what the greeting might mean. The most important passages figure in the account of the adoration of the shepherds. The Evangelist comments: "Mary kept all these things, pondering them in her heart" (Lk 2:19). At the conclusion of the narrative of the twelve-year-old Jesus we read once again: "His mother kept all these things in her heart" (Lk 2:51). Mary's memory is first of all a retention of the events in remembrance, but it is more than that: It is an interior conversation with all that has happened. Thanks to this conversation, she penetrates into the interior dimension, she sees the events in their inter-connectedness, and she learns to understand them.

It is on just this sort of "recollection" that the Gospel of John is based, even as the Gospel takes the concept of memory to a new depth by conceiving it as the memory of the "we" of the disciples, of the Church. This remembering is no mere psychological or intellectual process; it is a pneumatic event [i.e., an event imbued with the Pneuma, or the Holy Spirit]. The Church's remembering is not merely a private affair; it transcends the sphere of our own human understanding and knowing. It is a being-led by the Holy Spirit, who shows us the connectedness of Scripture, the connection between word and reality, and, in doing that, leads us "into all the truth."

This also has some fundamental implications for the concept of inspiration. The Gospel emerges from human remembering and presupposes the communion of those who remember, in this case very concretely the school of John and, before that, the community of disciples. But because the author thinks and writes with the memory of the Church, the "we" to which he belongs opens beyond the personal and is guided in its depths by the Spirit of God, who is the Spirit of truth. In this sense, the Gospel itself opens up a path of understanding, which always remains bound to the scriptural word, and yet from generation to generation can lead, and is meant to lead, ever anew into the depth of all the truth.

This means that the Gospel of John, because it is a

"pneumatic Gospel," does not simply transmit a stenographic transcript of Jesus' words and ways; it escorts us, in virtue of understanding-through-remembering, beyond the external into the depth of words and events that come from God and lead back to him. As such, the Gospel is "remembering," which means that it remains faithful to what really happened and is not a "Jesus poem," not a violation of the historical events. Rather, it truly shows us who Jesus was, and thereby it shows us someone who not only was, but is; who can always say "I am" in the present tense. "Before Abraham was, *I am*" (Jn 8:58). It shows us the real Jesus, and we can confidently make use of it as a source of information about him.

Before we turn to the great Johannine figurative discourses, two further general observations about the distinctive character of John's Gospel may be helpful. Whereas Bultmann thought the Fourth Gospel was rooted in Gnosticism and was therefore alien to the soil of the Old Testament and of Judaism, recent scholarship has given us a new and clearer appreciation of the fact that John stands squarely on the foundation of the Old Testament. "Moses . . . wrote of me" (Jn 5:46), Jesus says to his adversaries. But already at the beginning—when John recounts the calling of the disciples—Philip had said to Nathanael: "We have found him of whom Moses in the law and also the prophets wrote" (Jn 1:45). Providing an explanation and a basis for this claim is ultimately the aim of Jesus' discourses. He does not break the Torah, but brings its whole meaning to light and wholly fulfills it. But the connection between Jesus and Moses appears most prominently, one might say programmatically, at the end of the prologue; this passage gives us the key to understanding the Fourth Gospel: "And from his fullness have we all received, grace upon grace. For the law was given through Moses; grace and truth came through Jesus Christ. No one has ever seen God; it is the only Son, who is nearest to the Father's heart, who has made him known" (Jn 1:16–18).

We began this book with Moses' prophecy: "The Lord your God will raise up for you a prophet like me from among you, from your brethren—him you shall heed" (Deut 18:15). We saw that the Book of Deuteronomy, which contains this prophecy, ends with the observation: "and there has not arisen a prophet since in Israel like Moses, whom the Lord knew face to face" (Deut 34:10). Until that hour, the great promise had remained unfulfilled. Now He is here, the one who is truly close to the Father's heart, the only one who has seen him, who sees him and who speaks out of this seeing—the one of whom it is therefore fittingly said: "him you shall heed" (Mk 9:7; Deut 18:15). The promise to Moses is fulfilled superabundantly, in the overflowingly lavish way in which God is accustomed to bestow his gifts. The One who has come is more than Moses, more than a prophet. He is the Son. And that is why grace and truth now come to light, not in order to destroy the Law, but to fulfill it.

The second observation concerns the liturgical character of John's Gospel. It has a rhythm dictated by Israel's calendar of religious festivals. The major feasts of the People of God articulate the inner structure of Jesus' path and at the same time display the foundation on which the edifice of his message rises.

Right at the beginning of Jesus' activity we read of the "Passover of the Jews," which suggests the motif of the true

Temple, and thus of the Cross and Resurrection (cf. Jn 2: 13–25). The healing of the paralytic, which occasions Jesus' first major public discourse in Jerusalem, is once again connected with a "feast of the Jews" (Jn 5:1)—probably the "Feast of Weeks," Pentecost. The multiplication of the loaves and its interpretation in the "bread of life" discourse, which is the great eucharistic discourse in John's Gospel, occur in the context of Passover (cf. Jn 6:4). Jesus' next major discourse, where he promises "rivers of living water" (Jn 7:38f.), is set at the time of the Feast of Tabernacles. Finally, we meet Jesus again in Jerusalem in wintertime at the Feast of the Dedication of the Temple (Hanukkah) (cf. Jn 10:22). Jesus' path is brought to completion during his last Passover (cf. Jn 12:1), when he himself becomes the true Paschal Lamb who pours out his blood on the Cross. We shall see, moreover, that Jesus' high-priestly prayer, which contains a subtle eucharistic theology in the form of a theology of his sacrifice on the Cross, is built up entirely in terms of the theological content of the Feast of the Atonement. This fundamentally important feast of Israel thus also feeds crucially into the crafting of Jesus' words and works. In the next chapter, furthermore, we shall see that the event of Jesus' Transfiguration recounted by the Synoptics is set in the framework of the Day of the Atonement and the Feast of Tabernacles and therefore reflects the same theological background. Only if we constantly keep in mind the liturgical context of Jesus' discourses, indeed of the whole structure of John's Gospel, will we be able to understand its vitality and depth.

All Jewish festivals, as we shall see below in greater detail, have a triple basis. The initial stratum is composed of feasts of nature religion, which connect with creation and with man's search for God through creation; this then develops into feasts of remembrance, of the recollection and making-present of God's saving deeds; finally, remembering increasingly takes on the form of hope for the coming definitive saving deed that is still awaited. Clearly, then, Jesus' discourses in John's Gospel are not disputes occasioned by metaphysical questions, but they contain the whole dynamic of salvation history and, at the same time, they are rooted in creation. They are ultimately pointers to the One who can simply say of himself: "I am." It is evident that Jesus' discourses direct us toward worship and in this sense toward "sacrament," at the same time embracing the questioning and seeking of all peoples.

After these introductory considerations, it is time to take a somewhat closer look at some of the principal images that we find in the Fourth Gospel.

The Principal Johannine Images

Water

Water is the primordial element of life and is therefore also one of the primordial symbols of humanity. It appears to man in various forms and hence with various meanings.

The first form is the spring, water that bursts forth fresh from the womb of the earth. The spring is origin, beginning, in its as yet unclouded and unspent purity. The spring thus figures as a truly creative element, as well as being a symbol of fruitfulness, of maternity.

A second form is flowing water. The great rivers—the

Nile, the Euphrates, and the Tigris—are the major, seemingly almost godlike sources of life in the vast lands surrounding Israel. In Israel it is the Jordan River that bestows life on the land. In connection with Jesus' Baptism, though, we saw that river symbolism shows another side as well: A river is deep, and so embodies danger; descent into the deep can therefore signify descent into death, just as ascent from it can signify rebirth.

The final form is the sea. It is a power that evokes admiration; its majesty calls forth amazement. Above all, though, it is feared in its guise as the counterpart to the earth, the domain of human life. The Creator has assigned the sea its limits, which it may not transgress: It is not permitted to swallow up the earth. The crossing of the Red Sea was above all a symbol of salvation for Israel, but of course it also points to the danger that proved to be the destiny of the Egyptians. If Christians consider the crossing of the Red Sea as a prefiguring of Baptism, there in the immediate foreground is the symbolism of death: It becomes an image of the mystery of the Cross. In order to be reborn, man must first enter with Christ into the "Red Sea," plunge with him down into death, in order thus to attain new life with the risen Lord.

But let us now turn from these general remarks about water symbolism in religious history to the Gospel of John. Water symbolism pervades the Gospel from beginning to end. We meet it for the first time in Jesus' conversation with Nicodemus in chapter 3. In order to be able to enter the Kingdom of God, man must be made new, he must become another person—he must be born again of water and the Spirit (cf. Jn 3:5). What does this mean?

Baptism, the gateway into communion with Christ, is

being interpreted for us here as rebirth. This rebirth—by analogy with natural birth from the begetting of the man and the conception of the woman—involves a double principle: God's spirit and "water, the 'universal mother' of natural life—which grace raises up in the sacrament to be a sister-image of the virginal Theotokos" (Rech, *Inbild,* II, p. 303).

Rebirth—to put it another way—involves the creative power of God's Spirit, but it also requires the sacrament of the maternal womb of the receiving and welcoming Church. Photina Rech cites Tertullian: Never was Christ without water (Tertullian, *De baptismo,* IX, 4). She then gives this somewhat enigmatic saying of the early Church writer its correct interpretation: "Christ never was, and never is, without the Ekklesia" (Rech, *Inbild,* II, p. 304). Spirit and water, heaven and earth, Christ and the Church, belong together. And that is how "rebirth" happens. In the sacrament, water stands for the maternal earth, the holy Church, which welcomes creation into herself and stands in place of it.

Immediately after the conversation with Nicodemus, we meet Jesus at Jacob's well in chapter 4. The Lord promises the Samaritan woman water that becomes in the one who drinks it a source springing up into eternal life (cf. Jn 4:14), so that whoever drinks it will never be thirsty again. In this scene, the symbolism of the well is associated with Israel's salvation history. Earlier, at the calling of Nathanael, Jesus had already revealed himself as the new and greater Jacob. In a nocturnal vision Jacob had seen the angels of God ascending and descending above the stone he was using for a pillow. Jesus prophesies to Nathanael that his disciples will see heaven open and the angels of God ascending and descending above him (cf. Jn 1:51). Here, at Jacob's well, we encounter Jacob as the great patriarch who by means of this well had provided water, the basic element of life. But there is a greater thirst in man—it extends beyond the water from the well, because it seeks a life that reaches out beyond the biological sphere.

We will come across this same inner tension in man once more when we come to the section on bread. Moses gave manna, bread from heaven. But it was still just earthly "bread." The manna is a promise: The new Moses is also expected to give bread. Once again, however, something greater than manna has to be given. Once again we see man reaching out into the infinite, toward another "bread" that will truly be "bread from heaven."

The promise of new water and the promise of new bread thus mirror each other. They both reflect the other dimension of life, for which man can only yearn. John distinguishes between *bios* and *zoé*—between biological life (*bios*) and the fullness of life (*zoé*) that is itself a source and so is not subject to the dying and becoming that mark the whole of creation. In the conversation with the Samaritan woman, then, water once again—though now in a different way—functions as the symbol of the Pneuma, the real life-force, which quenches man's deeper thirst and gives him plenitude of life, for which he is waiting without knowing it.

In the next chapter, chapter 5, water appears more or less in passing. It makes its appearance in the story of the man who has lain sick for thirty-eight years. He hopes to be healed by wading into the pool of Bethzatha, but there is no one to help him into the water. Jesus heals the man by his supreme authority; he accomplishes for the sick man the very thing the man had hoped to receive from the healing water. In chapter 7, which, according to a convincing hypothesis of modern exegesis, in all likelihood originally followed directly after chapter 5, we find Jesus attending the Feast of Tabernacles, which involves a solemn ritual of water libation. We will have to treat this in detail presently.

We come across water symbolism again in chapter 9, where Jesus heals the man born blind. The process of healing involves the sick man, on Jesus' instructions, washing in the Pool of Siloam. In this way he obtains his sight. "Siloam means, being translated: the One Sent" (Jn 9:7), as the Evangelist notes for the reader who knows no Hebrew. But this is more than a philological observation. It is a way of identifying the real cause of the miracle. For "the One Sent" is Jesus. When all is said and done, Jesus is the one through whom and in whom the blind man is cleansed so that he can gain his sight. The whole chapter turns out to be an interpretation of Baptism, which enables us to see. Christ is the giver of light, and he opens our eyes through the mediation of the sacrament.

Water appears with a similar, yet further shade of meaning in chapter 13—at the hour of the Last Supper—in connection with the washing of the feet. Jesus gets up from the table, takes off his upper garment, girds himself with a linen cloth, pours water into a bowl, and begins to wash the feet of the disciples (cf. Jn 13:4f.). The humility of Jesus, in making himself his followers' slave, is the purifying foot washing that renders us fit to take our places at God's table.

Finally, water appears before us again with a mysterious grandeur at the end of the Passion. Since Jesus is dead, his bones are not broken (Jn 19:31), but one of the soldiers "pierced his side with a spear, and at once there came out blood and water" (Jn 19:34). There is no doubt that John means to refer here to the two main sacraments of the Church—Baptism and the Eucharist—which spring forth from Jesus' opened heart and thus give birth to the Church from his side.

Now, John later goes back to the motif of blood and water in his First Letter and there gives it a new twist: "This is he who came by water and blood, Jesus Christ, not with the water only but with the water and the blood. . . . There are three witnesses, the Spirit, the water, and the blood; and these three are one" (1 Jn 5:6–8). Here John very obviously gives the motif a polemical turn against a form of Christianity that acknowledges Jesus' Baptism as a saving event but does not acknowledge his death on the Cross in the same way. He is responding to a form of Christianity that, so to speak, wants only the word, but not flesh and blood. Jesus' body and his death ultimately play no role. So all that is left of Christianity is mere "water"—without Jesus' bodiliness the word loses its power. Christianity becomes mere doctrine, mere moralism, an intellectual affair, but it lacks any flesh and blood. The redemptive character of Jesus' blood is no longer accepted. It disturbs the intellectual harmony.

Who could fail to recognize here certain temptations threatening Christianity in our own times? Water and blood belong together; Incarnation and Cross, Baptism, word, and sacrament are inseparable from one another. Not only that, but the *Pneuma* is needed to complete this triple testimony. Schnackenburg rightly points out that what is intended here is "the witness of the Spirit in the church and through the church, as in John 15:26, 16:10" (*Johannine Epistles,* p. 234).

Let us turn now to Jesus' words of revelation in the context of the Feast of Tabernacles that John transmits to us at 7:37–39. "On the last day of the feast, the great day, Jesus stood up and proclaimed, 'If anyone thirst, let him come to me and drink. He who believes in me, as the Scripture has said, "Out of his heart shall flow rivers of living water."'" In the background is the ritual of the feast, which prescribed that participants should draw water from the spring at Siloam in order to offer a water libation in the Temple on each of the seven days of the feast. On the seventh day, the priests processed seven times around the altar holding a golden water vessel before ritually pouring out its contents. These water rituals are in the first place indications of the origin of the feast in the nature religions: The feast began as an invocatory petition for rain, which was so vitally necessary in a land chronically threatened by drought. But the ritual was then transformed into a remembrance of a piece of salvation history, of the water from the rock that, in spite of all their doubts and fears, God gave the Jews as they wandered in the desert (cf. Num 20:1–13).

Finally, the gift of water from the rock increasingly became a motif of messianic hope. Moses had given Israel bread from heaven and water from the rock as the people wandered in the desert. On this pattern, the new Moses, the Messiah, was expected to give these two essential gifts of life as well. This messianic interpretation of the gift of water is reflected in Saint Paul's First Letter to the Corinthians: "All ate the same pneumatic food and all drank the same pneumatic drink; for they drank from the pneumatic rock that went with them. But the rock was Christ" (1 Cor 10:3f.).

In the words that Jesus speaks during the water ritual, he responds to this hope: He is the new Moses. He himself is the life-giving rock. Just as in the bread discourse he reveals himself as the true bread that comes from heaven, he shows himself here—just as he had done with the Samaritan woman—as the living water that is the goal of man's deeper thirst, the thirst for life, for "life in abundance" (Jn 10:10): This life is no longer conditioned by need that must constantly be satisfied, but it springs up from within, from deep inside itself. Jesus also answers the questions as to how one drinks this living water, how one gets to the well and draws from it, by saying, "He who believes in me . . ." Faith in Jesus is the way we drink the living water, the way we drink life that is no longer threatened by death.

But now we must listen more carefully to the text. It continues: "As the Scripture has said, 'Out of his body shall flow rivers of living water'" (Jn 7:38). Out of whose body? Since the earliest times there have been two different answers to this question. The tradition started by Origen, which is associated with Alexandria, though the great Latin Fathers Jerome and Augustine also subscribe to it, reads the text thus: "He who believes . . . out of his body . . ." The believer himself becomes a spring, an oasis out of which bubbles up fresh, uncontaminated water, the life-giving power of the Creator Spirit. Alongside this tradition there is another, albeit much less widespread, from Asia Minor, which is closer to John in its origins. It is documented by Justin (d. 165), Irenaeus, Hippolytus, Cyprian, and Ephraim of Syria. It punctuates the text differently: "He who thirsts, let him come to me, and let him who believes in me drink it. As the Scripture says: out of his body rivers will flow." "His body" is now applied to Christ: He is the source, the living rock, from which the new water comes.

From the purely linguistic point of view, the first interpretation is more convincing. It has accordingly been adopted by the majority of modern exegetes—along with the great Church Fathers. In terms of the content, though, there is more to be said for the second, "Asia Minor" interpretation, to which Schnackenburg, for example, subscribes, though it need not be considered to exclude the "Alexandrian" reading. An important key to the interpretation of this passage lies in the phrase "as the Scripture says." Jesus attaches great importance to being in continuity with the Scripture, in continuity with God's history with men. The whole Gospel of John, as well as the Synoptic Gospels and the entirety of the New Testament writings, justify faith in Jesus by showing that all the currents of Scripture come together in him, that he is the focal point in terms of which the overall coherence of Scripture comes to light—everything is waiting for him, everything is moving toward him.

But where does Scripture speak of this living spring? John is obviously not thinking of any one particular passage, but precisely of "the Scripture," of a vision that runs through its texts. We have just come across one of the principal clues: The story of the water issuing from the rock, a story that became an image of hope in Israel. Ezekiel 47:1–12 furnishes us with the second major clue, the vision of the new Temple: "And behold, water was issuing from below the threshold of the Temple toward the east" (Ezek 47:1). A good fifty years later Zechariah returned to this image: "On that day there shall be a fountain opened for the house of David and the inhabitants of Jerusalem to cleanse them from sin and uncleanness" (Zech 13:1), "On that day living waters shall flow out from Jerusalem" (Zech 14:8). The final chapter of the Bible reinterprets these images and at the same time manifests their full greatness for the first time: "Then he showed me the river of the water of life, bright as crystal, flowing from the throne of God and of the Lamb" (Rev 22:1).

Our brief consideration of the cleansing of the Temple has already shown us that John sees the risen Lord, his body, as the new Temple, which is awaited not just by the Old Testament, but by all peoples (cf. Jn 2:21). We thus have good reason to hear a reference to the new Temple echoing through Jesus' words about the streams of living waters: Yes, this Temple exists. The promised river of life that decontaminates the briny soil and allows the fullness of life to ripen and bear fruit really does exist. It is He who, in "loving to the end," endured the Cross and now lives with a life that can never again be threatened by death. It is the living Christ. Accordingly, Jesus' words during the Feast of Tabernacles not only point forward to the new Jerusalem where God himself lives and is the fountain of life, but also point immediately ahead to the body of the Crucified, out of which blood and water flow (cf. Jn 19:34). It shows the body of Jesus to be the real Temple, built not of stone nor by human hands; hence—because it signifies the living indwelling of God in the world—it is, and will remain, the source of life for all ages.

If one looks at history with a keen eye, one can see this river flowing through the ages from Golgotha, from Jesus crucified and risen. One can see that, wherever this river reaches, the earth is decontaminated and fruit-bearing trees grow up; one can see that life, real life, flows from this spring of love that has given itself and continues to give itself.

The application of this passage primarily to Christ—as we saw earlier—does not have to exclude a secondary interpretation referring to the believer. A saying from the apocryphal Gospel of Thomas (108) points in a direction compatible with John's Gospel: "Whoever drinks from my mouth shall become as I am" (Barrett, *Gospel,* p. 328). The believer becomes one with Christ and participates in his fruitfulness. The man who believes and loves with Christ becomes a well that gives life. That, too, is something that is wonderfully illustrated in history: The saints are oases around which life sprouts up and something of the lost paradise returns. And ultimately, Christ himself is always the well-spring who pours himself forth in such abundance.

Vine and Wine

Whereas water is a basic element of life for all creatures on earth, wheat bread, wine, and olive oil are gifts typical of Mediterranean culture. The creation Psalm 104 first of all mentions the grass that God has appointed for the cattle and then goes on to speak of the gifts God gives to men through the earth: the bread that man produces from the earth, the wine that gladdens his heart, and finally the oil that makes his face shine. It then returns to speak of the bread that strengthens man's heart (cf. Ps 104:14f.). Along with water, the three great gifts of the earth subsequently became the basic elements of the Church's sacraments, in which the fruits of creation are transformed into bearers of God's historical action, into "signs," in which he bestows upon us his special closeness.

Each of the three gifts has a special character that sets it apart from the others, so that each one functions as a sign in its own way. Bread, in its simplest form prepared from water and ground wheat—though the element of fire and human work clearly have a part to play—is the basic foodstuff. It belongs to the poor and the rich alike, but especially to the poor. It represents the goodness of creation and of the Creator, even as it stands for the humble simplicity of daily life. Wine, on the other hand, represents feasting. It gives man a taste of the glory of creation. In this sense, it forms part of the rituals of the Sabbath, of Passover, of marriage feasts. And it allows us to glimpse something of the definitive feast God will celebrate with man, the goal of all Israel's expectations: "On this mountain the LORD of hosts will make for all peoples a feast of fat things, a feast of wine on the lees, of fat things full of marrow, of wine on the lees well refined" (Is 25:6). Finally, oil gives man strength and beauty; it has the power to heal and nourish. It signifies a higher calling in the anointing of prophets, kings, and priests.

As far as I can see, olive oil does not figure in John's Gospel. The precious "oil of nard" that Mary of Bethany uses to anoint the Lord before he enters upon his Passion (cf. Jn 12:3) was thought to be of Oriental origin. In this scene, it appears, first, as a sign of the sacred extravagance of love and, second, as a reference to death and Resurrection. We come across bread in the scene of the multiplication of the loaves, which the Synoptics also document in great detail, and immediately after that in the great eucharistic discourse in John's Gospel. The gift of new wine occupies a central place in the wedding at Cana (cf. Jn 2:1–12), while in his Farewell

Discourses Jesus presents himself to us as the true vine (cf. Jn 15:1–10).

Let us focus on these two texts. The miracle of Cana seems at first sight to be out of step with the other signs that Jesus performs. What are we supposed to make of the fact that Jesus produces a huge surplus of wine—about 520 liters—for a private party? We need to look more closely to realize that this is not at all about a private luxury, but about something much greater. The first important detail is the timing. "On the third day there was a marriage at Cana in Galilee" (Jn 2:1). It is not quite clear what previous date this "third day" is related to—which shows all the more plainly that what matters to the Evangelist is precisely the symbolic time reference, which he gives us as a key to understanding the event.

In the Old Testament, the third day is the time for theophany, as, for example, in the central account of the meeting between God and Israel on Sinai: "On the morning of the third day there were thunders and lightnings. . . . The LORD descended upon it in fire"(Ex 19:16–18). At the same time what we have here is a prefiguring of history's final and decisive theophany: the Resurrection of Christ on the third day, when God's former encounters with man become his definitive irruption upon earth, when the earth is torn open once and for all and drawn into God's own life. What John is hinting at here, then, is that at Cana God first reveals himself in a way that carries forward the events of the Old Testament, all of which have the character of a promise and are now straining toward their definitive fulfillment. The exegetes have reckoned up the number of the preceding days in John's Gospel that are taken up with the calling of the disciples (e.g.,

Barrett, *Gospel*, p. 190). The conclusion is that this "third day" would be the sixth or seventh day since Jesus began calling the disciples. If it were the seventh day, then it would be, so to speak, the day of God's feast for humanity, an anticipation of the definitive Sabbath as described, for example, in the prophecy of Isaiah cited above.

There is another basic element of the narrative linked to this timing. Jesus says to Mary that his hour has not yet come. On an immediate level, this means that he does not simply act and decide by his own lights, but always in harmony with the Father's will and always in terms of the Father's plan. More particularly, the "hour" designates his "glorification," which brings together his Cross, his Resurrection, and his presence throughout the world in word and sacrament. Jesus' hour, the hour of his "glory," begins at the moment of the Cross, and its historical setting is the moment when the Passover lambs are slaughtered—it is just then that Jesus, the true lamb, pours out his blood. His hour comes from God, but it is solidly situated in a precise historical context tied to a liturgical date—and just so it is the beginning of the new liturgy in "spirit and truth." When at this juncture Jesus speaks to Mary of his hour, he is connecting the present moment with the mystery of the Cross interpreted as his glorification. This hour is not yet come; that was the first thing that had to be said. And yet Jesus has the power to anticipate this "hour" in a mysterious sign. This stamps the miracle of Cana as an anticipation of the hour, tying the two together intrinsically.

How could we forget that this thrilling mystery of the anticipated hour continues to occur again and again? Just as at his mother's request Jesus gives a sign that anticipates his hour, and at the same time directs our gaze toward it, so too he does the same thing ever anew in the Eucharist. Here, in response to the Church's prayer, the Lord anticipates his return; he comes already now; he celebrates the marriage feast with us here and now. In so doing, he lifts us out of our own time toward the coming "hour."

We thus begin to understand the event of Cana. The sign of God is overflowing generosity. We see it in the multiplication of the loaves; we see it again and again—most of all, though, at the center of salvation history, in the fact that he lavishly spends himself for the lowly creature, man. This abundant giving is his "glory." The superabundance of Cana is therefore a sign that God's feast with humanity, his self-giving for men, has begun. The framework of the event, the wedding, thus becomes an image that points beyond itself to the messianic hour: The hour of God's marriage feast with his people has begun in the coming of Jesus. The promise of the last days enters into the Now.

This links the story of Cana with Saint Mark's account of the question posed to Jesus by the disciples of John the Baptist and the Pharisees: Why don't your disciples fast? Jesus answers: "Can the wedding guests fast so long as the bridegroom is among them?" (Mk 2:18f.). Jesus identifies himself here as the "bridegroom" of God's promised marriage with his people and, by doing so, he mysteriously places his own existence, himself, within the mystery of God. In him, in an unexpected way, God and man become one, become a "marriage," though this marriage—as Jesus subsequently points out—passes through the Cross, through the "taking away" of the bridegroom.

There remain two aspects of the Cana story for us to ponder if we wish in some sense to explore its Christological depth—the self-revelation of Jesus and his "glory" that we encounter in the narrative. Water, set aside for the purpose of ritual purification, is turned into wine, into a sign and a gift of nuptial joy. This brings to light something of the fulfillment of the Law that is accomplished in Jesus' being and doing.

The Law is not denied, it is not thrust aside. Rather, its inner expectation is brought to fulfillment. Ritual purification in the end is just ritual, a gesture of hope. It remains "water," just as everything man does on his own remains "water" before God. Ritual purification is in the end never sufficient to make man capable of God, to make him really "pure" for God. Water becomes wine. Man's own efforts now encounter the gift of God, who gives himself and thereby creates the feast of joy that can only be instituted by the presence of God and his gift.

The historical study of comparative religion likes to claim the myth of Dionysus as a pre-Christian parallel to the story of Cana. Dionysus was the god who was supposed to have discovered the vine and also to have changed water into wine—a mythical event that was also celebrated liturgically. The great Jewish theologian Philo of Alexandria (ca. 13 B.C.–A.D. 45/50) gave this story a demythologizing reinterpretation: The true giver of wine, Philo says, is the divine Logos; he is the one who gives us the joy, the sweetness, and the cheerfulness of true wine. Philo then goes on to anchor his Logos theology onto a figure from salvation history, onto Melchisedek, who offered bread and wine. In Melchisedek it is the Logos who is acting and giving us the gifts that are essential for human living. By the same token, the Logos appears as the priest of a cosmic liturgy (Barrett, *Gospel,* p. 188).

Whether John had such a background in mind is doubtful, to say the least. But since Jesus himself in interpreting his mission referred to Psalm 110, which features the priesthood of Melchisedek (cf. Mk 12:35–37); since the Letter to the Hebrews, which is theologically akin to the Gospel of John, explicitly develops a theology of Melchisedek; since John presents Jesus as the Logos of God and as God himself; since, finally, the Lord gave bread and wine as the bearers of the New Covenant, it is certainly not forbidden to think in terms of such connections and so to see shining through the Cana story the mystery of the Logos and of his cosmic liturgy, which fundamentally transforms the myth of Dionysus, and yet also brings it to its hidden truth.

While the Cana story deals with the *fruit* of the vine and the rich symbolism that goes with it, in chapter 15—in the context of the Farewell Discourses—John takes up once more the ancient traditional image of the vine itself, and brings to fulfillment the vision that is presented there. In order to understand this discourse of Jesus, it is necessary to consider at least *one* foundational Old Testament text based on the vine motif and to ponder briefly a related parable in the Synoptics that takes up and refashions the Old Testament text.

Isaiah 5:1–7 presents us with a song about a vineyard. The Prophet probably sang it in the context of the Feast of Tabernacles, in the context of the cheerful atmosphere characteristic of this eight-day feast (cf. Deut 16:14). It is easy to imagine many different sorts of performances going on in the areas between the booths built of leaves and branches, and the Prophet himself mingling with the celebrating people and announcing a love song about his friend and his vineyard.

Everyone knew that "vineyard" was an image for a bride (cf. Song 2:15, 7:12f.), so they were expecting some entertainment suited to the festive atmosphere. And the song does start off on a good note: The friend had a vineyard on rich soil, planted choice grapes on it, and did everything he could to make them flourish. But then the mood suddenly changes: The vineyard is a disappointment, and instead of choice fruit, it produces nothing but inedible sour grapes, small and hard. The audience understands what that means: The bride was unfaithful, disappointing the trust and hope, disappointing the love that the friend had expected. How will the story continue? The friend hands over his vineyard to be plundered—he repudiates the bride, leaving her in the dishonor for which she has no one but herself to blame.

It suddenly becomes clear that the vineyard, the bride, is Israel—it is the very people who are present. God gave them the way of justice in the Torah, he loved them, he did everything for them, and they have answered him with unjust action and a regime of injustice. The love song has become a threat of judgment. It finishes with a gloomy prospect—that of God's abandonment of Israel, with no sign at this stage of any further promise. Isaiah points to the situation that the Psalmist later describes in a lament before God in deep anguish at its having come to pass: "Thou didst bring a vine out of Egypt; thou didst drive out the nations and plant it. Thou didst clear the ground for it. . . . Why then hast thou broken down its walls, so that all who pass along the way plunder its fruit?" (Ps 80:9–13). In the Psalm, lament leads into petition: "Have regard for this vine, the stock which thy right hand planted. . . . Restore us, O LORD God of hosts! let thy face shine, that we may be saved!" (Ps 80:16–20).

Despite everything that had happened to Israel since the Exile, it found itself again in essentially the same situation at the time when Jesus lived and spoke to the heart of his people. In a late parable, told on the eve of his Passion, he takes up the song of Isaiah in a modified form (cf. Mk 12:1–12). His discourse no longer uses the vine as the image of Israel, however. Rather, Israel is now represented by the tenants of a vineyard whose owner has gone on a journey and from a far country demands the fruits owed him. The history of God's constantly renewed struggle for and with Israel is depicted in a succession of "servants" who come at the owner's behest to collect the rent, the agreed-on portion of the fruits, from the tenants. The history of the Prophets, their sufferings, and the futility of their efforts appear through the narrative, which tells that the servants are manhandled, even killed.

Finally, the owner makes a last-ditch effort: He sends his "beloved son," who, being the heir, can also enforce the owner's claim to the rent in court and for that reason is entitled to hope for respect. Just the opposite happens. The tenants kill the son, precisely because he is the heir; his death, they think, will pave the way for them to take possession of the vineyard once and for all. Jesus continues the parable thus: "What will the owner of the vineyard do? He will come and destroy the tenants, and give the vineyard to others" (Mk 12:9).

At this point, as in Isaiah's song, the parable that seemed to be just a story about the past crosses over into the situation of the audience. History suddenly enters the present. The audience knows he is saying to them: Just as the Prophets were abused and killed, so now you want to kill me: I'm talking about *you* and about *me* (cf. verse 12).

The modern interpretation ends at this point. It thus relegates the parable to the past again; the parable, it seems, speaks only of what happened back then, of the rejection of Jesus' message by his contemporaries, of his death on the Cross. But the Lord always speaks in the present and with an eye to the future. He is also speaking with us and about us. If we open our eyes, isn't what is said in the parable actually a description of our present world? Isn't this precisely the logic of the modern age, of our age? Let us declare that God is dead, then we ourselves will be God. At last we no longer belong to anyone else; rather, we are simply the owners of ourselves and of the world. At last we can do what we please. We get rid of God; there is no measuring rod above us; we ourselves are our only measure. The "vineyard" belongs to us. What happens to man and the world next? We are already beginning to see it. . . .

Let us return to the text of the parable. When Isaiah arrived at this point, there was no promise in sight; in the Psalm, just as the threat was being fulfilled, suffering turned to prayer. This, again and again, is the situation of Israel, of the Church, and of humanity. Again and again we find ourselves in the darkness of trial and have no recourse but to call upon God: Raise us up again! But Jesus' words contain a promise—the beginning of an answer to the prayer: "take care of this vineyard." The Kingdom is handed over to other servants—this statement is both a threat of judgment and a promise. It means that the Lord stands by his vineyard, without being bound to its present servants. This threat-promise applies not only to the ruling classes, about whom and with whom Jesus is speaking. It continues to apply among the new People of God as well—not, of course, to the whole Church, but repeatedly to the particular churches, as the Risen Lord's words to the Church at Ephesus show: "Repent and do the works you did at first. If not, I will come to you and remove your lampstand from its place" (Rev 2:5).

The threat and promise that the vineyard will be handed over to other servants is followed, though, by a promise of a much more fundamental nature. The Lord cites Psalm 118:22f: "The stone which the builders rejected has become the cornerstone." The death of the son is not the last word. He is killed, but he does not remain in death, he does not remain "rejected." He becomes a new beginning. Jesus gives his audience to understand that he himself will be the Son who is killed; he foretells his Cross and Resurrection and prophesies that upon him, when he has been killed and has risen, God will erect a new building, a new Temple in the world.

The image of the vine is abandoned and replaced by the image of God's living building. The Cross is not an end, but a new beginning. The song of the vineyard does not end with the killing of the son. It opens the prospect that God will do something new. The affinity with John 2, which speaks of the destruction of the Temple and its reconstruction, is impossible to overlook. God does not fail; we may be unfaithful, but he is always faithful (cf. 2 Tim 2:13). He finds new and greater ways for his love. The indirect Christology of the early parables is transcended here into a fully open Christological statement.

The parable of the vine in Jesus' Farewell Discourses continues the whole history of biblical thought and language on the subject of the vine and discloses its ultimate depth. "I am the true vine," the Lord says (Jn 15:1). The word *true* is the first important thing to notice about this saying. Barrett makes the excellent observation that "fragments of meaning, obscurely hinted at by other vines, are gathered up and made explicit by him. He is the *true* vine" (*Gospel*, p. 473). But the really important thing about this saying is the opening: "I am." The Son identifies himself with the vine; he himself has become the vine. He has let himself be planted in the earth. He has entered into the vine: The mystery of the Incarnation, which John spoke of in the prologue to his Gospel, is taken up again here in a surprising new way. The vine is no longer merely a creature that God looks upon with love, but that he can still uproot and reject. In the Son, he himself has become the vine; he has forever identified himself, his very being, with the vine.

This vine can never again be uprooted or handed over to be plundered. It belongs once and for all to God; through the Son, God himself lives in it. The promise has become irrevocable, the unity indestructible. God has taken this great new step within history, and this constitutes the deepest content of the parable. Incarnation, death, and Resurrection come to be seen in their full breadth: "For the Son of God, Jesus Christ, whom we preached among you . . . was not Yes and No; but in him it is always Yes. For all the promises of God find their Yes in him" (2 Cor 1:19f.), as Saint Paul puts it.

The idea that through Christ the vine has become the Son himself is a new one, and yet the ground for it has been prepared in biblical tradition. Psalm 80:18 closely associates the "Son of Man" with the vine. Conversely: Although the Son has now himself become the vine, this is precisely his method for remaining one with his own, with all the scattered children of God whom he has come to gather (cf. Jn 11:52). The vine is a Christological title that as such embodies a whole ecclesiology. The vine signifies Jesus' inseparable oneness with his own, who through him and with him are all "vine," and whose calling is to "remain" in the vine. John does not make use of the Pauline image of the "Body of Christ." But the parable of the vine expresses substantially the same idea: the fact that Jesus is inseparable from his own, and that they are one with him and in him. In this sense, the discourse about the vine indicates the irrevocability of the gift God has given, never to take it back again. In becoming incarnate, God has bound himself. At the same time, though, the discourse speaks of the demands that this gift places upon us in ever new ways.

The vine, we said, can no longer be uprooted or handed over to be plundered. It does, however, constantly need purification. Purification, fruit, remaining, commandment, love, unity—these are the key words for this drama of being in and with the Son in the vine that the Lord's words place before our soul. Purification—the Church and the individual need constant purification. Processes of purification, which are as necessary as they are painful, run through the whole of history, the whole life of those who have dedicated themselves to Christ. The mystery of death and resurrection is ever present in these purifications. When man and his institutions climb too high, they need to be cut back; what has become too big must be brought back to the simplicity and poverty of the Lord himself. It is only by undergoing such processes of dying away that fruitfulness endures and renews itself.

The goal of purification is fruit, the Lord tells us. What sort of fruit is it that he expects? Let us begin by looking at the fruit that he himself has borne by dying and rising. Isaiah and the whole prophetic tradition spoke of how God expected grapes, and thus choice wine, from his vine. This was an image of the righteousness, the rectitude that consists in living within the Word and will of God. The same tradition says that what God finds instead are useless, small, sour grapes that he can only throw away. This was an image of life lived away from God's righteousness amid injustice, corruption, and violence. The vine is meant to bear choice grapes that through the process of picking, pressing, and fermentation will produce excellent wine.

Let us recall that the parable of the vine occurs in the context of Jesus' Last Supper. After the multiplication of the loaves he had spoken of the true bread from heaven that he would give, and thus he left us with a profound interpretation of the eucharistic bread that was to come. It is hard to believe that in his discourse on the vine he is not tacitly alluding to the new wine that had already been prefigured at Cana and which he now gives to us—the wine that would flow from his Passion, from his "love to the end" (Jn 13:1). In this sense, the parable of the vine has a thoroughly eucharistic background. It refers to the fruit that Jesus brings forth: his love, which pours itself out for us on the Cross and which is the choice new wine destined for God's marriage feast with man. Thus we come to understand the full depth and grandeur of the Eucharist, even though it is not explicitly mentioned here. The

Eucharist points us toward the fruit that we, as branches of the vine, can and must bear with Christ and by virtue of Christ. The fruit the Lord expects of us is love—a love that accepts with him the mystery of the Cross, and becomes a participation in his self-giving—and hence the true justice that prepares the world for the Kingdom of God.

Purification and fruit belong together; only by undergoing God's purifications can we bear the fruit that flows into the eucharistic mystery and so leads to the marriage feast that is the goal toward which God directs history. Fruit and love belong together: The true fruit is the love that has passed through the Cross, through God's purifications. "Remaining" is an essential part of all this. In verses 1–10 the word *remain* (in Greek *ménein*) occurs ten times. What the Church Fathers call *perseverantia*—patient steadfastness in communion with the Lord amid all the vicissitudes of life—is placed center stage here. Initial enthusiasm is easy. Afterward, though, it is time to stand firm, even along the monotonous desert paths that we are called upon to traverse in this life—with the patience it takes to tread evenly, a patience in which the romanticism of the initial awakening subsides, so that only the deep, pure Yes of faith remains. This is the way to produce good wine. After the brilliant illuminations of the initial moment of his conversion, Augustine had a profound experience of this toilsome patience, and that is how he learned to love the Lord and to rejoice deeply at having found him.

If the fruit we are to bear is love, its prerequisite is this "remaining," which is profoundly connected with the kind of faith that holds on to the Lord and does not let go. Verse 7 speaks of prayer as an essential element of this remaining:

Those who pray are promised that they will surely be heard. Of course, to pray in the name of Jesus is not to make an ordinary petition, but to ask for the essential gift that Jesus characterizes as "joy" in the Farewell Discourses, while Luke calls it the Holy Spirit (cf. Lk 11:13)—the two being ultimately the same. Jesus' words about remaining in his love already point ahead to the last verse of his high-priestly prayer (cf. Jn 17:26) and thus connect the vine discourse with the great theme of unity, for which the Lord prays to the Father at the Last Supper.

Bread

We have already dealt extensively with the bread motif in connection with Jesus' temptations. We have seen that the temptation to turn the desert rocks into bread raises the whole question of the Messiah's mission, and that through the devil's distortion of this mission Jesus' positive answer can already be glimpsed; this answer then becomes explicit once and for all in the gift of his body as bread for the life of the world on the eve of his Passion. We have also encountered the bread motif in our exposition of the fourth petition of the Our Father, where we tried to survey the different dimensions of this petition, and thus to explore the full range of the bread theme. At the end of Jesus' activity in Galilee, he performs the multiplication of the loaves; on one hand, it is an unmistakable sign of Jesus' messianic mission, while on the other, it is also the crossroads of his public ministry, which from this point leads clearly to the Cross. All three Synoptic Gospels tell of a miraculous feeding of five thousand men (cf. Mt 14:13–21; Mk 6:32–44; Lk 9:10b–17); Matthew and

Mark tell of an additional feeding of four thousand (cf. Mt 15:32–38; Mk 8:1–9).

The two stories have a rich theological content that we cannot enter into here. I will restrict myself to John's story of the multiplication of the loaves (cf. Jn 6:1–15), not in order to study it in depth, but rather to focus upon the interpretation that Jesus gives of this event in his great bread of life discourse the following day in the synagogue on the other side of the lake. One more qualification is in order: We cannot consider the details of this discourse, which the exegetes have discussed at length and analyzed thoroughly. I would merely like to draw out its principal message and, above all, to situate it in the context of the whole tradition to which it belongs and in terms of which it has to be understood.

The fundamental context in which the entire chapter belongs is centered upon the contrast between Moses and Jesus. Jesus is the definitive, greater Moses—the "prophet" whom Moses foretold in his discourse at the border of the Holy Land and concerning whom God said, "I will put my words in his mouth, and he shall speak to them all that I command him" (Deut 18:18). It is no accident, then, that the following statement occurs between the multiplication of the loaves and the attempt to make Jesus king: "This is indeed the prophet who is to come into the world!" (Jn 6:14). In a very similar vein, after the saying about the water of life on the Feast of Tabernacles, the people say: "This is really the prophet" (Jn 7:40). The Mosaic background provides the context for the claim that Jesus makes. Moses struck the rock in the desert and out flowed water; Jesus promises the water of life, as we have seen. The great gift, though, which stood out in the people's memory, was the manna. Moses gave bread from heaven; God himself fed the wandering people of Israel with heavenly bread. For a people who often went hungry and struggled to earn their daily bread, this was the promise of promises, which somehow said everything there was to say: relief of every want—a gift that satisfied hunger for all and forever.

Before we take up this idea, which is the key to understanding chapter 6 of John's Gospel, we must first complete the picture of Moses, because this is the only way to focus upon John's picture of Jesus. The central point from which we started in this book, and to which we keep returning, is that Moses spoke face-to-face with God, "as a man speaks to his friend" (Ex 33:11; cf. Deut 34:10). It was only because he spoke with God himself that Moses could bring God's word to men. But, although this immediate relationship with God is the heart and inner foundation of Moses' mission, a shadow lies over it. For when Moses says, "I pray thee, show me thy glory," at the very moment when the text affirms that he is God's friend who has direct access to him, he receives this answer: "While my glory passes by I will put you in a cleft of the rock, and I will cover you with my hand until I have passed by; then I will take away my hand, and you shall see my back; but my face shall not be seen" (Ex 33:18, 22f.). Even Moses sees only God's back—his face "shall not be seen." The limits to which even Moses is subject now become clear.

The saying at the end of the prologue is the decisive key to the image of Jesus in John's Gospel: "No one has ever seen God; it is the only Son, who is nearest to the Father's heart, who has made him known" (Jn 1:18). Only the one who is God sees God—Jesus. He truly speaks from his vision of the

Father, from unceasing dialogue with the Father, a dialogue that is his life. If Moses only showed us, and could only show us, God's back, Jesus, by contrast, is the Word that comes from God, from a living vision of him, from unity with him. Connected with this are two further gifts to Moses that attain their final form in Christ. First, God communicated his name to Moses, thereby making possible a relationship between himself and human beings; by handing on the name revealed to him, Moses acts as mediator of a real relationship between men and the living God. We have already reflected on this point in our consideration of the first petition of the Our Father. Now, in his high-priestly prayer Jesus stresses that he has revealed God's name, that he has brought to completion this aspect too of the work begun by Moses. When we consider the high-priestly prayer, we will have to investigate this claim more closely: In what sense has Jesus gone beyond Moses in revealing God's "name"?

The other gift to Moses—which is closely connected with the vision of God and the communication of his name, as well as with the manna—is the gift that gives Israel its identity as God's people in the first place: the Torah, the word of God that points out the way and leads to life. Israel realized with increasing clarity that this was Moses' fundamental and enduring gift, that what really set Israel apart was this knowledge of God's will and so of the right path of life. The great Psalm 119 is a single outburst of joy and gratitude for this gift. A one-sided view of the Law, arising from a one-sided interpretation of Pauline theology, prevents us from seeing this joy of Israel: the joy of knowing God's will, and so of being privileged to live in accordance with God's will.

This observation brings us back to the bread of life discourse, surprising as that may seem. For as Jewish thought developed inwardly, it became increasingly plain that the real bread from heaven that fed and feeds Israel is precisely the Law—the word of God. The Wisdom Literature presents the wisdom that is substantially accessible and present in the Law as "bread" (Prov 9:5); the rabbinic literature went on to develop this idea further (Barrett, *Gospel*, p. 290). This is the perspective from which we need to understand Jesus' dispute with the Jews assembled in the synagogue at Capernaum. Jesus begins by pointing out that they have failed to understand the multiplication of the loaves as a "sign," which is its true meaning. Rather, what interested them was eating and having their fill (cf. Jn 6:26). They have been looking at salvation in purely material terms, as a matter of universal well-being, and they have therefore reduced man, leaving God out altogether. But if they see the manna only as a means of satisfying their hunger, they need to realize that even the manna was not heavenly bread, but only earthly bread. Even though it came from "heaven," it was earthly food—or rather a food substitute that would necessarily cease when Israel emerged from the desert back into inhabited country.

But man hungers for more. He needs more. The gift that feeds man as man must be greater, must be on a wholly different level. Is the Torah this other food? It is in some sense true that in and through the Torah, man can make God's will his food (cf. Jn 4:34). So the Torah is "bread" from God, then. And yet it shows us only God's back, so to speak. It is a "shadow." "For the bread of God is that which comes down from heaven, and gives life to the world" (Jn 6:33). As the audience still does not understand, Jesus repeats himself even more unambiguously: "I am the bread of life; he who comes to me shall not hunger, and he who believes in me shall never thirst" (Jn 6:35).

The Law has become a *person.* When we encounter Jesus, we feed on the living God himself, so to speak; we truly eat "bread from heaven." By the same token, Jesus has already made it clear that the only work God demands is the work of believing in him. Jesus' audience had asked him: "What must we do, to be doing the works of God?" (Jn 6:28). The text uses here the Greek word *ergázesthai,* which means "to perform a work" (Barrett, *Gospel,* p. 287). Jesus' listeners are ready to work, to do something, to perform "works," in order to receive this bread. But it cannot be "earned" by human work, by one's own achievement. It can only come to us as a gift from God, as *God's work.* The whole of Pauline theology is present in this dialogue. The highest things, the things that really matter, we cannot achieve on our own; we have to accept them as gifts and enter into the dynamic of the gift, so to speak. This happens in the context of faith in Jesus, who is dialogue—a living relationship with the Father—and who wants to become Word and love in us as well.

But the question as to how we can "feed" on God, live on God, in such a way that he himself becomes our bread—this question is not yet fully answered by what has just been said. God becomes "bread" for us first of all in the Incarnation of the Logos: The Word takes on flesh. The Logos becomes one of us and so comes down to our level, comes into the sphere of what is accessible to us. Yet a further step is still needed beyond even the Incarnation of the Word. Jesus names this step in the concluding words of his discourse: His flesh is life "for" the world (Jn 6:51). Beyond the act of the Incarnation, this points to its intrinsic goal and ultimate realization: Jesus' act of giving himself up to death and the mystery of the Cross.

This is made even clearer in verse 53, where the Lord adds that he will give us his blood to "drink." These words are not only a manifest allusion to the Eucharist. Above all they point to what underlies the Eucharist: the sacrifice of Jesus, who sheds his blood for us, and in so doing steps out of himself, so to speak, pours himself out, and gives himself to us.

In this chapter, then, the theology of the Incarnation and the theology of the Cross come together; the two cannot be separated. There are thus no grounds for setting up an opposition between the Easter theology of the Synoptics and Saint Paul, on one hand, and Saint John's supposedly purely incarnational theology, on the other. For the goal of the Word's becoming-flesh spoken of by the prologue is precisely the offering of his body on the Cross, which the sacrament makes accessible to us. John is following here the same line of thinking that the Letter to the Hebrews develops on the basis of Psalm 40:6–8: "Sacrifices and offerings you did refuse—you have prepared a body for me" (Heb 10:5). Jesus becomes man in order to give himself and to take the place of the animal sacrifices, which could only be a gesture of longing, but not an answer.

Jesus' bread discourse, on one hand, points the main movement of the Incarnation and of the Paschal journey toward the sacrament, in which Incarnation and Easter are permanently present, but conversely, this has the effect of integrating the sacrament, the Holy Eucharist, into the larger context of God's descent to us and for us. On one hand, then, the Eucharist emphatically moves right to the center of Christian existence; here God does indeed give us the manna that humanity is waiting for, the true "bread of heaven"—the nourishment we can most deeply live upon as human beings. At the same time, however, the Eucharist is revealed as man's unceasing great encounter with God, in which the Lord gives himself as "flesh," so that in him, and by participating in his way, we may become "spirit." Just as he was transformed through the Cross into a new manner of bodiliness and of being-human pervaded by God's own being, so too for us this food must become an opening out of our existence, a passing through the Cross, and an anticipation of the new life in God and with God.

This is why at the conclusion of the discourse, which places such emphasis on Jesus' becoming flesh and our eating and drinking the "flesh and blood of the Lord," Jesus says: "it is the spirit that gives life, the flesh is of no avail" (Jn 6:63). This may remind us of Saint Paul's words: "The first man Adam became a living being; the last Adam became a life-giving spirit" (1 Cor 15:45). This in no way diminishes the realism of "becoming-flesh." Yet the Paschal perspective of the sacrament is underlined: Only through the Cross and through the transformation that it effects does this flesh become accessible to us, drawing us up into the process of transformation. Eucharistic piety needs to be constantly learning from this great Christological—indeed, cosmic—dynamism.

In order to understand the full depth of Jesus' bread discourse, we must finally take a brief look at one of the key sayings of John's Gospel. Jesus pronounces it on Palm Sunday as he looks ahead to the universal Church that will embrace Jews and Greeks—all the peoples of the world: "Unless a grain of wheat falls into the earth and dies, it remains alone; but if it dies, it bears much fruit" (Jn 12:24). What we call "bread" contains the mystery of the Passion. Before there can be bread, the seed—the grain of wheat—first has to be placed in the earth, it has to "die," and then the new ear can grow out of this death. Earthly bread can become the bearer of Christ's presence because it contains in itself the mystery of the Passion, because it unites in itself death and resurrection. This is why the world's religions used bread as the basis for myths of death and resurrection of the godhead, in which man expressed his hope for life out of death.

In this connection, Cardinal Christoph Schönborn reminds us of the conversion of the great British writer C. S. Lewis; Lewis, having read a twelve-volume work about these myths, came to the conclusion that this Jesus who took bread in his hands and said, "This is my body," was just "another corn divinity, a corn king who lays down his life for the life of the world." One day, however, he overheard a firm atheist remarking to a colleague that the evidence for the historicity of the Gospels was actually surprisingly good. The atheist then paused thoughtfully and said: "About the dying God. Rum thing. It almost looks as if it really happened once" (Schönborn, *Weihnacht*, pp. 23f.).

Yes, it really did happen. Jesus is no myth. He is a man of flesh and blood and he stands as a fully real part of history. We can go to the very places where he himself went. We can hear his words through his witnesses. He died and he is risen. It is as if the mysterious Passion contained in bread had waited for him, had stretched out its arms toward him; it is as if the myths had waited for him, because in him what they long for came to pass. The same is true of wine. It too contains the Passion in itself, for the grape had to be pressed in order to become wine. The Fathers gave this hidden language of the eucharistic gifts an even deeper interpretation. I would like to add just one example here. In the early Christian text called the Teaching of the Twelve Apostles, also known as the *Didache* (probably composed around the year 100), the following prayer is recited over the bread intended for the Eucharist: "As the bread was scattered on the mountains and brought into unity, so may the Church be gathered from the ends of the earth into your Kingdom" (IX, 4).

The Shepherd

The image of the shepherd, which Jesus uses to explain his mission both in the Synoptics and in the Gospel of John, has a long history behind it. In the ancient Near East, in royal inscriptions from both Sumer and the area of Babylonia and Assyria, the king refers to himself as the shepherd instituted by God. "Pasturing sheep" is an image of his task as a ruler. This image implies that caring for the weak is one of the tasks of the just ruler. One could therefore say that, in view of its origins, this image of Christ the Good Shepherd is a Gospel of Christ the King, an image that sheds light upon the kingship of Christ.

Of course, the immediate precedents for Jesus' use of this image are found in the Old Testament, where God himself appears as the Shepherd of Israel. This image deeply shaped Israel's piety, and it was especially in times of need that Israel found a word of consolation and confidence in it. Probably the most beautiful expression of this trustful devotion is Psalm 23: "The Lord is my shepherd . . . Even though I walk through the valley of the shadow of death, I fear no evil; for thou art with me" (Ps 23:1, 4). The image of God as Shepherd is more fully developed in chapters 34–37 of Ezekiel, whose vision is brought into the present and interpreted as a prophecy of Jesus' ministry both in the Synoptic shepherd parables and in the Johannine shepherd discourse. Faced with the self-seeking shepherds of his own day, whom he challenges and accuses, Ezekiel proclaims the promise that God himself will seek out his sheep and care for them. "And I will bring them out from the peoples, and gather them from the countries, and will bring them into their own land. . . . I myself will be the shepherd of my sheep, and I will make them lie down, says the Lord GOD. I will seek the lost, and I will bring back the strayed, and I will bind up the crippled, and I will strengthen the weak, and the fat and the strong I will watch over" (Ezek 34:13, 15–16).

Faced with the murmuring of the Pharisees and scribes over Jesus' table fellowship with sinners, the Lord tells the parable of the ninety-nine sheep who remained in the fold and the one lost sheep. The shepherd goes after the lost sheep, lifts it joyfully upon his shoulders, and brings it home. Jesus puts this parable as a question to his adversaries: Have you not read God's word in Ezekiel? I am only doing what God, the true Shepherd, foretold: I wish to seek out the sheep that are lost and bring the strayed back home.

At a late stage in Old Testament prophecy, the portrayal of the shepherd image takes yet another surprising and thought-provoking turn that leads directly to the mystery of Jesus Christ. Matthew recounts to us that on the way to the Mount of Olives after the Last Supper, Jesus tells his disciples that the prophecy foretold in Zechariah 13:7 is about to be fulfilled: "I will strike the shepherd, and the sheep of the flock will be scattered" (Mt 26:31). Zechariah does in fact present in this passage the vision of a Shepherd "who by God's will patiently suffers death and in so doing initiates the final turn of events" (Jeremias, *TDNT*, VI, pp. 500-1).

This surprising vision of the slain Shepherd, who through his death becomes the Savior, is closely linked to another image from the Book of Zechariah: "And I will pour out on the house of David and the inhabitants of Jerusalem a spirit of compassion and supplication. And they will look on him whom they have pierced. They shall mourn for him, as one mourns for an only child, and weep bitterly over him, as one weeps over a firstborn. . . . On that day the mourning in Jerusalem will be as great as the mourning for Hadad-Rimmon in the plain of Megiddo. . . . On that day there shall be a fountain opened for the house of David and the inhabitants of Jerusalem to cleanse them from sin and uncleanness" (Zech 12:10, 11; 13:1). Hadad-Rimmon was one of the dying and rising vegetation deities whom we encountered earlier when we were explaining that bread presupposes the death and resurrection of the grain. The death of the god, which is then followed by resurrection, was celebrated with wild ritual laments; these rituals impressed themselves upon those who witnessed them—as the Prophet and his audience evidently did—as the absolute archetype of grief and lamentation. For Zechariah, Hadad-Rimmon is one of the nonexistent divinities that Israel despises and unmasks as mythical dreams. And yet, through the ritual lamentation over him, he mysteriously prefigures someone who really does exist.

An inner connection with the Servant of God in Deutero-Isaiah is discernible here. In the writings of the later Prophets, we see the figure of the suffering and dying Redeemer, the Shepherd who becomes the lamb, even if some of the details are yet to be filled in. K. Elliger comments apropos of this: "On the other hand, however, his [Zechariah's] gaze penetrates with remarkable accuracy into a new distance and circles around the figure of the one who was pierced on the Cross at Golgotha. Admittedly, he does not clearly discern the figure of Christ, although the allusion to Hadad-Rimmon does come remarkably close to the mystery of the Resurrection, albeit no more than close . . . and above all without clearly seeing the real connection between the Cross and the fountain that cleanses sin and impurity" ("Das Buch," *ATD*, 25, p. 172). While in Matthew's Gospel, Jesus himself cites Zechariah 13:7—the image of the slain Shepherd—at the beginning of the Passion narrative, John, by contrast, concludes his account of the Lord's Crucifixion with an allusion to Zechariah 12:10: "They shall look on him whom they have pierced" (Jn 19:37). Now it becomes clear: the one who is slain and the Savior is Jesus Christ, the crucified one.

John associates this with Zechariah's prophetic vision of

the fountain that purifies from sin and impurity: Blood and water flow forth from Jesus' wounded side (cf. Jn 19:34). Jesus himself, the one pierced on the Cross, is the fountain of purification and healing for the whole world. John connects this further with the image of the Paschal Lamb, whose blood has purifying power: "Not a bone of him shall be broken" (Jn 19:36; cf. Ex 12:46). With that, the circle is closed, joining the end to the beginning of the Gospel, where the Baptist—catching sight of Jesus—said: "Behold, the Lamb of God, who takes away the sin of the world" (Jn 1:29). The image of the lamb, which in a different way plays a decisive role in the Book of Revelation, thus encompasses the entire Gospel. It also points to the deepest meaning of the shepherd discourse, whose center is precisely Jesus' act of laying down his life.

Surprisingly, the shepherd discourse does not begin with the words: "I am the Good Shepherd" (Jn 10:11), but with another image: "Truly, truly, I say to you, I am the door of the sheep" (Jn 10:7). Jesus has already said: "Truly, truly, I say to you, he who does not enter the sheep-fold by the door but climbs in by another way, that man is a thief and a robber; but he who enters by the door is the shepherd of the sheep" (Jn 10:1f.). This can only really mean that Jesus is establishing the criterion for those who will shepherd his flock after his ascension to the Father. The proof of a true shepherd is that he enters through Jesus as the door. For in this way it is ultimately Jesus who is the Shepherd—the flock "belongs" to him alone.

In practice, the way to enter through Jesus as the door becomes apparent in the appendix to the Gospel in chapter 21—when Peter is entrusted with Jesus' own office as Shepherd. Three times the Lord says to Peter: "Feed my lambs" (or sheep—cf. Jn 21:15–17). Peter is very clearly being appointed as the shepherd of Jesus' sheep and established in Jesus' office as shepherd. For this to be possible, however, Peter has to enter through the "door." Jesus speaks of this entry—or, better, this being allowed to enter through the door (cf. Jn 10:3)—when he asks Peter three times: Simon, son of John, do you love me? Notice first the utterly personal aspect of this calling: Simon is called by name—both by his own personal name, Simon, and by a name referring to his ancestry. And he is asked about the love that makes him one with Jesus. This is how he comes to the sheep "through Jesus": He takes them not as his own—Simon Peter's—but as *Jesus'* "flock." It is because he comes through the "door," Jesus, it is because he comes to them united with Jesus in love, that the sheep listen to his voice, the voice of Jesus himself—they are following not Simon, but Jesus, from whom and through whom Simon comes to them, so that when he leads them it is Jesus himself who leads.

The whole investiture scene closes with Jesus saying to Peter, "Follow me" (Jn 21:19). It recalls the scene after Peter's first confession, where Peter tries to dissuade the Lord from the way of Cross, and the Lord says to him, "Get behind me," and then goes on to invite everyone to take up his cross and "follow him" (cf. Mk 8:33ff.). Even the disciple who now goes ahead of the others as shepherd must "follow" Jesus. And as the Lord declares to Peter after conferring upon him the office of shepherd, this includes accepting the cross, being prepared to give his life. This is what it means in practice when Jesus says: "I am the door." This is how Jesus himself remains the shepherd.

Let us return to the shepherd discourse in chapter 10 of John's Gospel. It is only in the second part that Jesus declares: "I am the Good Shepherd" (Jn 10:11). He takes upon himself all the historical associations of the shepherd image, which he then purifies, and brings to its full meaning. Four essential points receive particular emphasis. First, the thief "comes only to steal and kill and destroy" (Jn 10:10). He regards the sheep as part of his property, which he owns and exploits for himself. All he cares about is himself; he thinks the world revolves around him. The real Shepherd does just the opposite. He does not take life, but gives it: "I came that they may have life, and have it abundantly" (Jn 10:10).

This is Jesus' great promise: to give life in abundance. Everyone wants life in abundance. But what is it? What does life consist in? Where do we find it? When and how do we have "life in abundance"? When we live like the prodigal son, squandering the whole portion God has given us? When we live like the thief and the robber, taking everything for ourselves alone? Jesus promises that he will show the sheep where to find "pasture"—something they can live on—and that he will truly lead them to the springs of life. We are right to hear echoes of Psalm 23 in this: "He makes me lie down in green pastures. He leads me beside still waters. . . . Thou preparest a table before me in the presence. . . . Surely goodness and mercy shall follow me all the days of my life" (Ps 23:2, 5f.). There is an even more immediate echo of the shepherd discourse from Ezekiel: "I will feed them with good pasture, and upon the mountain country of Israel shall be their pasture" (Ezek 34:14).

But what does all this mean? We know what sheep live

on, but what does man live on? The Fathers saw Ezekiel's reference to the mountain country of Israel and the shady and well-watered pastures on its uplands as an image of the heights of Holy Scripture, of the life-giving food of God's word. Although this is not the historical sense of the text, in the end the Fathers saw correctly and, above all, they understood Jesus himself correctly. Man lives on truth and on being loved: on being loved by the truth. He needs God, the God who draws close to him, interprets for him the meaning of life, and thus points him toward the path of life. Of course, man needs bread, he needs food for the body, but ultimately what he needs most is the Word, love, God himself. Whoever gives him *that* gives him "life in abundance," and also releases the energies man needs to shape the earth intelligently and to find for himself and for others the goods that we can have only in common with others.

In this sense, there is an inner connection between the bread discourse in chapter 6 and the shepherd discourse: In both cases the issue is what man lives on. Philo, the great Jewish philosopher of religion and contemporary of Jesus, said that God, the true Shepherd of his people, had appointed his "firstborn Son," the Logos, to the office of Shepherd (Barrett, *Gospel,* p. 374). The Johannine shepherd discourse is not immediately connected with the understanding of Jesus as Logos, and yet—in the specific context of the Gospel of John—the point the discourse is making is that Jesus, being the incarnate Word of God himself, is not just the Shepherd, but also the food, the true "pasture." He gives life by giving himself, for he *is* life (cf. Jn 1:4, 3:36, 11:25).

This brings us to the second motif in the shepherd discourse. It reveals the novelty that leads us beyond Philo—not by means of new ideas, but by means of a new event, the Incarnation and Passion of the Son: "The Good Shepherd lays down his life for the sheep" (Jn 10:11). Just as the bread discourse does not merely allude to the word, but goes on to speak of the Word that became flesh and also gift "for the life of the world" (Jn 6:51), so too the shepherd discourse revolves completely around the idea of Jesus laying down his life for the "sheep." The Cross is at the center of the shepherd discourse. And it is portrayed not as an act of violence that takes Jesus unawares and attacks him from the outside, but as a free gift of his very self: "I lay down my life, that I may take it again. No one takes it from me, but I lay it down of my own accord" (Jn 10:17f.). Here Jesus interprets for us what happens at the institution of the Eucharist: He transforms the outward violence of the act of crucifixion into an act of freely giving his life for others. Jesus does not give *something,* but rather he gives himself. And that is how he gives life. We will have to return to these ideas and explore them more deeply when we speak of the Eucharist and the Paschal event.

A third essential motif of the Shepherd discourse is the idea that the shepherd and his flock know each other: "He calls his own sheep by name and leads them out. . . . The sheep follow him, for they know his voice" (Jn 10:3f.). "I am the Good Shepherd; I know my own and my own know me, as the Father knows me and I know the Father; and I lay down my life for the sheep" (Jn 10:14f.). These verses present two striking sets of interrelated ideas that we need to consider if we are to understand what is meant by "knowing." First of all, knowing and belonging are interrelated. The

Shepherd knows the sheep because they belong to him, and they know him precisely because they are his. Knowing and belonging (the Greek text speaks of the sheep as the Shepherd's "own," *ta ídia*) are actually one and the same thing. The true shepherd does not "possess" the sheep as if they were a thing to be used and consumed; rather, they "belong" to him, in the context of their knowing each other, and this "knowing" is an inner acceptance. It signifies an inner belonging that goes much deeper than the possession of things.

Let us illustrate this with an example from our own lives. No human being "belongs" to another in the way that a thing does. Children are not their parents' "property"; spouses are not each other's "property." Yet they do "belong" to each other in a much deeper way than, for example, a piece of wood or a plot of land, or whatever else we call "property." Children "belong" to their parents, yet they are free creatures of God in their own right, each with his own calling and his own newness and uniqueness before God. They belong to each other, not as property, but in mutual responsibility. They belong to each other precisely by accepting one another's freedom and by supporting one another in love and knowledge—and in this communion they are simultaneously free and one for all eternity.

In the same way, the "sheep," who after all are people created by God, images of God, do not belong to the shepherd as if they were *things*—though that is what the thief and robber thinks when he takes possession of them. Herein lies the distinction between the owner, the true Shepherd, and the robber. For the robber, for the ideologues and the dictators, human beings are merely a thing that they possess. For the true Shepherd, however, they are free in relation to truth and love; the Shepherd proves that they belong to him precisely by knowing and loving them, by wishing them to be in the freedom of the truth. They belong to him through the oneness of "knowing," through the communion in the truth that the Shepherd himself is. This is why he does not *use* them, but gives his life for them. Just as Logos and Incarnation, Logos and Passion belong together, so too knowing and self-giving are ultimately one.

Let us listen once more to these decisive words: "I am the good shepherd; I know my own and my own know me, as the Father knows me and I know the Father; and I lay down my life for the sheep" (Jn 10:14f.). This statement contains a second set of interrelated ideas that we need to consider. The mutual knowing of shepherd and sheep is interwoven with the mutual knowing of Father and Son. The knowing that links Jesus with "his own" exists within the space opened up by his "knowing" oneness with the Father. Jesus' "own" are woven into the Trinitarian dialogue; we will see this again when we consider the high-priestly prayer. This will help us to see that Church and Trinity are mutually interwoven. This interpenetration of two levels of knowing is crucial for understanding the essence of the "knowing" of which John's Gospel speaks.

Applying all of the above to the world in which we live, we can say this: It is only in God and in light of God that we rightly know man. Any "self-knowledge" that restricts man to the empirical and the tangible fails to engage with man's true depth. Man knows himself only when he learns to understand himself in light of God, and he knows others only when he sees the mystery of God in them. For the shepherd in Jesus' service, this means that he has no right to bind men to himself, to his own little "I." The mutual knowing that binds him to the "sheep" entrusted to his care must have a different goal: It must enable them to lead one another into God, toward God; it must enable them to encounter each other in the communion formed around knowing and loving God. The shepherd in Jesus' service must always lead beyond himself in order to enable others to find their full freedom; and therefore he must always go beyond himself into unity with Jesus and with the Trinitarian God.

Jesus' own "I" is always opened into "being with" the Father; he is never alone, but is forever receiving himself from and giving himself back to the Father. "My teaching is not mine"; his "I" is opened up into the Trinity. Those who come to know him "see" the Father; they enter into this communion of his with the Father. It is precisely this transcendent dialogue, which encounter with Jesus involves, that once more reveals to us the true Shepherd, who does not take possession of us, but leads us to the freedom of our being by leading us into communion with God and by giving his own life.

Let us turn to the last principal motif of the shepherd discourse: the motif of unity. The shepherd discourse in Ezekiel emphasizes this motif: "The word of the LORD came to me: 'Son of Man, take a stick and write on it, "For Judah, and the children of Israel associated with him"; then take another stick and write upon it, "For Joseph (the stick of Ephraim) and all the house of Israel associated with him"; and join them together into one stick, that they may become one in your hand. . . . "Thus says the Lord GOD: Behold, I will take the people of Israel from the nations . . . and I will make them one nation in the land, upon the mountains of Israel . . . And they shall be no longer two nations, and no longer divided into two kingdoms''''' (Ezek 37:15–17, 21f.). God is the Shepherd who reunites divided and scattered Israel into a single people.

Jesus' shepherd discourse takes up this vision, while very decidedly enlarging the scope of the promise: "I have other sheep, that are not of this fold; I must bring them also, and they will heed my voice. So there shall be one flock, one Shepherd" (Jn 10:16). Jesus the Shepherd is sent not only to gather the scattered sheep of the house of Israel, but to gather together all "the children of God who are scattered abroad" (Jn 11:52). In this sense, Jesus' promise that there will be one Shepherd and one flock is equivalent to the risen Lord's missionary command in Matthew's Gospel: "Go therefore and make all nations my disciples" (Mt 28:19); the same idea appears again in the Acts of the Apostles, where the risen Lord says: "You shall be my witnesses in Jerusalem and in all Judea and Samaria and to the end of the earth" (Acts 1:8).

This brings to light the inner reason for this universal mission: There is only one Shepherd. The Logos who became man in Jesus is the Shepherd of all men, for all have been created through the one Word; however scattered they may be, yet as coming from him and bound toward him they are one. However widely scattered they are, all people can become one through the true Shepherd, the Logos who became man in order to lay down his life and so to give life in abundance (cf. Jn 10:10).

From very early on—the evidence goes back to the third century—the vision of the shepherd became a typical image of the Christian world. In the surrounding culture, the Christian people encountered the figure of a man carrying a sheep, which to an overstressed urban society expressed the popular dream of the simple life. But the Christian people were immediately able to reinterpret this figure in light of Scripture. Psalm 23 is an example that comes to mind directly: "The LORD is my shepherd, I shall not want; he makes me lie down in green pastures. . . . Even though I walk through the valley of the shadow of death, I fear no evil. . . . Surely goodness and mercy shall follow me all the days of my life; and I shall dwell in the house of the LORD for ever." They recognized Christ as the Good Shepherd who leads us through life's dark valleys; the Shepherd who himself walked through the valley of the shadow of death; the Shepherd who also knows the way through the night of death and does not abandon me in this final solitude, but leads me out of this valley of death into the green pastures of life, to the place of "light, happiness and peace" (Roman Canon). Clement of Alexandria expressed this trust in the Shepherd's guidance in verses that convey something of the hope and confidence felt by the early Church in the midst of frequent sufferings and constant persecutions: "Lead, holy Shepherd, your spiritual sheep: Lead, king, your pure children. Christ's footsteps are the way to heaven" (*Paedogogus*, III, 12, 101; Van der Meer, *Menschensohn*, p. 23).

But naturally, Christians were also reminded of the parable of the shepherd who follows after the lost sheep, lifts it onto his shoulders, and brings it home, as well as the shepherd discourse of John's Gospel. For the Church Fathers, the two texts flowed into each other. The Shepherd who sets off to seek the lost sheep is the eternal Word himself, and the sheep that he lovingly carries home on his shoulders is humanity, the human existence that he took upon himself. In his Incarnation and Cross he brings home the stray sheep, humanity; he brings me home, too. The incarnate Logos is the true "sheep-bearer"—the Shepherd who follows after us through the thorns and deserts of our life. Carried on his shoulders, we come home. He gave his life for us. He himself is life.

CHAPTER NINE

Two Milestones on Jesus' Way: Peter's Confession and the Transfiguration

Peter's Confession

All three Synoptic Gospels present Jesus' question to the disciples about who the people think he is and who they themselves consider him to be (Mk 8:27–30; Mt 16:13–20; Lk 9:18–21) as an important milestone on his way. In all three Gospels, Peter answers in the name of the Twelve with a confession that is markedly different from the opinion of the "people." In all three Gospels, Jesus then foretells his Passion and Resurrection, and continues this announcement of his own destiny with a teaching about the way of discipleship, the way to follow him, the Crucified. In all three Gospels, however, he also interprets this "following" on the way of the Cross from an essentially anthropological standpoint: It is the indispensable way for man to "lose his life," without which it is impossible for him to find it (Mk 8:31–9:1; Mt 16:21–28; Lk 9:22–27). And finally, in all three Gospels there follows the account of the Transfiguration of Jesus, which once again interprets Peter's confession and takes it deeper, while at the same time connecting it with the mystery of Jesus' death and Resurrection (Mk 9:2–13; Mt 17:1–13; Lk 9:28–36).

Only Matthew immediately follows Peter's confession with the bestowal upon Peter of the power of the keys—of the power to bind and loose—and this is connected with Jesus' promise to build his Church upon Peter as on a rock. Parallel passages concerning this commission and this promise are found in Luke 22:31f. in the context of the Last Supper and in John 21:15–19 after Jesus' Resurrection.

It should be pointed out that John, too, places a similar confession on Peter's lips, which once again is presented as a decisive milestone on Jesus' way, giving the circle of the Twelve its full weight and profile for the first time (Jn 6:68f.). As we study Peter's confession in the Synoptics, we will also need to take this text into account, since, despite all the differences, it does reveal some basic elements in common with the Synoptic tradition.

These somewhat schematic observations should have made it clear that Peter's confession can be properly understood only in the context of Jesus' prophecy of the Passion and his words about the way of discipleship. These three elements—Peter's words and Jesus' twofold answer—belong inseparably together. Equally indispensable for understanding Peter's confession is the attestation of Jesus in the Transfiguration scene by the Father himself and by the Law and the Prophets. In Mark's Gospel, the story of the Transfiguration is preceded by what seems to be a promise of the Parousia. On one hand, this promise is connected with what Jesus says about the way of discipleship. At the same time, however, it leads to Jesus' Transfiguration, and as such, it interprets in its own way both discipleship and the promise of the Parousia. According to Mark and Luke, Jesus' words about discipleship are addressed to all—in contrast to the prediction of the Passion, which is communicated only to the witnesses. They thus bring an ecclesiological note into the whole context; they open up the horizon of the whole situation, so that we see beyond the journey to Jerusalem that Jesus has just begun, toward all God's people (cf. Lk 9:23). Indeed, these words about following the Crucified One address fundamental issues of human existence as such.

John has placed them in the context of Palm Sunday and he links them with the question the Greeks ask about Jesus, thus emphasizing the universal character of these sayings. Here too they are associated with Jesus' destiny on the Cross, which is thus presented as something intrinsically necessary and free from all contingency (cf. Jn 12:24f.). The saying about the death of the grain of wheat, moreover, connects Jesus' statement about losing one's life in order to find it with the mystery of the Eucharist, which in turn had provided the context for Peter's confession—placed by John at the end of the story of the multiplication of the loaves and Jesus' interpretation of it in his eucharistic discourse.

Let us turn our attention now to the individual components of this great tapestry woven of event and word. Matthew and Mark identify the theater of the event as the region of Caesarea Philippi (present-day Banias), a sanctuary of Pan established by Herod the Great that was located at the source of the Jordan. Herod's son Philip subsequently made this place the capital of his dominion and named it after Caesar Augustus and himself.

Tradition has located the scene at a place where a wall of rock overhangs the waters of the Jordan and thus powerfully illustrates Jesus' words about Peter as the rock. Mark and Luke, each in his own way, introduce us into what might be called the interior location of the event. Mark says that Jesus asked his question "on the way"; it is clear that the way Mark is speaking of is the one leading to Jerusalem. To be on the way among "the villages of Caesarea Philippi" (Mk 8:27) means to be starting the ascent to Jerusalem—to the center of salvation history, to the place where Jesus' destiny would be fulfilled in the Cross and the Resurrection, but also where the Church had its origin after these events. Peter's confession and hence the words of Jesus that follow it are located at the beginning of this way.

The great period of preaching in Galilee is at an end and we are at a decisive milestone: Jesus is setting out on the journey to the Cross and issuing a call to decision that now clearly distinguishes the group of disciples from the people who merely listen, without accompanying him on his way—a decision that clearly shapes the disciples into the beginning of Jesus' new family, the future Church. It is characteristic of this community to be "on the way" with Jesus—what that way involves is about to be made clear. It is also characteristic that this community's decision to accompany Jesus rests upon a realization—on a "knowledge" of Jesus that at the same time gives them a new insight into God, the one God in whom they believe as children of Israel.

In Luke—and this is entirely in keeping with his portrait

of the figure of Jesus—Peter's confession is connected with a prayer event. Luke begins his account of the story with a deliberate paradox: "As he was praying alone, the disciples were with him" (Lk 9:18). The disciples are drawn into his solitude, his communion with the Father that is reserved to him alone. They are privileged to see him as the one who—as we reflected at the beginning of this book—speaks face-to-face with the Father, person to person. They are privileged to see him in his utterly unique filial being—at the point from which all his words, his deeds, and his powers issue. They are privileged to see what the "people" do not see, and this seeing gives rise to a recognition that goes beyond the "opinion" of the people. This seeing is the wellspring of their faith, their confession; it provides the foundation for the Church.

Here we may identify the interior location of Jesus' twofold question. His inquiry about the opinion of the people and the conviction of the disciples presupposes two things. On one hand, there is an external knowledge of Jesus that, while not necessarily false, is inadequate. On the other hand, there is a deeper knowledge that is linked to discipleship, to participation in Jesus' way, and such knowledge can grow only in that context. All three Synoptics agree in recounting the opinion of the people that Jesus is John the Baptist, or Elijah, or some other of the Prophets returned from the dead; Luke has just told us that Herod, having heard about such accounts of Jesus' person and activity, felt a wish to see him. Matthew adds an additional variation: the opinion of some that Jesus is Jeremiah.

The common element in all these ideas is that Jesus is classified in the category "prophet," an interpretative key drawn from the tradition of Israel. All the names that are mentioned as interpretations of the figure of Jesus have an eschatological ring to them, the expectation of a radical turn of events that can be associated both with hope and with fear. While Elijah personifies hope for the restoration of Israel, Jeremiah is a figure of the Passion, who proclaims the failure of the current form of the Covenant and of the Temple that, so to speak, serves as its guarantee. Of course, he is also the bearer of the promise of a New Covenant that is destined to rise from the ashes. By his suffering, by his immersion in the darkness of contradiction, Jeremiah bears this twofold destiny of downfall and renewal in his own life.

These various opinions are not simply mistaken; they are greater or lesser approximations to the mystery of Jesus, and they can certainly set us on the path toward Jesus' real identity. But they do not arrive at Jesus' identity, at his newness. They interpret him in terms of the past, in terms of the predictable and the possible, not in terms of himself, his uniqueness, which cannot be assigned to any other category. Today, too, similar opinions are clearly held by the "people" who have somehow or other come to know Christ, who have perhaps even made a scholarly study of him, but have not encountered Jesus himself in his utter uniqueness and otherness. Karl Jaspers spoke of Jesus alongside Socrates, the Buddha, and Confucius as one of the four paradigmatic individuals. He thus acknowledged that Jesus is of fundamental significance in the search for the right way to be human. Yet for all that, Jesus remains one among others grouped within a common category, in terms of which they can be explained and also delimited.

Today it is fashionable to regard Jesus as one of the great religious founders who were granted a profound experience of God. They can thus speak of God to other people who have been denied this "religious disposition," as it were, drawing them into their own experience of God. However, we are still dealing here with a *human* experience of God that reflects his infinite reality in the finitude and limitation of a human spirit: It can therefore never amount to more than a partial, not to mention time- and space-bound, translation of the divine. The word *experience* thus indicates on one hand a real contact with the divine, while also acknowledging the limitation of the receiving subject. Every human subject can capture only a particular fragment of the reality that is there to be perceived, and this fragment then requires further interpretation. Someone who holds this opinion can certainly love Jesus; he can even choose him as a guide for his own life. Ultimately, though, this notion of Jesus' "experience of God" remains purely relative and needs to be supplemented by the fragments of reality perceived by other great men. It is man, the individual subject, who ends up being himself the measure: The individual decides what he is going to accept from the various "experiences," what he finds helpful and what he finds alien. There is no definitive commitment here.

Standing in marked contrast to the opinion of the people is the "recognition" of the disciples, which expresses itself in acknowledgment, in confession. How is this confession worded? Each of the three Synoptics formulates it differently, and John's formula is different again. According to Mark, Peter simply says to Jesus: "You are the Messiah [the Christ]" (Mk 8:29). According to Luke, Peter calls him "the

Christ [the anointed one] of God" (Lk 9:20), and according to Matthew he says: "You are the Christ [the Messiah], the Son of the living God" (Mt 16:16). In John's Gospel, finally, Peter's confession is as follows: "You are the Holy One of God" (Jn 6:69).

One could be tempted to construct a history of the evolution of the Christian confession from these various versions. There is no doubt that the diversity of the texts does reflect a process of development through which something at first only tentatively grasped gradually emerges into full clarity. Among recent Catholic exegetes, Pierre Grelot has offered the most radical interpretation of the contrasts between the texts: What he sees is not evolution, but contradiction (*Les Paroles de Jésus Christ*). According to Grelot, Peter's simple confession of Jesus' Messiahship as transmitted by Mark is doubtless an accurate record of the historical moment; for, he continues, we are still dealing here with a purely "Jewish" confession that saw Jesus as a political Messiah in accordance with the ideas of the time. Only the Markan account, he argues, is logically consistent, because only a political messianism would explain Peter's protest against the prophecy of the Passion, a protest that Jesus sharply rejects, as once he rejected Satan's offer of lordship over the world: "Get behind me, Satan! For you are not on the side of God, but of men" (Mk 8:33). This brusque rebuff, says Grelot, makes sense only if it applies also to the confession that went before, and declares this too to be false. Placed after the theologically mature version of the confession in Matthew's Gospel, the rebuff no longer makes sense.

The conclusion that Grelot draws from this is one that

he shares with those exegetes who disagree with his rather negative interpretation of the Markan text: namely, that Matthew's version of the confession represents a post-Resurrection saying, since, in the view of the great majority of commentators, it was only after the Resurrection that such a confession could be formulated. Grelot goes on to connect this with his special theory of an appearance of the Risen Lord to Peter, which he places alongside the encounter with the Lord that Paul regarded as the foundation of his own apostolate. Jesus' words to Peter, Blessed are you, Simon Bar Jona, "for *flesh and blood* has not *revealed* this to you, but my Father who is in heaven" (Mt 16:17), have a remarkable parallel in the Letter to the Galatians: "But when he who had set me apart before I was born, and had called me through his grace, was pleased to *reveal* his Son to me, in order that I might preach him among the Gentiles, I did not confer with *flesh and blood*" (Gal 1:15f.; cf. 1:11f.: "The gospel which was preached by me is not man's gospel. For I did not receive it from man, nor was I taught it, but it came through a revelation of Jesus Christ"). Common to both the Pauline text and to Jesus' commendation of Peter are the reference to Revelation and the declaration that this knowledge does not derive "from flesh and blood."

Grelot now concludes from all this that Peter, like Paul, was honored with a special appearance of the risen Christ (to which several New Testament texts do in fact refer) and that, just like Paul, who was also granted such an appearance, he received his specific commission on that occasion. Peter's mission was to the Church of the Jews, while Paul's was to the Church of the Gentiles (Gal 2:7). The promise to Peter,

Grelot maintains, properly belongs to the risen Christ's appearance to him, and its content has to be seen as a strict parallel to the commission that Paul received from the exalted Lord. There is no need to enter here into a detailed discussion of this theory, especially since this book, being a book about Jesus, is primarily concerned with the Lord himself, and deals with the topic of the Church only insofar as it is necessary for a correct understanding of the figure of Jesus.

Anyone who reads Galatians 1:11–17 attentively can easily recognize not only the parallels but also the differences between the two texts. Paul clearly intends in this passage to emphasize the independence of his apostolic commission, which is not derived from the authority of others, but is granted by the Lord himself; what is at stake here for him is precisely the universality of his mission and the specificity of his path as one engaged in building up the Church of the Gentiles. But Paul also knows that if his ministry is to be valid, he needs *communio* (*koinonia*) with the original Apostles (cf. Gal 2:9), and that without this *communio* he would be running in vain (cf. Gal 2:2). For this reason, after three years in Arabia and Damascus following his conversion, he went up to Jerusalem in order to see Peter (Cephas); thereafter he also met James, the brother of the Lord (cf. 1:18f.). For the same reason, fourteen years later, this time together with Barnabas and Titus, he traveled to Jerusalem and received the sign of *communio* from the "pillars," James, Cephas, and John, who extended to him the right hand of fellowship (cf. Gal 2:9). First Peter, and then later the three pillars, are thus presented as the guarantors of *communio,* as its indispensable reference points, who vouch for the correctness and unity of the Gospel and so of the nascent Church.

But this also brings to light the indisputable significance of the historical Jesus, of his preaching and of his decisions. The Risen Lord called Paul and gave him his own authority and his own commission, but the same Lord had previously chosen the Twelve, had entrusted Peter with a special commission, had gone with them to Jerusalem, had suffered there on the Cross, and had risen on the third day. The first Apostles guarantee this continuity (Acts 1:21f.), and this continuity explains why the commission given to Peter is actually fundamentally different from the commission given to Paul.

The special commission of Peter figures not only in Matthew, but in different forms (though always with the same substance) in Luke and John and even in Paul. In his passionate apologia in the Letter to the Galatians, Paul very clearly presupposes Peter's special commission; this primacy is in fact attested by the whole spectrum of the tradition in all of its diverse strands. To trace it back purely to a personal Easter appearance, and thus to place it in an exact parallel to Paul's mission, is simply not justified by the New Testament data.

But it is now time to return to Peter's confession of Christ and so to our actual topic. We saw that Grelot presents the confession of Peter transmitted in Mark as completely "Jewish," and hence bound to be repudiated by Jesus. There is, however, no such repudiation in the text, in which Jesus merely forbids the disciples to speak openly of this confession, given that it would undoubtedly have been misinterpreted in the public climate of Israel and would necessarily have led on one hand to false hopes in him and on the other hand to political action against him. Only after this prohibition does the explanation of what "Messiah" really means then follow: The true Messiah is the "Son of Man," who is condemned to death as the precondition for his entrance into glory as the one who rose from death after three days.

Scholars speak of two types of confessional formula in relation to early Christianity, the "substantive" and the "verbal"; perhaps it would be clearer to speak of an "ontological" and a "salvation history" type of confession. All three forms of Peter's confession transmitted to us by the Synoptics are "substantive"—you *are* the Christ, the Christ of God, the Christ, the Son of the living God. The Lord always sets a "verbal" confession alongside these substantive statements: the prophetic announcement of the Paschal Mystery of Cross and Resurrection. The two types of confession belong together, and each one is incomplete and ultimately unintelligible without the other. Without the concrete history of salvation, Christ's titles remain ambiguous: not only the word "Messiah," but also "Son of the living God." For this title is equally capable of being understood in a sense that is opposed to the mystery of the Cross.

Conversely, the bald "salvation history" statement remains without its full depth unless it is made clear that he who suffered here is the Son of the living God, who is equal to God (cf. Phil 2:6), but emptied himself and became like a slave, abasing himself to death, even death on the Cross (cf. Phil 2:7f.). It is therefore only the combination of Peter's confession and Jesus' teaching of the disciples that furnishes us with the full, essential Christian faith. By the same token, the great creedal statements of the Church always linked the two dimensions together.

Yet we know that through all the centuries, right up to the present, Christians—while in possession of the right confession—need the Lord to teach every generation anew that his way is not the way of earthly power and glory, but the way of the Cross. We know and we see that even today Christians—ourselves included—take the Lord aside in order to say to him: "God forbid it, Lord! This shall never happen to you!" (Mt 16:22). And because we doubt that God really will forbid it, we ourselves try to prevent it by every means in our power. And so the Lord must constantly say to us, too: "Get behind me, Satan!" (Mk 8:33). The whole scene thus remains uncomfortably relevant to the present, because in the end we do in fact constantly think in terms of "flesh and blood," and not in terms of the Revelation that we are privileged to receive in faith.

We must return once more to the titles of Christ used in the confessions. The first important point is that the respective form of the title must be read within the total context of the individual Gospels and the specific form in which they have been handed down. In this regard, there is always an important connection with the trial of Jesus, in which the confession of the disciples reappears in the form of question and accusation. In Mark, the high priest's question takes up the title Christ (Messiah) and extends it: "Are you the Messiah, the Son of the Blessed?" (Mk 14:61). This question implies that such interpretations of the figure of Jesus had found their way from the circle of the disciples into public knowledge. The linking of the titles "Christ" (Messiah) and

"Son" was in keeping with biblical tradition (cf. Ps 2:7; Ps 110). Looked at from this perspective, the difference between Mark's and Matthew's versions of the confession now appears only relative and far less significant than Grelot and other exegetes would claim. According to Luke, as we have seen, Peter confesses Jesus as "the Anointed One [Christ, Messiah] of God." Here we see again what the old man Simeon had known concerning the child Jesus, it having been revealed to him that this child was the Anointed One (Christ) of the Lord (cf. Lk 2:26). The rulers of the people present a counterimage of this when they mock Jesus under the Cross, saying, "He saved others; let him save himself, if he is the Christ of God, his Chosen One!" (Lk 23:35). There is thus an arc stretching from Jesus' childhood up over the confession at Caesarea Philippi and down to the Cross. Taken together, the three texts display the unique sense in which the "Anointed One" belongs to God.

There is, however, another incident from the Gospel of Luke that is important for the disciples' faith in Jesus: the story of the abundant catch of fish that ends with the calling of Simon Peter and his companions into discipleship. These experienced fishermen have caught nothing during the whole night, and now Jesus instructs them to put out to sea again in broad daylight and cast out their nets. This seems to make little sense according to the practical knowledge of these men, but Simon answers: "Master, we toiled all night and took nothing! But at your word I will let down the nets" (Lk 5:5). This is followed by the overflowing catch of fish, which profoundly alarms Peter. He falls at Jesus' feet in the posture of adoration and says: "Depart from me, for I am a sinful man,

O Lord" (Lk 5:8). In what has just happened, Peter recognizes the power of God himself working through Jesus' words, and this direct encounter with the living God in Jesus shakes him to the core of his being. In the light of this presence, and under its power, man realizes how pitifully small he is. He cannot bear the awe-inspiring grandeur of God—it is too enormous for him. Even in terms of all the different religions, this text is one of the most powerful illustrations of what happens when man finds himself suddenly and directly exposed to the proximity of God. At that point, he can only be alarmed at himself and beg to be freed from the overwhelming power of this presence. This inner realization of the proximity of God himself in Jesus suddenly breaks in upon Peter and finds expression in the title that he now uses for Jesus: "Kyrios" (Lord). It is the designation for God that was used in the Old Testament as a substitute for the unutterable divine name given from the burning bush. Whereas before putting out from the shore, Peter called Jesus *epistata,* which means "master," "teacher," "rabbi," he now recognizes him as the Kyrios.

We find a similar situation in the story of how Jesus approaches the disciples' boat across the storm-tossed lake. Peter now asks the Lord to bid him walk upon the waters as well—toward Jesus. When he is about to sink, he is rescued by the outstretched hand of Jesus, who then also gets into the boat. But just at this moment the wind subsides. And now the same thing happens that we saw in the story about the abundant haul of fish: The disciples in the boat fall down before Jesus, in an expression at once of terror and adoration, and they confess: "Truly you are the Son of God" (Mt 14:

22–33). These and other experiences, found throughout the Gospels, lay a clear foundation for Peter's confession as reported in Matthew 16:16. In various ways, the disciples were repeatedly able to sense in Jesus the presence of the living God himself.

Before we attempt to put together a complete picture out of all of these pieces of mosaic, we still must cast a brief glance at the confession of Peter in John's Gospel. Jesus' eucharistic discourse, which John places after the multiplication of the loaves, could be considered as a public continuation of Jesus' No to the tempter's invitation to transform stones into bread—the temptation, that is, to see his mission in terms of generating material prosperity. Jesus draws attention instead to the relationship with the living God and to the love that comes from him; therein lies the truly creative power that gives meaning, and also provides bread. Jesus thus interprets his own mystery, his own self, in light of his gift of himself as the living bread. The people do not like this; many go away. Jesus thereupon asks the Twelve: Do you want to leave me as well? Peter answers: "Lord, to whom shall we go? You have the words of eternal life, and we have believed, and have come to know, that you are the Holy One of God" (Jn 6:68f.).

We will need to ponder this version of Peter's confession more closely in the context of the Last Supper. It clearly reveals Jesus' priestly mystery (Psalm 106:16 calls Aaron "the holy one of God"). This title points backward to the eucharistic discourse and it points forward, along with this discourse, to the mystery of Jesus' Cross; it is thus anchored in the Paschal Mystery, in the heart of Jesus' mission, and it indicates what makes the figure of Christ completely different from the then current forms of messianic hope. The Holy One of God—that also reminds us, however, of how Peter quails when brought face-to-face with the proximity of the holy after the abundant catch of fish, when he dramatically experiences his wretchedness as a sinner. We find ourselves immersed in the context of the disciples' experience of Jesus, which we have tried to understand on the basis of certain key moments of their journey in fellowship with him.

So what firm conclusion can we draw from all this? The first thing to say is that the attempt to arrive at a historical reconstruction of Peter's original words and then to attribute everything else to posterior developments, and possibly to post-Easter faith, is very much on the wrong track. Where is post-Easter faith supposed to have come from if Jesus laid no foundation for it before Easter? Scholarship overplays its hand with such reconstructions.

It is during Jesus' trial before the Sanhedrin that we see what was actually scandalous about him: not a political messianism—that had manifested itself with Barabbas and would do so again with Bar-Kokhba. Both men gained a following and both movements were put down by the Romans. What scandalized people about Jesus was exactly what we have already seen in connection with Rabbi Neusner's conversation with the Jesus of the Sermon on the Mount: He seemed to be putting himself on an equal footing with the living God himself. This was what the strictly monotheistic faith of the Jews was unable to accept. This was the idea to which even Jesus could only slowly and gradually lead people. This was also what permeated his entire message—while preserving unbroken unity with faith in the one God; this was what was new, characteristic, and unique about his message. The fact that Jesus' trial was then presented to the Romans as the trial of a political Messiah reflects the pragmatism of the Sadducees. But even Pilate sensed that something completely different was really at stake here—that anyone who really seemed to be a politically promising "king" would never have been handed over to him to be condemned.

But we have stepped too far ahead here. Let us go back to the confessions of the disciples. What do we see when we put together the complete mosaic of texts? Now, the disciples have recognized that Jesus does not fit into any of the existing categories, that he is more than, and different from, "one of the Prophets." From the Sermon on the Mount, from his mighty deeds and his authority to forgive sins, from the sovereign manner of his preaching and his way of handling the traditions of the Law—from all of this they were able to recognize that Jesus was more than one of the Prophets. He is *the* Prophet who, like Moses, speaks face-to-face with God as with a friend; he is the Messiah, but in a different sense from that of a mere bearer of some commission from God.

In him, the great messianic words are fulfilled in a disconcerting and unexpected way: "You are my Son; today I have begotten you" (Ps 2:7). At certain key moments, the disciples came to the astonishing realization: This is God himself. They were unable to put all this together into a perfect response. Instead they rightly drew upon the Old Testament's words of promise: Christ, the Anointed One, Son of God, Lord. These are the key words on which their confession focused, while still tentatively searching for a way forward. It could arrive at its complete form only when Thomas, touching the wounds of the Risen Lord, cried out, in amazement: "My Lord and my God" (Jn 20:28). In the end, however, these words send us upon a never-ending journey. They are so vast that we can never grasp them completely, and they always surpass us. Throughout her entire history, the pilgrim Church has been exploring them ever more deeply. Only by touching Jesus' wounds and encountering his Resurrection are we able to grasp them, and then they become our mission.

The Transfiguration

All three Synoptic Gospels create a link between Peter's confession and the account of Jesus' Transfiguration by means of a reference to time. Matthew and Mark say: "And after six days Jesus took with him Peter and James, and John his brother" (Mt 17:1; Mk 9:2). Luke writes: "Now about eight days after these sayings" (Lk 9:28). Clearly, this means that the two events, in each of which Peter plays a prominent role, are interrelated. We could say that in both cases the issue is the divinity of Jesus as the Son; another point, though, is that in both cases the appearance of his glory is connected with the Passion motif. Jesus' divinity belongs with the Cross—only when we put the two together do we recognize Jesus correctly. John expressed this intrinsic interconnectedness of Cross and glory when he said that the Cross is Jesus' "exaltation," and that his exaltation is accomplished in no other way than in the Cross. But now we must try to delve somewhat more deeply into this remarkable time reference. There are two different interpretations, though they do not have to be considered mutually exclusive.

J.-M. van Cangh and M. van Esbroeck have explored the connection with the calendar of Jewish festivals. They point out that only five days separate two major Jewish feasts that occur in the fall. First there is the feast of *Yom ha-Kippurim*, the great Day of Atonement; the celebration of the weeklong Feast of Tabernacles (*Sukkoth*) follows six days afterward. This would mean that Peter's confession fell on the great Day of Atonement and should be interpreted theologically against the backdrop of this feast, on which, for the one time in the year, the high priest solemnly pronounced the name YHWH in the Temple's Holy of Holies. This context would give added depth to Peter's confession of Jesus as the Son of the living God. Jean Daniélou, by contrast, sees the Evangelists' references to the timing of the Transfiguration exclusively in relation to the Feast of Tabernacles, which—as we have seen—lasted an entire week. On this reading, Matthew, Mark, and Luke would all be in agreement about the chronology of the event. The six or eight days would then designate the weeklong Feast of Tabernacles itself; Jesus' Transfiguration would accordingly have taken place on the last day of the feast, which was both its high point and the synthesis of its inner meaning.

Both interpretations have in common the idea that Jesus' Transfiguration is linked with the Feast of Tabernacles. We will see that this connection actually comes to light in the text itself and that it makes possible a deeper understanding of the whole event. In addition to the specific elements of these accounts, we may observe here a fundamental trait of Jesus' life, which receives particularly thorough treatment in John's Gospel. As we saw in chapter 8, the great events of Jesus' life are inwardly connected with the Jewish festival calendar. They are, as it were, liturgical events in which the liturgy, with its remembrance and expectation, becomes reality—becomes life. This life then leads back to the liturgy and from the liturgy seeks to become life again.

Our analysis of the connections between the Transfiguration story and the Feast of Tabernacles illustrates once again the fact that all Jewish feasts contain three dimensions. They originate from celebrations of nature religion and thus tell of Creator and creation; they then become remembrances of God's actions in history; finally, they go on from there to become feasts of hope, which strain forward to meet the Lord who is coming, the Lord in whom God's saving action in history is fulfilled, thereby reconciling the whole of creation. We will see how these three dimensions of Jewish feasts are further deepened and refashioned as they become actually present in Jesus' life and suffering.

Contrasting with this liturgical interpretation of the timing of the Transfiguration is an alternative account that is insistently maintained by H. Gese (*Zur biblischen Theologie*). This interpretation holds that there is insufficient evidence for the claim that the text alludes to the Feast of Tabernacles. Instead, it reads the whole text against the background of Exodus 24—Moses' ascent of Mount Sinai. Now, this chapter, which recounts how God seals the Covenant with Israel, is indeed an essential key to interpreting the story of the Transfiguration. There we read: "The glory of the LORD dwelt on Mount Sinai, and the cloud covered it six days. And on the seventh day he called to Moses out of the midst of the cloud" (Ex 24:16). The Exodus text, unlike the Gospels, mentions the seventh day. This is not necessarily an argument against connecting it with the story of the Transfiguration. Nevertheless, I do consider the first idea—that the timing is derived from the Jewish festival calendar—to be more convincing. It should be pointed out, though, that it is not at all unusual for different typological connections to converge in the events occurring along Jesus' way. This makes it plain that Moses and the Prophets all speak of Jesus.

Let us turn now to the text of the Transfiguration narrative itself. There we are told that Jesus took Peter, James, and John and led them up onto a high mountain by themselves (Mk 9:2). We will come across these three again on the Mount of Olives (Mk 14:33) during Jesus' agony in the garden, which is the counterimage of the Transfiguration, although the two scenes are inextricably linked. Nor should we overlook the connection with Exodus 24, where Moses takes Aaron, Nadab, and Abihu with him as he climbs the mountain—though seventy of the elders of Israel are also included.

Once again the mountain serves—as it did in the Sermon on the Mount and in the nights spent by Jesus in prayer—as the locus of God's particular closeness. Once again we need to keep together in our minds the various mountains of Jesus' life: the mountain of the temptation; the mountain of his great preaching; the mountain of his prayer; the mountain of the Transfiguration; the mountain of his agony; the mountain of the Cross; and finally, the mountain of the Risen Lord, where he declares—in total antithesis to the offer of world dominion through the devil's power: "All power in heaven and on earth is given to me" (Mt 28:18). But in the background we also catch sight of Sinai, Horeb, Moriah—the mountains of Old Testament revelation. They are all at one and the same time mountains of passion and of Revelation, and they also refer in turn to the Temple Mount, where Revelation becomes liturgy.

When we inquire into the meaning of the mountain, the first point is of course the general background of mountain symbolism. The mountain is the place of ascent—not only outward, but also inward ascent; it is a liberation from the burden of everyday life, a breathing in of the pure air of creation; it offers a view of the broad expanse of creation and its beauty; it gives one an inner peak to stand on and an intuitive sense of the Creator. History then adds to all this the experience of the God who speaks, and the experience of the Passion, culminating in the sacrifice of Isaac, in the sacrifice of the lamb that points ahead to the definitive Lamb sacrificed on Mount Calvary. Moses and Elijah were privileged to receive God's Revelation on the mountain, and now they are conversing with the One who is God's Revelation in person.

"And he was transfigured before them," Mark says quite simply, going on to add somewhat awkwardly, as if stammering before the Mystery: "And his clothes became radiant, intensely white, as no one on earth could bleach them" (Mk 9:2–3). Matthew has rather more elevated words at his command: "His face shone like the sun, and his clothes became white as light" (Mt 17:2). Luke is the only one of the Evangelists who begins his account by indicating the purpose of Jesus' ascent: He "went up on the mountain to pray" (Lk 9: 28). It is in the context of Jesus' prayer that he now explains the event that the three disciples are to witness: "And as he was praying, the appearance of his face was altered, and his clothing became dazzling white" (Lk 9:29). The Transfiguration is a prayer event; it displays visibly what happens when Jesus talks with his Father: the profound interpenetration of his being with God, which then becomes pure light. In his oneness with the Father, Jesus is himself "light from light." The reality that he is in the deepest core of his being, which Peter tried to express in his confession—that reality becomes perceptible to the senses at this moment: Jesus' being in the light of God, his own being-light as Son.

At this point Jesus' relation to the figure of Moses as well as the differences between the two become apparent: "As he came down from the mountain, Moses did not know that the skin of his face shone because he had been talking with God" (Ex 34:29–35). Because Moses has been talking with God, God's light streams upon him and makes him radiant. But the light that causes him to shine comes upon him from the outside, so to speak. Jesus, however, shines from within; he does not simply receive light, but he himself is light from light.

Yet Jesus' garment of white light at the Transfiguration speaks of our future as well. In apocalyptic literature, white garments are an expression of heavenly beings—the garments of angels and of the elect. In this vein the Apocalypse of John—the Book of Revelation—speaks of the white garments that are worn by those who have been saved (cf. especially 7:9, 13; 19:14). But it also tells us something new: The garments of the elect are white because they have washed them in the blood of the Lamb (cf. Rev 7:14); this means that through Baptism they have been united with Jesus' Passion, and his Passion is the purification that restores to us the original garment lost through our sin (cf. Lk 15:22). Through

Baptism we are clothed with Jesus in light and we ourselves become light.

At this point Moses and Elijah appear and talk with Jesus. What the Risen Lord will later explain to the disciples on the road to Emmaus is seen here in visible form. The Law and the Prophets speak with Jesus; they speak of Jesus. Only Luke tells us—at least in a brief allusion—what God's two great witnesses were talking about with Jesus: They "appeared in glory and spoke of his departure [his exodus], which he was about to accomplish at Jerusalem" (Lk 9:31). Their topic of conversation is the Cross, but understood in an inclusive sense as Jesus' Exodus, which had to take place in Jerusalem. Jesus' Cross is an Exodus: a departure from this life, a passage through the "Red Sea" of the Passion, and a transition into glory—a glory, however, that forever bears the mark of Jesus' wounds.

This is a clear statement that the Law and the Prophets are fundamentally about the "hope of Israel," the Exodus that brings definitive liberation; but the content of this hope is the suffering Son of Man and Servant of God, who by his suffering opens the door into freedom and renewal. Moses and Elijah are themselves figures of the Passion and witnesses of the Passion. They speak with the transfigured Jesus about what they said while on earth, about the Passion of Jesus. But by speaking of these things with Jesus during his Transfiguration they make it apparent that this Passion brings salvation; that it is filled with the glory of God; that the Passion is transformed into light, into freedom and joy.

At this point, we need to jump ahead to the conversation that the three disciples have with Jesus as they come down from the "high mountain." Jesus is talking with them about his coming Resurrection from the dead, which of course presupposes the Cross. The disciples ask instead about the return of Elijah, which is foretold by the scribes. This is Jesus' reply: "Elijah does come first to restore all things. And how is it written of the Son of Man that he should suffer many things and be treated with contempt? But I tell you that Elijah has come, and they did to him whatever they pleased, as it is written of him" (Mk 9:12–13). Jesus' words confirm the expectation of Elijah's return. At the same time, however, he completes and corrects the common picture of it. He tacitly identifies the Elijah who will return as John the Baptist: the return of Elijah has already happened in the work of the Baptist.

John had come to reassemble Israel in preparation for the advent of the Messiah. But if the Messiah himself is the suffering Son of Man, and if it is only as such that he opens the way to salvation, then the work of Elijah that prepares his way must also somehow bear the mark of the Passion. And it does: "They did to him whatever they pleased, as it is written of him" (Mk 9:13). Jesus recalls the destiny that actually befell the Baptist, but his reference to Scripture is probably also an allusion to the traditions of the day foretelling the martyrdom of Elijah. Elijah was considered "the only one who, though persecuted, escaped martyrdom; but when he returns . . . he too has to undergo death" (Pesch, *Markusevangelium*, II, p. 80).

The hoped-for salvation and the Passion are thus joined together intimately and then developed into a picture of the redemption that accords with Scripture's deepest intention, although in terms of the prevailing expectations of the day it constitutes a startling novelty. Scripture had to be read anew with the suffering Christ, and so it must ever be. We constantly have to let the Lord draw us into his conversation with Moses and Elijah; we constantly have to learn from him, the Risen Lord, to understand Scripture afresh.

Let us return to the Transfiguration story itself. The three disciples are shaken by the enormousness of what they have seen. They are overcome by "fear of God," as we have seen them be on other occasions when they have experienced God's closeness in Jesus, when they have sensed their own wretchedness and have been practically paralyzed by fear. "They were terrified" (Mk 9:6), says Mark. And yet Peter begins to speak, although he is so dazed that "he did not know what to say" (Mk 9:6): "Rabbi, it is good that we are here. Let us make three tents, one for you and one for Moses and one for Elijah" (Mk 9:5).

These words, which Peter speaks in a sort of ecstasy, in the midst of fear yet also in the joy of God's closeness, have been the object of much discussion. Do they have something to do with the Feast of Tabernacles, on the final day of which the Transfiguration took place? H. Gese contests this and argues that the real point of reference in the Old Testament is Exodus 33:7ff., which describes the "ritualization of the Sinai event." According to this text, Moses goes "outside the camp" to pitch the Tent of Meeting, on which the pillar of cloud then descends. There the Lord and Moses spoke "face to face, as a man speaks to his friend" (Ex 33:11). On this interpretation, then, Peter's intention is to give permanence to the event of Revelation and erect tents of meeting; the account of the cloud overshadowing the disciples could confirm this reading. It is perfectly possible that the Transfiguration account does contain a reminiscence of the Exodus text; both Jewish and early Christian exegesis customarily interweave different scriptural references so that they converge and complement each other. Nevertheless, the proposal to set up *three* tents of meeting argues against such a connection, or at least makes it appear secondary.

The connection with the Feast of Tabernacles becomes convincing if we take account of the messianic interpretation of the feast in the Judaism of Jesus' day. Jean Daniélou (in *The Bible and the Liturgy*) has made a convincing study of this aspect and linked it with the testimony of the Fathers, who were still quite familiar with the traditions of Judaism and reread them in a Christian context. The Feast of Tabernacles exhibits the same three-dimensional structure that we have seen to be typical of major Jewish feasts generally: a celebration originally borrowed from nature religion becomes at the same time a feast in remembrance of God's saving deeds in history, and remembrance in turn becomes hope for definitive redemption. Creation, history, and hope become interlinked. If at one time, during the Feast of Tabernacles with its water libation, there had been a prayer for the rain needed in a drought-stricken land, the feast very quickly developed into the remembrance of Israel's wandering through the desert, when the Jews lived in tents (tabernacles, *sukkoth*) (cf. Lev 23:43). Daniélou cites Harald Riesenfeld: "The huts were thought of, not only as a remembrance of the protection of God in the desert, but also as a prefiguration of the *sukkoth* in which the just are to dwell in the age to come. Thus, it seems that a very exact eschatological symbolism was attached to the most characteristic rite of the Feast of Tabernacles, as this was celebrated in Jewish times" (*Bible and Liturgy*, pp. 334f.). In the New Testament, a mention of the eternal tabernacles of the righteous in the life to come occurs in Luke (Lk 16:9). "The manifestation of the glory of Jesus," to quote Daniélou, "appears to Peter to be the sign that the times of the Messiah have arrived. And one of the qualities of these messianic times was to be the dwelling of the just in the tents signified by the huts of the Feast of Tabernacles" (*Bible and Liturgy*, p. 340). By experiencing the Transfiguration during the Feast of Tabernacles, Peter, in his ecstasy, was able to recognize "that the realities prefigured by the Feast were accomplished . . . the scene of the Transfiguration marks the fact that the messianic times have come" (pp. 340f.). It is only as they go down from the mountain that Peter has to learn once again that the messianic age is first and foremost the age of the Cross and that the Transfiguration—the experience of becoming light from and with the Lord—requires us to be burned by the light of the Passion and so transformed.

These connections also shed new light on the meaning of the fundamental claim of the prologue to John's Gospel, where the Evangelist sums up the mystery of Jesus: "And the Word became flesh and pitched his tent among us" (Jn 1:14). Indeed, the Lord has pitched the tent of his body among us and has thus inaugurated the messianic age. Following this line of thought, Gregory of Nyssa reflected on the connection between the Feast of Tabernacles and the Incarnation in a magnificent text. He says that the Feast of Tabernacles, though constantly celebrated, remained unfulfilled. "For the true Feast of Tabernacles had not yet come. According to the words of the Prophet, however [an allusion to Psalm 118:27], God, the Lord of all things, has revealed himself to us in order to complete the construction of the tabernacle of our ruined habitation, human nature" (*De anima, PG* 46, 132B, cf. Daniélou, *Bible and Liturgy,* pp. 344f.).

Let us return from these broad vistas to the story of the Transfiguration. "And a cloud overshadowed them, and a voice came out of the cloud, 'This is my beloved Son; listen to him'" (Mk 9:7). The holy cloud, the *shekinah,* is the sign of the presence of God himself. The cloud hovering over the Tent of Meeting indicated that God was present. Jesus is the holy tent above whom the cloud of God's presence now stands and spreads out to "overshadow" the others as well. The scene repeats that of Jesus' Baptism, in which the Father himself, speaking out of the cloud, had proclaimed Jesus as Son: "You are my beloved Son; with you I am well pleased" (Mk 1:11).

The solemn proclamation of Sonship, however, is now followed by the command "Listen to him." At this point, we are reminded of the link with Moses' ascent of Mount Sinai, which we saw at the beginning to be the background of the Transfiguration story. On the mountain, Moses received the Torah, God's teaching word. Now we are told in reference to Jesus: "Listen to him." H. Gese has provided a perceptive commentary on this scene: "Jesus himself has become the divine Word of revelation. The Gospels could not illustrate it any more clearly or powerfully: Jesus himself is the Torah" (*Zur biblischen Theologie,* p. 81). This one command brings the theophany to its conclusion and sums up its deepest meaning. The disciples must accompany Jesus back down the mountain and learn ever anew to "listen to him."

If we learn to understand the content of the Transfiguration story in these terms—as the irruption and inauguration of the messianic age—then we are also able to grasp the obscure statement that Mark's Gospel inserts between Peter's confession and the teaching on discipleship, on one hand, and the account of the Transfiguration, on the other: "Truly, I say to you, there are some standing here who will not taste death until they see the dominion of God [the Kingdom of God] come with power" (Mk 9:1). What does this mean? Is Jesus predicting that some of the bystanders will still be alive at the time of his Parousia, at the definitive inbreaking of the Kingdom of God? If not, then what?

Rudolf Pesch (*Markusevangelium*, II, 2, pp. 66f.) has convincingly argued that the placing of this saying immediately before the Transfiguration clearly relates it to this event. Some—that is to say, the three disciples who accompany Jesus up the mountain—are promised that they will personally witness the coming of the Kingdom of God "in power." On the mountain the three of them see the glory of God's Kingdom shining out of Jesus. On the mountain they are overshadowed by God's holy cloud. On the mountain—in the conversation of the transfigured Jesus with the Law and the Prophets—they realize that the true Feast of Tabernacles has come. On the mountain they learn that Jesus himself is the living Torah, the complete Word of God. On the mountain they see the "power" (*dynamis*) of the Kingdom that is coming in Christ.

Yet equally, through the awe-inspiring encounter with God's glory in Jesus, they must learn what Paul says to the disciples of all ages in the First Letter to the Corinthians:

"We preach Christ crucified, a stumbling block to Jews and folly to Gentiles, but to those who are called, both Jews and Greeks, Christ the power [*dynamis*] of God and the wisdom of God" (1 Cor 1:23f.). This "power" (*dynamis*) of the coming Kingdom appears to them in the transfigured Jesus, who speaks with the witnesses of the Old Covenant about the necessity of his Passion as the way to glory (cf. Lk 24:26f.). They personally experience the anticipation of the Parousia, and that is how they are slowly initiated into the full depth of the mystery of Jesus.

CHAPTER TEN

Jesus Declares His Identity

Already during Jesus' lifetime, people tried to interpret his mysterious figure by applying to him categories that were familiar to them and that were therefore considered apt for deciphering his mystery: He is seen as John the Baptist, as Elijah or Jeremiah returning, or as the Prophet (cf. Mt 16:14; Mk 8:28; Lk 9:19). In his confession, Peter uses—as we have seen—other, loftier titles: Messiah, Son of the living God. The effort to express the mystery of Jesus in titles that explained his mission, indeed, his essence, continued after Easter. Increasingly, three fundamental titles began to emerge: "Christ" (Messiah), "Kyrios" (Lord), and "Son of God."

The first title, taken by itself, made little sense outside of Semitic culture. It quickly ceased to function as a title and was joined with the name of Jesus: Jesus Christ. What began as an interpretation ended up as a name, and therein lies a deeper message: He is completely one with his office; his task and his person are totally inseparable from each other. It was thus right for his task to become a part of his name.

This leaves the two titles "Kyrios" and "Son," which both point in the same direction. In the development of the Old Testament and of early Judaism, "Lord" had become a paraphrase for the divine name. Its application to Jesus therefore claimed for him a communion of being with God himself; it identified him as the living God present among us. Similarly, the title "Son of God" connected him with the being of God himself. Of course, the question as to exactly what sort of ontological connection this might be inevitably became the object of strenuous debate from that moment on, as faith strove to prove, and to understand clearly, its own rational content. Is he "Son" in a derivative sense, referring to some special closeness to God, or does the term "Son" imply that within God himself there is Father and Son, that the Son is truly "equal to God," true God from true God? The First Council of Nicea (325) summed up the result of this fierce debate over Jesus' Sonship in the word *homooúsios,* "of the same substance"—the only philosophical term that was incorporated into the Creed. This philosophical term serves, however, to safeguard the reliability of the *biblical* term. It tells us that when Jesus' witnesses call him "the Son," this statement is not meant in a mythological or political sense—those being the two most obvious interpretations given the context of the time. Rather, it is meant to be understood quite literally: Yes, in God himself there is an eternal dialogue between Father and Son, who are both truly one and the same God in the Holy Spirit.

The exalted Christological titles contained in the New Testament are the subject of an extensive literature. The debate surrounding them falls outside the scope of this book, which seeks to understand Jesus' earthly path and his preaching, not their theological elaboration in the faith and reflection of the early Church. What we need to do instead is to attend somewhat more closely to the titles that Jesus applies to himself, according to the evidence of the Gospels. There are two. Firstly, his preferred self-designation is "Son of Man"; secondly, there are texts—especially in the Gospel of John—where he speaks of himself simply as the "Son." The title "Messiah" Jesus did not actually apply to himself; in a few passages in John's Gospel we find the title "Son of God" on his lips. Whenever messianic or other related titles are applied to him, as for example by the demons he casts out, or by Peter in his confession, he enjoins silence. It is true, of course, that the messianic title "King of the Jews," is placed over the Cross—publicly displayed before the whole world. And it is permissible to place it there—in the three languages of the world of that time (cf. Jn 19:19f.)—because now there is no longer any chance of its being misunderstood. The Cross is his throne, and as such it gives the correct interpretation of this title. *Regnavit a ligno Deus*—God reigns from the wood of the Cross, as the ancient Church sang in celebration of this new kingship.

Let us now turn to the two "titles" that Jesus used for himself, according to the Gospels.

The Son of Man

Son of Man—this mysterious term is the title that Jesus most frequently uses to speak of himself. In the Gospel of Mark alone the term occurs fourteen times on Jesus' lips. In fact, in the whole of the New Testament, the term "Son of Man" is found only on Jesus' lips, with the single exception of the vision of the open heavens that is granted to the dying Stephen: "Behold, I see the heavens opened, and the Son of Man standing at the right hand of God" (Acts 7:56). At the moment of his death, Stephen sees what Jesus had foretold during his trial before the Sanhedrin: "You will see the Son of Man seated at the right hand of Power, and coming with the clouds of heaven" (Mk 14:62). Stephen is therefore actually "citing" a saying of Jesus, the truth of which he is privileged to behold at the very moment of his martyrdom.

This is an important finding. The Christology of the New Testament writers, including the Evangelists, builds not on the title "Son of Man," but on the titles that were already beginning to circulate during Jesus' lifetime: "Messiah" (Christ), "Kyrios" (Lord), "Son of God." The designation "Son of Man" is typical for Jesus' own sayings; in the preaching of the Apostles, its content is transferred to the other titles, but this particular title is not used. This is actually a clear finding. And yet a huge debate has developed around it in modern exegesis; anyone who tries to get to the bottom of it finds himself in a graveyard of mutually contradictory hypotheses. A discussion of this debate lies outside the scope of this book. Nevertheless, we do need to consider the main lines of the argument.

Three sets of "Son of Man" statements are commonly distinguished. The first group consists of sayings concerning the Son of Man who is to come, sayings in which Jesus does not point to himself as the Son of Man, but distinguishes between the one who is to come and himself. The second group comprises sayings about the earthly activity of the Son of Man, while the third speaks of his suffering and Resurrection. The predominant trend among exegetes is to regard only the first group—if any—as authentic sayings of Jesus; this reflects the conventional interpretation of Jesus' preaching in terms of imminent eschatology. The second group, which includes sayings about the authority of the Son of Man to forgive sins, about his lordship over the Sabbath, and about his having neither possessions nor home, is said to have developed—according to one main line of argument—in early Palestinian tradition. This would point to quite an early origin, but not as far back as Jesus himself. Finally, the most recent sayings would be those concerning the death and Resurrection of the Son of Man. In Mark's Gospel, they occur at intervals during Jesus' journey up to Jerusalem, and naturally, according to this theory, could only have been created after the events in question—perhaps even by the Evangelist Mark himself.

Splitting up the Son of Man sayings in this way is the result of a certain kind of logic that meticulously classifies the different aspects of a title. While that might be appropriate for rigorous professorial thinking, it does not suit the complexity of living reality, in which a multilayered whole clamors for expression. The fundamental criterion for this type of interpretation rests, however, on the question as to what we can safely attribute to Jesus, given the circumstances of his life and his cultural world. Very little, apparently! Real claims to authority or predictions of the Passion do not seem to fit. The sort of toned-down apocalyptic expectation that was in circulation at the time can be "safely" ascribed to him—but nothing more, it would seem. The problem is that this approach does not do justice to the powerful impact of the Jesus-event. Our reflections on Jülicher's exegesis of the parables have already led us to the conclusion that no one would have been condemned to the Cross on account of such harmless moralizing.

For such a radical collision to occur, provoking the extreme step of handing Jesus over to the Romans, something dramatic must have been said and done. The great and stirring events come right at the beginning; the nascent Church could only slowly come to appreciate their full significance, which she came to grasp as, in "remembering" them, she gradually thought through and reflected on these events. The anonymous community is credited with an astonishing level of theological genius—who were the great figures responsible for inventing all this? No, the greatness, the dramatic newness, comes directly from Jesus; within the faith and life of the community it is further developed, but not created. In fact, the "community" would not even have emerged and survived at all unless some extraordinary reality had preceded it.

The term "Son of Man," with which Jesus both concealed his mystery and, at the same time, gradually made it accessible, was new and surprising. It was not in circulation as a title of messianic hope. It fits exactly with the method of Jesus' preaching, inasmuch as he spoke in riddles and parables so as to lead gradually to the hidden reality that can truly be discovered only through discipleship. In both Hebrew and Aramaic usage, the first meaning of the term "Son of Man" is simply "man." That simple word blends together with a mysterious allusion to a new consciousness of mission in the term "Son of Man." This becomes apparent in a saying about the Sabbath that we find in the Synoptics. It reads as follows in Mark: "The Sabbath was made for man, not man for the Sabbath. So the Son of Man is Lord even of the Sabbath" (Mk 2:27f.). In Matthew and Luke, the first sentence is missing. They record Jesus as saying simply: "The Son of Man is Lord of the Sabbath" (Mt 12:8; Lk 6:5). Perhaps the explanation is that Matthew and Luke omit the first sentence for fear that it will be abused. Be that as it may, it is clear that according to Mark the two sentences belong together and interpret one another.

To say that the Sabbath is for man, and not man for the Sabbath, is not simply an expression of the sort of modern liberal position that we spontaneously read into these words. We saw in our examination of the Sermon on the Mount that this is exactly how *not* to understand Jesus' teaching. In the Son of Man, man is revealed as he truly ought to be. In terms of the Son of Man, in terms of the criterion that Jesus himself is, man is free and he knows how to use the Sabbath properly as the day of freedom deriving from God and destined for God. "The Son of Man is Lord of the Sabbath." The magnitude of Jesus' claim—which is an authoritative interpretation of the Law because he himself is God's primordial Word—becomes fully apparent here. And it also becomes apparent what sort of new freedom devolves upon man as a result—a freedom that has nothing to do with mere caprice. The important thing about this Sabbath saying is the overlapping of "man" and "Son of Man"; we see how this teaching, in itself quite ordinary, becomes an expression of the special dignity of Jesus.

"Son of Man" was not used *as a title* at the time of Jesus. But we find an early hint of it in the Book of Daniel's vision of four beasts and the "Son of Man" representing the history of the world. The visionary sees the succession of dominant secular powers in the image of four great beasts that come up out of the sea—that come "from below," and thus represent a power based mainly on violence, a power that is "bestial." He thus paints a dark, deeply disturbing picture of world history. Admittedly, the vision does not remain entirely negative. The first beast, a lion with the wings of an eagle, has its wings plucked out: "It was lifted up from the ground and made to stand on two feet like a man, and the heart of a man was given to it" (Dan 7:4). Power can be humanized, even in this age of the world; power can receive a human face. This is only a relative salvation, however, for history continues and becomes darker as it progresses.

But then—after the power of evil has reached its apogee—something totally different happens. The seer perceives as if from afar the real Lord of the world in the image of the Ancient of Days, who puts an end to the horror. And now "with the clouds of heaven there came one like a son of man . . . And to him was given dominion and glory and a kingdom, that all peoples, nations, and languages should serve him; his dominion is an everlasting dominion . . . and his kingdom one that shall not be destroyed" (Dan 7:13f.). The beasts from the depths are confronted by the man from above. Just as the beasts from the depths represent hitherto existing secular kingdoms, the image of the "Son of Man," who comes "with the clouds of heaven," prophesies a totally new kingdom, a kingdom of "humanity," characterized by the real power that comes from God himself. This kingdom also signals the advent of true universality, the definitive positive shape of history that has all along been the object of silent longing. The "Son of Man" who comes from above is thus the antithesis of the beasts from the depths of the sea; as such, he stands not for an individual figure, but for the "kingdom" in which the world attains its goal.

It is widely held among exegetes that this text rests upon an earlier version in which "Son of Man" indicated an individual figure. We do not possess this version, though; it remains a conjecture. The frequently cited texts from 4 Ezra 13 and the Ethiopian Book of Enoch that do portray the Son of Man as an individual figure are more recent than the New Testament and therefore cannot be regarded as one of its sources. Of course, it would have seemed obvious to connect the vision of the Son of Man with messianic hope and with the figure of the Messiah himself, but we have no textual evidence that this was done dating from before Jesus' public ministry. The conclusion therefore remains that the book of Daniel uses the image of the Son of Man to represent the coming kingdom of salvation—a vision that was available for Jesus to build on, but which he reshapes by connecting this expectation with his own person and his work.

Let us turn now to the scriptural passages themselves. We saw that the first group of sayings about the Son of Man refers to his future coming. Most of these occur in Jesus' discourse about the end of the world (cf. Mk 13:24–27) and in his trial before the Sanhedrin (cf. Mk 14:62). Discussion of them therefore belongs in the second volume of this book. There is just one important point that I would like to make here: They are sayings about Jesus' future glory, about his coming to judge and to gather the righteous, the "elect." We must not overlook, however, that they are spoken by a man who stands before his judges, accused and mocked: In these very words glory and the Passion are inextricably intertwined.

Admittedly, they do not expressly mention the Passion, but that is the reality in which Jesus finds himself and in which he is speaking. We encounter this connection in a uniquely concentrated form in the parable about the Last Judgment recounted in Saint Matthew's Gospel (25:31–46), in which the Son of Man, in the role of judge, identifies himself with those who hunger and thirst, with the strangers, the naked, the sick, the imprisoned—with all those who suffer in this world—and he describes behavior toward them as behavior toward himself. This is no mere fiction about the judge of the world, invented after the Resurrection. In becoming incarnate, he accomplished this identification with the utmost literalism. He is the man without property or home who has no place to lay his head (cf. Mt 8:19; Lk 9:58). He is the prisoner, the accused, and he dies naked on the Cross. This identification of the Son of Man who judges the world with those who suffer in every way presupposes the judge's identity with the earthly Jesus and reveals the inner unity of Cross and glory, of earthly existence in lowliness and future authority to judge the world. The Son of Man is one person alone, and that person is Jesus. This identity shows us the way, shows us the criterion according to which our lives will one day be judged.

It goes without saying that critical scholarship does not regard any of these sayings about the coming Son of Man as the genuine words of Jesus. Only two texts from this group, in the version reported in Luke's Gospel, are classified—at least by some critics—as authentic sayings of Jesus that may "safely" be attributed to him. The first one is Luke 12:8f.: "I tell you, every one who acknowledges me before men, the Son of man also will acknowledge before the angels of God; but he who denies me before men will be denied before the angels of God." The second text is Luke 17:24ff.: "For as the lightning flashes and lights up the sky from one side to the other, so will the Son of man be in his day. But first he must suffer many things and be rejected by this generation." The reason why these texts are looked upon with approval is that they seem to distinguish between the Son of Man and Jesus; especially the first saying, it is argued, makes it quite clear that the Son of Man is not identical with the Jesus who is speaking.

Now, the first thing to note in this regard is that the most ancient tradition, at any rate, did not understand it in that way. The parallel text in Mark 8:38 ("For whoever is ashamed of me and my words in this adulterous and sinful generation, of him will the Son of Man also be ashamed, when he comes in the glory of his Father with the holy angels") does not state the identification explicitly, but the structure of the sentence makes it crystal clear. In Matthew's version of the same text, the term Son of Man is missing. This makes even clearer the identity of the earthly Jesus with the judge who is to come: "So every one who acknowledges me before men, I also will acknowledge before my Father who is in heaven; but whoever denies me before men, I also will deny before my Father who is in heaven" (Mt 10:32f.). But even in the Lukan text, the identity is perfectly clear from the overall content. It is true that Jesus speaks in the riddle form that is characteristic of him, leaving the listener to take the final step toward understanding. But there is a functional identification in the parallelism of confession and denial—now and at the judgment, before Jesus and before the Son of Man—and this only makes sense on the basis of ontological identity.

The judges of the Sanhedrin actually understood Jesus properly: he did not correct them by saying something like: "But you misunderstand me; the coming Son of Man is someone else." The inner unity between Jesus' lived *kénosis* (cf. Phil 2:5–11) and his coming in glory is the constant motif of his words and actions; this is what is authentically new about Jesus, it is no invention—on the contrary, it is the epitome of his figure and his words. The individual texts have to be seen in context—they are not better understood in isolation. Even if Luke 12:8f. might appear to lend itself to a different interpretation, the second text is much clearer: Luke 17:24ff. unambiguously identifies the two figures. The Son of Man will not come here or there, but will appear like a flash of lightning from one end of heaven to the other, so that everyone will behold him, the Pierced One (cf. Rev 1:7); before that, however, he—this same Son of Man—will have to suffer much and be rejected. The prophecy of the Passion and the announcement of future glory are inextricably interwoven. It is clearly one and the same person who is the subject of both: the very person, in fact, who, as he speaks these words, is already on the way to his suffering.

Similarly, the sayings in which Jesus speaks of his present activity illustrate both aspects. We have already briefly examined his claim that, as Son of Man, he is Lord of the Sabbath (cf. Mk 2:28). This passage exactly illustrates something that Mark describes elsewhere: "They were dismayed at his teaching, for he taught them as one who had authority, and not as the scribes" (Mk 1:22). Jesus places himself on the side of the Lawgiver, God; he is not an interpreter, but the Lord.

This becomes clearer still in the account of the paralytic, whose friends lower him from the roof to the Lord's feet on a stretcher. Instead of speaking a word of healing, as the paralytic and his friends were expecting, Jesus says first of all to the suffering man: "My son, your sins are forgiven" (Mk 2:5). Forgiving sins is the prerogative of God alone, as the scribes rightly object. If Jesus ascribes this authority to the Son of Man, then he is claiming to possess the dignity of God himself and to act on that basis. Only after the promise of forgiveness does he say what the sick man was hoping to hear: "'But that you may know that the Son of man has authority on earth to forgive sins'—he said to the paralytic—'I say to you, rise, take up your pallet and go home'" (Mk 2:10–11). This divine claim is what leads to the Passion. In that sense, what Jesus says about his authority points toward his suffering.

Let us move on now to the third group of Jesus' sayings about the Son of Man: the predictions of his Passion. We have already seen that the three Passion predictions in Mark's Gospel, which recur at intervals in the course of Jesus' journey, announce with increasing clarity his approaching destiny and its inner necessity. They reach their inner center and their culmination in the statement that follows the third prediction of the Passion and the closely connected discourse on ruling and serving: "For the Son of man also came not to be served but to serve, and to give his life as a ransom for many" (Mk 10:45).

This saying incorporates a citation from the Suffering Servant Songs (cf. Is 53) and thus weaves another strand of

Old Testament tradition into the picture of the Son of Man. Jesus, while on one hand identifying himself with the coming judge of the world, also identifies himself here with the suffering and dying Servant of God whom the Prophet foretells in his Songs. The unity of suffering and "exaltation," of abasement and majesty, becomes visible. Service is the true form of rule and it gives us an insight into God's way of being Lord, of "God's lordship." In suffering and in death, the life of the Son of Man becomes sheer "pro-existence." He becomes the Redeemer and bringer of salvation for the "many": not only for the scattered children of Israel, but for all the scattered children of God (cf. Jn 11:52), for humanity. In his death "for many," he transcends the boundaries of place and time, and the universality of his mission comes to fulfillment.

Earlier exegesis considered the blending together of Daniel's vision of the coming Son of Man with the images of the Suffering Servant of God transmitted by Isaiah to be the characteristically new and specific feature of Jesus' idea of the Son of Man—indeed, as the center of his self-understanding overall. It was quite right to do so. We must add, though, that the synthesis of Old Testament traditions that make up Jesus' image of the Son of Man is more inclusive still, and it brings together even more strands and currents of Old Testament tradition.

First of all, Jesus' answer to the question as to whether he is the Messiah, the Son of the Blessed, combines Daniel 7 with Psalm 110: Jesus presents himself as the one who sits "at the right hand of Power," corresponding to what the Psalm prophesies of the future priest-king. Furthermore, the third prediction of the Passion, which speaks of the rejection of the Son of Man by the scribes, elders, and high priests (cf. Mk 8:31), blends in the passage from Psalm 118:22 concerning the stone rejected by the builders that has become the chief cornerstone. This also establishes a connection with the parable of the unjust vintners, in which the Lord cites these words in order to prophesy his rejection, his Resurrection, and the new communion that will follow. This connection with the parable also brings to light the identity between the "Son of Man" and the "beloved Son" (Mk 12:1–12). Finally, the Wisdom Literature provides another of the currents present here. The second chapter of the Book of Wisdom depicts the enmity of the "ungodly" against the righteous man: "He boasts that God is his father. . . . If the righteous man is God's son, he will help him. . . . Let us condemn him to a shameful death" (Wis 2:16–20). V. Hampel holds that Jesus' words about the "ransom for many" are derived not from Isaiah 53:10–12, but from Proverbs 21:18 and Isaiah 43:3 (cited in Schnackenburg, *Jesus in the Gospels,* p. 59). This strikes me as very unlikely. The actual reference point is and remains Isaiah 53; other texts demonstrate only that this basic vision may be linked to a wide range of references.

Jesus lived by the whole of the Law and the Prophets, as he constantly told his disciples. He regarded his own being and activity as the unification and interpretation of this "whole." John later expressed this in his prologue, where he wrote that Jesus himself is "the Word." "Jesus Christ is the 'Yes' to all that God promised," is how Paul puts it (cf. 2 Cor 1:20). The enigmatic term "Son of Man" presents us in concentrated form with all that is most original and distinctive about the figure of Jesus, his mission, and his being. He comes from God and he is God. But that is precisely what makes him—having assumed human nature—the bringer of true humanity.

According to the Letter to the Hebrews, he says to his Father, "A body hast thou prepared for me" (Heb 10:5). In saying this, he transforms a citation from the Psalms that reads: "My ears hast thou opened" (Ps 40:6). In the context of the Psalm, this means that what brings life is obedience, saying Yes to God's Word, not holocausts and sin offerings. Now the one who is himself the Word takes on a body, he comes from God as a man, and draws the whole of man's being to himself, bearing it into the Word of God, making it "ears" for God and thus "obedience," reconciliation between God and man (2 Cor 5:18–20). Because he is wholly given over to obedience and love, loving to the end (cf. Jn 13:10), he himself becomes the true "offering." He comes from God and hence establishes the true form of man's being. As Paul says, whereas the first man was and is earth, he is the second, definitive (ultimate) man, the "heavenly" man, "life-giving spirit" (1 Cor 15:45–49). He comes, and he is at the same time the new "Kingdom." He is not just one individual, but rather he makes all of us "one single person" (Gal 3:28) with himself, a new humanity.

What Daniel glimpsed from afar as a collective ("like a Son of Man") now becomes a person, but this person, existing as he does "for the many," transcends the bounds of the individual and embraces "many," becomes with the many "one body and one spirit" (cf. 1 Cor 6:17). This is the "discipleship" to which he calls us: that we should let ourselves be drawn into his new humanity and from there into communion with God. Let us listen once more to what Paul has to say about this: "Just as the one [the first man, Adam] from the earth was earthly, so too is his posterity. And just as the one who comes from heaven is heavenly, so too is his posterity" (cf. 1 Cor 15:48).

The title "Son of Man" continued to be applied exclusively to Jesus, but the new vision of the oneness of God and man that it expresses is found throughout the entire New Testament and shapes it. The new humanity that comes from God is what being a disciple of Jesus Christ is all about.

The Son

At the beginning of this chapter, we saw briefly that the two titles "Son of God" and "Son" (without further qualification) need to be distinguished; their origin and significance are quite different, even though the two meanings overlapped and blended together as the Christian faith took shape. Since I have already dealt quite extensively with the whole question in my *Introduction to Christianity,* I offer only a brief summary here as an analysis of the term "Son of God."

The term "Son of God" derives from the political theology of the ancient Near East. In both Egypt and Babylon the king was given the title "son of God"; his ritual accession to the throne was considered to be his "begetting" as the son of God, which the Egyptians may really have understood in the sense of a mysterious origination from God, while the Babylonians apparently viewed it more soberly as a juridical act, a divine adoption. Israel took over these ideas in two ways, even as Israel's faith reshaped them. Moses received from God himself the commission to say to Pharaoh: "Thus says YHWH, Israel is my firstborn son, and I say to you, 'Let my son go that he may serve me'" (Ex 4:22f.). The nations are God's great family, but Israel is the "firstborn son," and as such, belongs to God in a special way, with all that firstborn status means in the ancient Middle East. With the consolidation of the Davidic kingship, the royal ideology of the ancient Near East was transferred to the king on Mount Zion.

The discourse in which Nathan prophesies to David the promise that his house will endure forever includes the following: "I will raise up your offspring after you, who shall come forth from your body, and I will establish his kingdom. . . . I will be his father, and he shall be my son. When he commits iniquity, I will chasten him . . . but I will not take my steadfast love from him" (2 Sam 7:12ff.; see Ps 89:27f., 37f.). These words then become the basis for the ritual installation of the kings of Israel, a ritual that we encounter in Psalm 2:7f.: "I will tell of the decree of the LORD: He said to me, 'You are my son, today I have begotten you. Ask of me, and I will make the nations your heritage, and the ends of the earth your possession.'"

Three things are evident here. Israel's privileged status as God's firstborn son is personified in the king; he embodies the dignity of Israel in person. Secondly, this means that the ancient royal ideology, the myth of divine begetting, is discarded and replaced by the theology of election. "Begetting" consists in election; in *today's* enthronement of the king, we see a summary expression of God's act of election, in which Israel and the king who embodies it become God's "son."

Thirdly, however, it becomes apparent that the promise of dominion over the nations—a promise taken over from the great kings of the East—is out of all proportion to the actual reality of the king on Mount Zion. He is only an insignificant ruler with a fragile power who ends up in exile, and afterward can be restored only for a brief time in dependence on the superpowers of the day. In other words, the royal oracle of Zion from the very beginning had to become a word of hope in a future king, a word that pointed far beyond the present moment, far beyond what the king seated upon his throne could regard as "today" and "now."

The early Christians very quickly adopted this word of hope and came to see the Resurrection of Jesus as its actual fulfillment. According to Acts 13:32f., Paul, in his stirring account of salvation history culminating in Christ, says to the Jews assembled in the synagogue of Antioch in Pisidia: "What God promised to the fathers, this he has fulfilled to us their children by raising Jesus; as also it is written in the second psalm, 'Thou art my Son, today I have begotten thee.'" We may safely assume that the discourse recounted here in the Acts of the Apostles is a typical example of early missionary preaching to the Jews, in which we encounter the nascent Church's Christological reading of the Old Testament. Here, then, we see a third stage in the refashioning of the political theology of the ancient Near East. In Israel, at the time of the Davidic kingship, it had merged with the Old Covenant's theology of election; as the Davidic kingship developed, moreover, it had increasingly become an expression of hope in the king who was to come. Now, however, Jesus' Resurrection is recognized by faith as the long-awaited "today" to which the Psalm refers. God has now appointed his king, and has truly given him possession of the peoples of the earth as a heritage.

But this "dominion" over the peoples of the earth has lost its political character. This king does not break the peoples with an iron rod (cf. Ps 2:9)—he rules from the Cross, and does so in an entirely new way. Universality is achieved through the humility of communion in faith; this king rules by faith and love, and in no other way. This makes possible an entirely new and definitive way of understanding God's words: "You are my son, today I have begotten you." The term "son of God" is now detached from the sphere of political power and becomes an expression of a special oneness with God that is displayed in the Cross and Resurrection. How far this oneness, this divine Sonship, actually extends cannot, of course, be explained on the basis of this Old Testament context. Other currents of biblical faith and of Jesus' own testimony have to converge in order to give this term its full meaning.

Before we move on to consider Jesus' simple designation of himself as "the Son," which finally gives the originally political title "Son of God" its definitive, Christian significance, we must complete the history of the title itself. For it is part of that history that the Emperor Augustus, under whose dominion Jesus was born, transferred the ancient Near Eastern theology of kingship to Rome and proclaimed himself the "Son of the Divine Caesar," the son of God (cf. P. W. v. Martitz, *TDNT,* VIII, pp. 334–40, esp. p. 336). While Augustus himself took this step with great caution, the cult of the Roman emperors that soon followed involved the full claim to divine sonship, and the worship of the emperor in Rome as a god was made binding throughout the empire.

At this particular historical moment, then, the Roman emperor's claim to divine kingship encounters the Christian belief that the risen Christ is the true Son of God, the Lord of all the peoples of the earth, to whom alone belongs worship in the unity of Father, Son, and Spirit. Because of the title "Son of God," then, the fundamentally apolitical Christian faith, which does not demand political power but acknowledges the legitimate authorities (cf. Rom 13:1–7), inevitably collides with the total claim made by the imperial political power. Indeed, it will always come into conflict with totalitarian political regimes and will be driven into the situation of martyrdom—into communion with the Crucified, who reigns solely from the wood of the Cross.

A clear distinction needs to be made between the term "Son of God," with its complex prehistory, and the simple term "the Son," which essentially we find only on the lips of Jesus. Outside the Gospels, it occurs five times in the Letter to the Hebrews (cf. 1:2, 1:8, 3:6, 5:8, 7:28), a letter that is related to the Gospel of John, and it occurs once in Paul (cf. 1 Cor 15:28). It also occurs five times in the First Letter of John and once in the Second Letter of John, harking back to Jesus' self-testimony in the Gospel of John. The decisive testimony is that of the Gospel of John (where we find the word eighteen times) and the Messianic *Jubelruf* (joyful shout) recorded by Matthew and Luke (see below), which is typically—and correctly—described as a Johannine text within the framework of the Synoptic tradition. To begin with, let us examine this messianic *Jubelruf:* "At that time Jesus declared, 'I thank thee, Father, Lord of heaven and earth, that thou hast hidden these things from the wise and understanding and revealed them to babes [to little ones]; yea, Father, for such was thy gracious will. All things have been delivered to me by my Father; and no one knows the Son except the Father, and no one knows the Father except the Son and any one to whom the Son wills to reveal him" (Mt 11:25–27; Lk 10:21–22).

Let us begin with this last sentence, which is the key to the whole passage. Only the Son truly "knows" the Father. Knowing always involves some sort of equality. "If the eye were not sunlike, it could never see the sun," as Goethe once said, alluding to an idea of Plotinus. Every process of coming to know something includes in one form or another a process of assimilation, a sort of inner unification of the knower with the known. This process differs according to the respective level of being on which the knowing subject and the known object exist. Truly to know God presupposes communion with him, it presupposes oneness of being with him. In this sense, what the Lord himself now proclaims in prayer is identical with what we hear in the concluding words of the prologue of John's Gospel, which we have quoted frequently: "No one has ever seen God; it is the only Son, who is nearest to the Father's heart, who has made him known" (Jn 1:18). This fundamental saying—it now becomes plain—is an explanation of what comes to light in Jesus' prayer, in his filial dialogue. At the same time, it also becomes clear what "the Son" is and what this term means: perfect communion in knowledge, which is at the same time communion in being. Unity in knowing is possible only because it is unity in being.

Only the "Son" knows the Father, and all real knowledge of the Father is a participation in the Son's filial knowledge of him, a revelation that he grants ("he has made him known," John tells us). Only those to whom the Son "wills to reveal him" know the Father. But to whom does the Son will to reveal him? The Son's will is not arbitrary. What we read in Matthew 11:27 about the Son's will to reveal the Father brings us back to the initial verse 25, where the Lord thanks the Father for having revealed it to the the little ones. We have already noted the unity of *knowledge* between Father and Son. The connection between verses 25 and 27 now enables us to see their unity of *will*.

The will of the Son is one with the will of the Father. This is, in fact, a motif that constantly recurs throughout the Gospels. The Gospel of John places particular emphasis on the fact that Jesus unites his own will totally with the Father's will. The act of uniting and merging the two wills is presented dramatically on the Mount of Olives, when Jesus draws his human will up into his filial will and thus into unity with the will of the Father. The third petition of the Our Father has its proper setting here. When we pray it, we are asking that the drama of the Mount of Olives, the struggle of Jesus' entire life and work, be brought to completion in us; that together with him, the Son, we may unite our wills with the Father's will, thus becoming sons in our turn, in union of will that becomes union of knowledge.

This enables us to understand the opening of Jesus' *Jubelruf*, which on first sight may seem strange. The Son wills to draw into his filial knowledge all those whom the Father wills should be there. This is what Jesus means when he says in the bread of life discourse at Capernaum: "No one can come to me unless the Father who sent me so wills" (Jn 6:44). But whom does the Father will? Not "the wise and understanding," the Lord tells us, but the simple.

Taken in the most straightforward sense, these words reflect Jesus' actual experience: It is not the Scripture experts, those who are professionally concerned with God, who recognize him; they are too caught up in the intricacies of their detailed knowledge. Their great learning distracts them from simply gazing upon the whole, upon the reality of God as he reveals himself—for people who know so much about the complexity of the issues, it seems that it just cannot be so simple. Paul describes this same experience and then goes on to reflect upon it: "For the word of the cross is folly to those who are perishing, but to us who are being saved it is the power of God. For it is written, 'I will destroy the wisdom of the wise, and the cleverness of the clever I will thwart' [Is 29:14]. . . . For consider your call, brethren; not many of you were wise according to worldly standards, not many were powerful, not many were of noble birth; but God chose what is foolish in the world to shame the wise, God chose what is weak in the world to shame the strong . . . so that no human being might boast in the presence of God" (1 Cor 1:18f., 26–29). "Let no one deceive himself. If any one among you thinks that he is wise in this age, let him become a fool that he may become wise" (1 Cor 3:18). What, though, is meant by "becoming a fool," by being "a little one," through which we are opened up for the will, and so for the knowledge, of God?

The Sermon on the Mount provides the key that discloses the inner basis of this remarkable experience and also the path of conversion that opens us up to being drawn into the Son's filial knowledge: "Blessed are the pure in heart, for they shall see God" (Mt 5:8). Purity of heart is what enables us to see. Therein consists the ultimate simplicity that opens up our life to Jesus' will to reveal. We might also say that our will has to become a filial will. When it does, then we can see. But to be a son is to be in relation: it is a relational concept. It involves giving up the autonomy that is closed in upon itself; it includes what Jesus means by saying that we have to become like children. This also helps us understand the paradox that is more fully developed in John's Gospel: While Jesus subordinates himself as Son entirely to the Father, it is this that makes him fully equal with the Father, truly equal to and truly one with the Father.

Let us return to the *Jubelruf*. The equality in being that we saw expressed in verses 25 and 27 (of Mt 11) as oneness in will and in knowledge is now linked in the first half of verse 27 with Jesus' universal mission and so with the history of the world: "All things have been delivered to me by my Father." When we consider the Synoptic *Jubelruf* in its full depth, what we find is that it actually already contains the entire Johannine theology of the Son. There too, Sonship is presented as mutual knowing and as oneness in willing. There too, the Father is presented as the Giver who has delivered "everything" to the Son, and in so doing has made him the Son, equal to himself: "All that is mine is thine, and all that is thine is mine" (Jn 17:10). And there too, this fatherly giving then extends into the creation, into the "world": "God so loved the world that he gave his only Son" (Jn 3:16). On one hand, the word *only* here points back to the prologue to John's

Gospel, where the Logos is called "the only Son, who is God" (Jn 1:18). On the other hand, however, it also recalls Abraham, who did not withhold his son, his "only" son from God (Gen 22:2, 12). The Father's act of "giving" is fully accomplished in the love of the Son "to the end" (Jn 13:1), that is, to the Cross. The mystery of Trinitarian love that comes to light in the term "the Son" is perfectly one with the Paschal Mystery of love that Jesus brings to fulfillment in history.

Finally, Jesus' prayer is seen also by John to be the interior locus of the term "the Son." Of course, Jesus' prayer is different from the prayer of a creature: It is the dialogue of love within God himself—the dialogue that God *is*. The term "the Son" thus goes hand in hand with the simple appellation "Father" that the Evangelist Mark has preserved for us in its original Aramaic form in his account of the scene on the Mount of Olives: "Abba."

Joachim Jeremias has devoted a number of in-depth studies to demonstrating the uniqueness of this form of address that Jesus used for God, since it implied an intimacy that was impossible in the world of his time. It expresses the "unicity" of the "Son." Paul tells us that Jesus' gift of participation in his Spirit of Sonship empowers Christians to say: "Abba, Father" (Rom 8:15; Gal 4:6). Paul makes it clear that this new form of Christian prayer is possible only through Jesus, through the only-begotten Son.

The term "Son," along with its correlate "Father (Abba)," gives us a true glimpse into the inner being of Jesus—indeed, into the inner being of God himself. Jesus' prayer is the true origin of the term "the Son." It has no prehistory, just as the Son himself is "new," even though Moses and the Prophets prefigure him. The attempt has been made to use postbiblical literature—for example, the Odes of Solomon (dating from the second century A.D.)—as a source for constructing a pre-Christian, "Gnostic" prehistory of this term, and to argue that John draws upon that tradition. If we respect the possibilities and limits of the historical method at all, this attempt makes no sense. We have to reckon with the originality of Jesus. Only he is "the Son."

"I Am"

The sayings of Jesus that the Gospels transmit to us include—predominantly in John, but also (albeit less conspicuously and to a lesser degree) in the Synoptics—a group of "I am" sayings. They fall into two different categories. In the first type, Jesus simply says "I am" or "I am he" without any further additions. In the second type, figurative expressions specify the content of the "I am" in more detail: I am the light of the world, the true vine, the Good Shepherd, and so on. If at first sight the second group appears to be immediately intelligible, this only makes the first group even more puzzling.

I would like to consider just three passages from John's Gospel that present the formula in its strictest and simplest form. I would then like to examine a passage from the Synoptics that has a clear parallel in John.

The two most important expressions of this sort occur in Jesus' dispute with the Jews that immediately follows the words in which he presents himself as the source of living water at the Feast of Tabernacles (cf. Jn 7:37f.). This led to division among the people; some started asking themselves whether he might really be the awaited Prophet after all, whereas others pointed out that no prophet is supposed to come from Galilee (cf. Jn 7:40, 52). At this point, Jesus says to them: "You do not know whence I come or whither I am going. . . . You know neither me nor my Father" (Jn 8:14, 19). He makes his point even clearer by adding: "You are from below, I am from above; you are of this world, I am not of this world" (Jn 8:23). It is here that the crucial statement comes: "You will die in your sins unless you believe that I am he" (Jn 8:24).

What does this mean? We want to ask: What are you, then? Who are you? And that, in fact, is just how the Jews respond: "Who are you?" (Jn 8:25). So what does it mean when Jesus says "I am he"? Exegesis understandably set out in search of the origins of this saying in order to make sense of it, and we will have to do the same in our own efforts to understand. Various possibilities have been suggested: typical Revelation discourses from the East (E. Norden), the Mandaean scriptures (E. Schweitzer), although these are much later than the books of the New Testament.

By now most exegetes have come to realize that we should look not just anywhere and everywhere for the spiritual roots of this saying, but rather in the world where Jesus was at home, in the Old Testament and in the Judaism of his lifetime. Scholars have since brought to light an extensive background of Old Testament texts, which we need not examine here. I would like to mention just the two essential texts on which the matter hinges.

The first one is Exodus 3:14—the scene with the burning bush. God calls from the bush to Moses, who in his turn asks the God who thus calls him: "What is your name?" In answer, he is given the enigmatic name YHWH, whose meaning the divine speaker himself interprets with the equally enigmatic statement: "I am who I am." The manifold interpretations of this statement need not occupy us here. The key point remains: This God designates himself simply as the "I am." He just *is*, without any qualification. And that also means, of course, that he is *always* there—for human beings, yesterday, today, and tomorrow.

At the great time of hope for a new Exodus at the end of the Babylonian exile, Deutero-Isaiah took up once again the message of the burning bush and developed it in a new direction: "'You are my witnesses,' says the LORD, 'and my servant whom I have chosen, that you may know and believe me and understand that I am he. Before me no god was formed, nor shall there be any after me. I, I am YHWH, and besides me there is no savior'" (Is 43:10f.). "That you may know and believe me and understand that I am he"—the old formula *'ani YHWH* is now abbreviated to *'ani hu'*—"I he," "I am he." The "I am" has become more emphatic, and while it remains a mystery, it has also become clearer.

During the time when Israel was deprived of land and Temple, God—according to the traditional criteria—could not compete with other gods, for a god who had no land and could not be worshiped was not a god at all. It was during this period that the people learned to understand fully what was different and new about Israel's God: that in fact he was not just Israel's god, the god of one people and one land, but quite simply God, the God of the universe, to whom all lands, all heaven and earth belong; the God who is master of all; the God who has no need of worship based on sacrifices of goats and bulls, but who is truly worshiped only through right conduct.

Once again: Israel came to recognize that its God was simply "God" without any qualification. And so the "I am" of the burning bush found its true meaning once more: This God simply *is*. When he says "I am," he is presenting himself precisely as the one who is, in his utter oneness. At one level, this is of course a way of setting him apart from the many divinities of the time. On the other hand, its primary meaning was entirely positive: the manifestation of his indescribable oneness and singularity.

When Jesus says "I am he," he is taking up this story and referring it to himself. He is indicating his oneness. In him, the mystery of the one God is personally present: "I and the Father are one." H. Zimmerman has rightly emphasized that when Jesus says "I am," he is not placing himself *alongside* the "I" of the Father ("Das absolute 'Ich bin,'" p. 6), but is pointing to the Father. And yet precisely by so doing, he is also speaking of himself. At issue here is the inseparability of Father and Son. Because he is the Son, he has every right to utter with his own lips the Father's self-designation. "He who sees me, sees the Father" (Jn 14:9). And conversely: Because this is truly so, Jesus is entitled to speak the words of the Father's self-revelation in his own name as Son.

The issue at stake in the whole of the dispute in which this verse occurs is precisely the oneness of Father and Son. In order to understand this correctly, we need above all to recall our reflections on the term "the Son" and its rootedness in the Father-Son dialogue. There we saw that Jesus is wholly "relational," that his whole being is nothing other than relation to the Father. This relationality is the key to understanding the use Jesus makes of the formulae of the burning bush and Isaiah. The "I am" is situated completely in the relatedness between Father and Son.

After the Jews ask the question "Who are you?"—which is also our question—Jesus' first response is to point toward the one who sent him and from whom he now speaks to the world. He repeats once again the formula of revelation, the "I am he," but now he expands it with a reference to future history: "When you have lifted up the Son of man, then you will know that I am he" (Jn 8:28). On the Cross, his Sonship, his oneness with the Father, becomes visible. The Cross is the true "height." It is the height of "love to the end" (Jn 13:1). On the Cross, Jesus is exalted to the very "height" of the God who is love. It is there that he can be "known," that the "I am he" can be recognized.

The burning bush is the Cross. The highest claim of revelation, the "I am he," and the Cross of Jesus are inseparably one. What we find here is not metaphysical speculation, but the self-revelation of God's reality in the midst of history for us. "Then you will know that I am he"—when is this "then" actually realized? It is realized repeatedly throughout history, starting on the day of Pentecost, when the Jews are "cut to the heart" by Peter's preaching (cf. Acts 2:37) and, as the Acts of the Apostles reports, three thousand people are baptized and join the communion of the Apostles (cf. Acts 2:41). It is realized in the fullest sense at the end of history, when, as the seer of the Book of Revelation says, "Every eye will see him, every one who pierced him" (Rev 1:7).

At the end of the disputes reported in chapter 8 of John's Gospel, Jesus utters once again the words "I am," now expanded and interpreted in another direction. The question "Who are you?" remains in the air, and it includes the question "Where do you come from?" This leads the discussion on to the Jews' descent from Abraham and, finally, to the Fatherhood of God himself: "Abraham is our father. . . We were not born of fornication; we have *one* Father, even God" (Jn 8:39, 41).

By tracing their origin back beyond Abraham to God as their Father, Jesus' interlocutors give the Lord the opportunity to restate his own origin with unmistakable clarity. In Jesus' origin we see the perfect fulfillment of the mystery of Israel, to which the Jews have alluded by moving beyond descent from Abraham to claim descent from God himself.

Abraham, Jesus tells us, not only points back beyond himself to God as Father, but above all he points ahead to Jesus, the Son: "Your father Abraham rejoiced that he was to see my day; he saw it and was glad" (Jn 8:56). At this point, when the Jews object that Jesus could hardly have seen Abraham, he answers: "Before Abraham came into existence, I am" (Jn 8:58). "I am"—once again, the simple "I am" stands before us in all its mystery, though now defined in contrast to Abraham's "coming into existence." Jesus' "I am" stands in contrast to the world of birth and death, the world of coming into being and passing away. Schnackenburg correctly points out that what is involved here is not just a temporal category, but "a fundamental distinction of nature." We have here a clear statement of "Jesus' claim to a totally unique mode of being which transcends human categories" (Barrett, *Gospel*, II, pp. 80f.).

Let us turn now to the story recounted by Mark about Jesus walking on the water immediately after the first multiplication of the loaves (cf. Mk 6:45–52), a story that closely resembles the parallel account in the Gospel of John (cf. Jn 6:16–21). H. Zimmermann has produced a painstaking analysis of the text ("Das absolute 'Ich bin,'" pp. 12f.). We will follow the main lines of his account.

After the multiplication of the loaves, Jesus makes the disciples get into the boat and sail to Bethsaida. He himself, however, withdraws to pray "on the mountain." The disciples, in their boat in the middle of the lake, can make no headway because the wind is against them. While he is praying, the Lord sees them, and comes toward them over the waters. Understandably, the disciples are terrified when they see Jesus walking on the water; they cry out in "total confusion." But Jesus kindly speaks words of consolation to them: "Take heart, it is I [I am he]; have no fear!" (Mk 6:50).

At first sight, this instance of the words "I am he" seems to be a simple identifying formula by means of which Jesus enables his followers to recognize him, so as to calm their fear. This interpretation does not go far enough, however. For at this point Jesus gets into the boat and the wind ceases; John adds that they then quickly reached the shore. The remarkable thing is that only now do the disciples really begin to fear; they were utterly astounded, as Mark vividly puts it (cf. Mk 6:51). But why? After their initial fright at seeing a ghost, the disciples' fear does not leave them, but reaches its greatest intensity at the moment when Jesus gets into the boat and the wind suddenly subsides.

Obviously, their fear is of the kind that is typical of

"theophanies"—the sort of fear that overwhelms man when he finds himself immediately exposed to the presence of God himself. We have already met an instance of this fear after the abundant catch of fish, where Peter, instead of joyfully thanking Jesus, is terrified to the depths of his soul, falls at Jesus' feet, and says: "Depart from me, for I am a sinful man" (Lk 5:8). It is this "divine terror" that comes over the disciples here. For walking on the waters is a divine prerogative: God "alone stretched out the heavens, and trampled the waves of the sea," we read in the book of Job (Job 9:8; cf. Ps 76:20 in the Septuagint version; Is 43:16). The Jesus who walks upon the waters is not simply the familiar Jesus; in this new Jesus they suddenly recognize the presence of God himself.

The calming of the storm is likewise an act that exceeds the limits of man's abilities and indicates the power of God at work. Similarly, in the earlier account of Jesus calming the storm on the Sea of Galilee, the disciples ask one another: "Who is this that even wind and water obey him?" (Mk 4:41). In this context too, the "I am" has something different about it. It is more than just a way for Jesus to identify himself. The mysterious "I am he" of the Johannine writings seems to find an echo here too. At any rate, there is no doubt that the whole event is a theophany, an encounter with the mystery of Jesus' divinity. Hence Matthew quite logically concludes his version of the story with an act of adoration (*proskynesis*) and the exclamation of the disciples: "Truly, you are the Son of God" (Mt 14:33).

Let us move on now to the sayings in which the "I am" is given a specific content by the use of some image. In John there are seven such sayings; the fact that there are seven is hardly accidental. "I am the Bread of Life," "the Light of the World," "the Door," "the Good Shepherd," "the Resurrection and the Life," "the Way, the Truth, and the Life," "the True Vine." Schnackenburg rightly points out that we could add to these principal images the image of the spring of water—even though it does not literally form part of an "I am" saying, there are nevertheless other sayings in which Jesus presents himself as this spring of water (cf. Jn 4:14, 6:35, 7:38; cf. also 19:34). We have already considered some of these images in detail in the chapter on John. Let it suffice here, then, to summarize briefly the meaning that all these Johannine sayings of Jesus have in common.

Schnackenburg draws our attention to the fact that all these images are "variations on the single theme, that Jesus has come so that human beings may have life, and have it in abundance (cf. Jn 10:10). His only gift is life, and he is able to give it because the divine life is present in him in original and inexhaustible fullness" (Barrett, *Gospel*, II, p. 88). In the end, man both needs and longs for just one thing: life, the fullness of life—"happiness." In one passage in John's Gospel, Jesus calls this one simple thing for which we long "perfect joy" (Jn 16:24).

This one thing that is the object of man's many wishes and hopes also finds expression in the second petition of the Our Father: thy Kingdom come. The "Kingdom of God" is life in abundance—precisely because it is not just private "happiness," not individual joy, but the world having attained its rightful form, the unity of God and the world.

In the end, man needs just one thing, in which everything else is included; but he must first delve beyond his superficial wishes and longings in order to learn to recognize what it is that he truly needs and truly wants. He needs God. And so we now realize what ultimately lies behind all the Johannine images: Jesus gives us "life" because he gives us God. He can give God because he himself is one with God, because he is the Son. He himself is the gift—he *is* "life." For precisely this reason, his whole being consists in communicating, in "pro-existence." This is exactly what we see in the Cross, which is his true exaltation.

Let us look back. We have found three terms in which Jesus at once conceals and reveals the mystery of his person: "Son of Man," "Son," "I am he." All three of these terms demonstrate how deeply rooted he is in the Word of God, Israel's Bible, the Old Testament. And yet all these terms receive their full meaning only in him; it is as if they had been waiting for him.

All three of them bring to light Jesus' originality—his newness, that specific quality unique to him that does not derive from any further source. All three are therefore possible only on his lips—and central to all is the word "Son," corresponding to the prayer-term "Abba, Father" that he addresses to God. None of these three terms as such could therefore be straightforwardly adopted as a confessional statement by the "community," by the Church in its early stages of formation.

Instead, the nascent Church took the substance of these three terms, centered on "Son," and applied it to the other term "Son of God," thereby freeing it once and for all from its former mythological and political associations. Placed on the foundation of Israel's theology of election, "Son of God" now acquires a totally new meaning, which Jesus had anticipated by speaking of himself as the Son and as the "I am."

This new meaning then had to go through many difficult stages of discernment and fierce debate in order to be fully clarified and secured against attempts to interpret it in light of polytheistic mythology and politics. For this purpose the First Council of Nicea (A.D. 325) adopted the word *consubstantial* (in Greek, *homooúsios*). This term did not Hellenize the faith or burden it with an alien philosophy. On the contrary, it captured in a stable formula exactly what had emerged as incomparably new and different in Jesus' way of speaking with the Father. In the Nicene Creed, the Church joins Peter in confessing to Jesus ever anew: "You are the Christ, the Son of the living God" (Mt 16:16).

GLOSSARY
(PREPARED BY DOUBLEDAY)

Apocalypse: n. Genre focused on eschatology and/or visions of heavenly mysteries. See *eschatology*. Adjective: *apocalyptic.*

Apocryphal: adj. Designates writings not included in the Church's canon of Holy Scripture.

Aramaic: n. A Semitic language, a dialect of which was probably spoken by Jesus. The New Testament preserves several of his words in Aramaic.

Babylonian Exile: n. See *exile.*

Babylonian Talmud: n. Best-known version of the Talmud, whose composition goes back to Jews living in Babylon in the third century A.D.

Book of Enoch: n. Collection of five apocryphal texts. Usually refers to apocalyptic 1 Enoch, the whole of which is preserved only in Ethiopic. See *apocryphal, apocalypse.*

Byzantine liturgy: n. Liturgy of the Eastern Orthodox and of Christians of the same tradition in communion with Rome.

Cathedra: n. Latinized form of Greek for "chair." Refers here to the "chair" of a teacher, with a connotation of "professorial chair" that German readers will hear in the word *cathedra.*

Cephas: n. Aramaic term meaning "rock." The name conferred by Jesus upon Simon Peter.

Christology: n. Branch of theology dealing with the person and work of Jesus Christ. Also the set of claims about Jesus as Messiah and divine Son reflected in the New Testament. Adjective: *Christological.*

Church Fathers: n. See *Fathers of the Church.*

Communio: n. Latin for "fellowship." Connotes here a deep interconnection. Greek equivalent is *koinonia.*

Community: n. Often refers here to the early church contexts in and for which the New Testament books are thought to have been written.

Consubstantial: adj. Possessing numerically one and the same being or substance. Christ, as Son, is consubstantial with the Father, just as all three persons of the Trinity are consubstantial with one another. Greek equivalent is *homooúsios.*

Decalogue: n. The Ten Commandments.

Deutero-Isaiah: n. Anonymous prophet to whom Isaiah 40–55 is ascribed.

Eastern Church: n. The Eastern Orthodox Church and the Churches of the same tradition in communion with Rome.

Ecclesial: adj. Pertaining to the Church or reflecting the mind of the Church.

Ecclesiology: n. Branch of theology dealing with the Church. Also refers here to the claims about the Church's nature and mission reflected in the New Testament. Adjective: *ecclesiological.*

Ekklesia: n. Transliteration of Greek for "Church."

Embolism: n. A prayer of the Mass immediately following the Our Father that begins: "Deliver us, Lord."

Epiphany: n. Liturgical feast traditionally celebrated on January 6. Associated with the adoration of the magi, a symbol of the revelation of Christ to the nations. See *feast, liturgy.*

Eschatological: adj. See *eschatology*.

Eschatology: n. Doctrine about, or content of, the end times. Refers also to the ultimate truth and fullness Christ brings us as the Kingdom of God in person.

Eschaton: n. Greek term referring to final state of the world after the Second Coming of Christ.

Exaltation: n. Christ's elevation on the Cross and in his Resurrection.

Exalted: adj. See *exaltation*.

Exile: n. The deportation of the Jews from their homeland, especially the sixth-century B.C. deportation to Babylon.

Ezra, 4: n. Apocryphal apocalyptic work thought to date from the end of the first century A.D.

Farewell Discourses: n. Discourses of Jesus found in John 13:31–17:26.

Fathers of the Church: n. Saintly theologians writing between the first and eighth centuries A.D. who are main sources of Catholic doctrine.

Feast: n. A liturgical celebration commemorating some particular event. See *liturgy*.

Form criticism: n. An exegetical method that analyzes the literary genre of a biblical text in terms of its sociological context with the aim of reconstructing the process of oral and written tradition leading from the actual historical events to the text's final form.

Fourfold sense of Scripture: n. An ancient doctrine holding that, beyond its literal meaning, Scripture has a "spiritual" sense, traditionally subdivided into three parts: allegorical (concerning the fulfillment of the Old Testament history in Christ), tropological (how we should live our lives), and anagogical (about the ultimate end of history).

Gate liturgy: n. A special liturgy having to do with entrance through the Temple gates in Jerusalem.

Gnosticism: n. Complex intellectual-spiritual movement roughly contemporaneous with Christianity that identified matter with evil and taught a secret knowledge (gnosis) to liberate man's divine spark from it. Adjective: *gnostic.*

Hermeneutic: adj. Pertaining to interpretation, here of Scripture.

Herodian Temple: n. Temple at Jerusalem under Herod the Great (74 B.C.–A.D. 4), who embellished it but also staffed it in conformity to his politics.

Herodians: n. Sect or party mentioned by the New Testament among Jesus' adversaries.

High-priestly prayer: n. Jesus' prayer to the Father at the Last Supper. See John 17.

Historicity: n. Here, the historical factuality or reliability of the Gospels.

History of salvation: n. The sequence of God's historical interventions recorded in the Bible. Underscores that revelation is a matter of historical action, and not simply of ideas.

Homooúsios: adj. Possessing numerically one and the same being or substance. Christ, as Son, is *homooúsios* with the Father, just as all three persons of the Trinity are *homooúsios* with one another. Synonymous with *consubstantial.*

Icon: n. In the Eastern Church, an image, painted according to strict theological and artistic rules, of a sacred personage. See *Eastern Church.*

Iconographic: adj. Here, pertaining to traditional icon motifs. See *icon.*

Incarnation: n. The act whereby the Son of God became man. Adjective: *incarnational.* The adjective can also connote an emphasis on the goodness of material creation.

Kénosis: n. The self-emptying of Christ to the point of the Cross.

Koine: n. Hellenistic form of Greek in which the New Testament was written.

Koinonia: n. Greek for "fellowship." Connotes here a deep interconnection. Latin equivalent is *communio.*

Kyrios: n. Greek for "Lord." Used in the Greek translation of the Old Testament as a name for God and in the Greek New Testament as a name for God and Christ.

Latin Fathers: n. Latin-speaking Fathers of the Church such as Augustine. See *Fathers of the Church.*

Liturgy: n. Ritual worship of God, especially in the Temple or synagogue (for Jews) or in a church (for Christians). More specifically, the ritual of the Eucharist or the Mass.

Logos: n. Greek for "reason," "rationality," or "meaning." Also Jesus as the Word of God (see John 1:1). When used in that sense here it appears with uppercase *L.*

Magisterium: n. The office and exercise of formulating doctrine in the Catholic Church.

Mandaean scriptures: n. Sacred texts of dualistc sect (Mandaeans) dating back to early Christian era.

Mishnah: n. Basic text of rabbinic teaching composed around A.D. 200.

Modernist: n. Adherent of an early-twentieth-century liberal movement in the Catholic Church called Modernism that challenged the origin of Church teaching in an objective divine self-revelation.

Mosaic (uppercase *M*): adj. Of or pertaining to Moses.

Nicea, Council of: n. Assembly in A.D. 325 that officially sealed belief in Jesus' full divinity.

Odes of Solomon: n. Forty-two poems attributed to Solomon dating from the early Christian era.

Ontology: n. Refers here to what things *are*, as distinct from what they *do* or *have*. Adjective: *ontological*.

Paraclete: n. From Greek for "advocate," "one who comforts." Refers in John's Gospel to the Holy Spirit.

Parousia: n. Greek term used to refer to Christ's Second Coming at the end of time.

Paschal lamb: n. The Passover lamb.

Paschal Mystery: n. Jesus' death, descent into hell, and Resurrection, understood as fulfillment of the Jewish Passover.

Pneuma: n. New Testament term for the Holy Spirit. Adjective: *pneumatic*. The adjective also connotes the divine life the Spirit gives the whole man, body and soul.

Pro-existence: n. Jesus' mode of existing for others in substitution for them. See *substitution*.

Redaction: n. Technical term for composition or version of a biblical text.

Roman Liturgy: n. Properly speaking, the liturgy of the Roman Church. Also the liturgy of the overwhelming majority of Catholics in the West.

Salvation history: n. See *history of salvation*.

Sanhedrin: n. Highest Jewish tribunal at the time of Jesus.

Satrap: n. Ruler of a province of the Persian Empire.

Septuagint: n. Greek translation of the Old Testament made by Jewish scholars in Alexandria around the middle of the third century B.C.

Shekinah: n. Hebrew for "dwelling." The special indwelling of divine presence.

Sicarian: n. From the Greek for "bandit" or "robber." Terroristic wing of the Zealot party.

Songs of the Suffering Servant: n. Passages in Isaiah 42, 49, 50, and 53 referring to the Suffering Servant of God. See *Suffering Servant of God.*

Suffering Servant of God: n. Mysterious figure appearing in chapters 42, 49, 50, and 53 of Isaiah thought to foreshadow Christ's vicarious suffering for the sins of the world.

Substitution: n. Christ's representing man before the Father and suffering vicariously for its sins.

Table fellowship: n. Here Jesus' eating with sinners and tax collectors (see Mk 2:15ff.) continued in the Eucharist.

Talmud: n. Commentary on the Mishnah paired with the Bible as the core text of Jewish teaching. See *Mishnah.*

Tent of Meeting: n. Tent serving as a movable temple during Israel's desert pilgrimage.

Theophany: n. An appearance of a god or of God, such as to Moses on Mount Sinai.

Theotokos: n. Greek for "God-bearer." Title of the Virgin Mary.

(Throne) Accession Psalms: n. Psalms (e.g., 47, 93, 95–99) featuring the theme of God's kingship.

Torah: n. The divine Law recorded in the first five books of the Bible.

Trinitarian: adj. Pertaining to the Holy Trinity.

Troparia: n. Poetic hymns in the Byzantine liturgy pertinent to the feast of the day. See *Byzantine liturgy, feast.*

Vulgate: n. Latin translation of the Bible made by Saint Jerome in the late fourth and early fifth centuries.

Wisdom Literature: n. Collective title for Ecclesiastes, Job, Proverbs, the Song of Solomon (or: Song of Songs), some Psalms, and, in the Catholic Bible, Sirach, Tobit, and Wisdom. These writings reflect on the great questions of human existence in the light of faith.

YHWH: n. Transliteration of the consonants of the Hebrew proper name of God.

BIBLIOGRAPHY

As explained in the Foreword, this book presupposes historical-critical exegesis and makes use of its findings, but it seeks to transcend this method and to arrive at a genuinely theological interpretation of the scriptural texts. It is not the aim here to enter into the debates of historical-critical research. I have therefore made no attempt to compile a comprehensive Bibliography, which would in any case be impossible. The titles of works cited in the book are briefly indicated in the text in parentheses; full bibliographical details are given below.

First of all, the following texts figure among the more important recent books on Jesus.

Joachim Gnilka. *Jesus von Nazareth. Botschaft und Geschichte.* Herder, Freiburg, 1990.

Klaus Berger. *Jesus.* Pattloch, Munich, 2004. On the basis of thorough exegetical knowledge, the author presents the figure and the message of Jesus in dialogue with the questions of the present time.

Heinz Schürmann. *Jesus. Gestalt und Geheimnis.* Ed. Klaus Scholtissek. Bonifatius, Paderborn, 1994. A collection of essays.

John P. Meier. *A Marginal Jew: Rethinking the Historical Jesus.* Doubleday, New York, 1991–2001. This several-volume work by an American exegete is in many respects a model of historical-critical exegesis, in which the significance and the limits of the method emerge clearly. It is worth reading the review by Jacob Neusner of volume 1, "Who Needs the Historical Jesus?" in: *Chronicles,* July 1993, pp. 32–34.

Thomas Söding. *Der Gottessohn aus Nazareth. Das Menschsein Jesu im Neuen Testament.* Herder, Freiburg, 2006. The book does not attempt to reconstruct the historical Jesus, but it presents the faith testimony of the various New Testament writings.

Rudolf Schnackenburg. *Jesus in the Gospels: A Biblical Christology.* Trans. O. C. Dean Jr. Westminster John Knox Press, Louisville, 1995. Schnackenburg followed this work, which is quoted in the Foreword of the present book, with a final, small, and very personal publication, *Freundschaft mit Jesus* (Freiburg, 1995), in which he "puts less emphasis on what can be recognized . . . than on the effects that Jesus brought about in the souls and hearts of men and women"—thereby, in Schnackenburg's own words, attempting "a balancing act between reason and experience" (pp. 7f.).

In the exegesis of the Gospels I rely principally on the individual volumes of *Herders Theologischer Kommentar zum Neuen Testament,* which unfortunately remains incomplete.

Extensive material on the Jesus story can be found in the six-volume work *La storia di Gesù,* Rizzoli, Milan, 1983–1985.

Chapter One: The Baptism of Jesus

Paul Evdokimov. *The Art of the Icon: A Theology of Beauty.* Oakwood Publications, Redondo Beach, Calif., 1990. On the theology of icons and patristic texts.

Joachim Jeremias. "Amnos." In: *Theological Dictionary of the New Testament.* Eerdmans, Grand Rapids, Mich., 1964, vol. 1, pp. 338–40.

Joachim Gnilka. *Das Matthäusevangelium. Erster Teil.* Herder, Freiburg, 1986.

Romano Guardini. *Das Wesen des Christentums—Die menschliche Wirklichkeit des Herrn. Beiträge zu einer Psychologie Jesu.* Matthias Grünewald, Mainz, 1991.

Chapter Two: The Temptations of Jesus

This chapter to a large extent comports with what I wrote in my book *Unterwegs zu Jesus Christus* (Augsburg, 2003), pp. 84–99, on Jesus' temptation. Further bibliography is indicated there.

Vladimir Soloviev. *The Antichrist.* Trans. W. J. Barnes and H. H. Haynes. Floris Classics, Edinburgh, 1982.

Joachim Gnilka. *Das Matthäusevangelium. Erster Teil.* Herder, Freiburg, 1986.

Chapter Three: The Gospel of the Kingdom of God

Adolf von Harnack. *What Is Christianity?* Trans. Thomas Bailey Sanders. Fortress Press, Philadelphia, 1986.

Jürgen Moltmann. *Theology of Hope: On the Ground and the Implications of a Christian Eschatology.* Trans. James W. Leitch. SCM Press Ltd., London, 1967.

Peter Stuhlmacher. *Biblische Theologie des Neuen Testaments,* vol. 1: *Grundlegung. Von Jesus zu Paulus;* vol. 2: *Von der Paulusschule bis zur Johannesoffenbarung.* Vandenhoeck & Ruprecht, Göttingen, 1992–1999.

Chapter Four: The Sermon on the Mount

Jacob Neusner. *A Rabbi Talks with Jesus.* McGill-Queen's University Press, Montreal, 2000.

Joachim Gnilka. *Das Matthäusevangelium. Erster Teil.* Herder, Freiburg, 1986.

Karl Elliger. *Das Buch der zwölf Kleinen Propheten,* vol. 2. Vol. 25 of *Das Alte Testament Deutsch.* Vandenhoeck & Ruprecht, Göttingen, 1964 (5th ed.).

Erich Dinkler. *Signum Crucis. Aufsätze zum Neuen Testament und zur christlichen Archäologie.* Mohr, Tübingen, 1967, pp. 1–54 (on the sign *taw*).

Bernard of Clairvaux. *Sermones in Cantica Canticorum,* 26:5. See Bernard of Clairvaux, *On the Song of Songs,* vol. 2, trans. Kilian Walsh (Kalamazoo, Mich., 1976), p. 63. Cf. on this text and its background Henri de Lubac, *Histoire et Esprit. L'Intelligence de l'Ecriture selon Origène* (Paris, 1950).

For Friedrich Nietzsche's critique of Christianity, on which an extensive literature exists, I refer to Henri de Lubac, *The Drama of Atheist Humanism,* trans. Edith M. Riley (Cleveland, 1963), esp. pp. 18–60.

For the section "Compromise and Prophetic Radicalism" I am indebted for the essential insights to two hitherto unpublished essays that Professor Olivier Artus prepared for the Pontifical Biblical Commission (Paris, 2003 and 2004). For the dialectic between the two types of law—casuistic and apodictic—he refers particularly to Frank Crüsemann, *Die Tora* (Munich, 1992).

Chapter Five: The Lord's Prayer

The literature on the Our Father is vast. For my exegesis I draw principally upon Joachim Gnilka, *Das Matthäusevangelium. Erster Teil* (Freiburg, 1986).

For the various interdisciplinary references some initial indications may be found in Florian Trenner, ed., *Vater unser im Himmel* (Munich, 2004).

On the Jewish background: Meinrad Limbeck, *Von Jesus beten lernen. Das Vaterunser auf dem Hintergrund des Alten Testamentes* (Stuttgart, 1980).

Jakob Josef Petuchowski and Michael Brocke. *The Lord's Prayer and Jewish Liturgy.* Burns & Oates, London, 1978.

From the great wealth of spiritual commentary I would single out the too little regarded late work by Romano Guardini, *Gebet und Wahrheit. Meditationen über das Vaterunser* (Würzburg, 1960; Mainz, 1988 [3rd ed.]).

Reinhold Schneider. *Das Vaterunser.* Herder, Freiburg, 1947; 1979 (6th ed.).

Peter-Hans Kolvenbach, S.J. *Der österliche Weg. Exerzitien zur Lebenserneuerung.* Herder, Freiburg, 1988, pp. 63–104.

Carlo Maria Martini. *Non sprecate parole. Esercizi spirituali con il Padre nostro.* Portalupi Editore, Casale Monferrato, 2005.

Among the commentaries on the Our Father by the Church Fathers, one of which I am particularly fond and which I therefore quote quite often is the one by Saint Cyprian of Carthage (c. 200–258), *De dominica oratione,* in: *Thasci Caecilli Cypriani Opera Omnia, CSEL* III 1, pp. 265–294. For an English edition, see *The Fathers of the Church: A New Translation,* vol. 36, trans. and ed. Roy J. Deferrari (New York, 1958).

On Revelation 12–13, cf., for example, Gianfranco Ravasi, *Apocalisse* (Casale Monferrato, 2000 [2nd ed.]), pp. 108–30.

Chapter Six: The Disciples

André Feuillet. *Études d'exégèse et de théologie biblique. Ancien Testament.* Gabalda, Paris, 1975.

Rudolf Pesch. *Das Markusevangelium. Erster Teil.* Herder, Freiburg, 1976.

Heinrich Schlier. *Der Brief an die Epheser. Ein Kommentar.* Patmos, Düsseldorf, 1958 (2nd ed.).

Eugen Biser. *Einweisung in das Christentum.* Patmos, Düsseldorf, 1997.

Chapter Seven: The Message of the Parables

Joachim Jeremias. *The Parables of Jesus.* Trans. S. H. Hooke. SCM Press, London, 1963, rev. ed.

Adolf Jülicher. *Die Gleichnisreden Jesu.* 2 vols. Mohr, Tübingen, 1899; 1910 (2nd ed.).

Charles H. Dodd. *The Parables of the Kingdom.* Nisbet, London, 1938 (4th ed.).

Helmut Kuhn. *"Liebe." Geschichte eines Begriffs.* Kösel, Munich, 1975.

Pierre Grelot. *Les Paroles de Jésus Christ.* Introduction à la Bible, Nouveau Testament, 7. Desclée, Paris, 1986.

Saint Augustine. "Sermon 2." In: *Sermons 1–19.* Trans. Matthew O'Connell. New City Press, Hyde Park, N.Y., 1991.

Chapter Eight: The Principal Images of John's Gospel

General reading

Rudolf Bultmann. *The Gospel of John: A Commentary.* Trans. G. R. Beasley-Murray. Blackwell, Oxford, 1971.

Martin Hengel. *The Son of God: The Origin of Christology and the History of Jewish-Hellenistic Religion.* Trans. John Bowden. Fortress Press, Philadelphia, 1976.

Martin Hengel. *The Johannine Question.* Trans. John Bowden. SCM Press, London, 1989.

Rudolf Pesch. *Antisemitismus in der Bibel? Das Johannesevangelium auf dem Prüfstand.* Sankt Ulrich, Augsburg, 2005.

Henri Cazelles. "Johannes. Ein Sohn des Zebedäus. 'Priester' und Apostel." In: *Internationale Katholische Zeitschrift Communio* 31 (2002), pp. 479–84.

Peter Stuhlmacher. *Biblische Theologie des Neuen Testaments,* vol. 1: *Grundlegung. Von Jesus zu Paulus;* vol. 2: *Von der Paulusschule bis zur Johannesoffenbarung.* Vandenhoeck & Ruprecht, Göttingen, 1992–1999.

Ulrich Wilckens. *Theologie des Neuen Testaments.* Neukirchener Verlag, Neukirchen-Vluyn, 2005, esp. vol. 1, pt. 4, pp. 155–58.

Ingo Broer. *Einleitung in das Neue Testament.* Die Neue Echter-Bibel, Ergänzungsband 2/1. Echter, Würzburg, 1998.

From among all the literature on Saint John's Gospel my principal source has been the three-volume commentary by Rudolf Schnackenburg, trans. David Smith and G. A. Kon (New York, 1982), from Herder's Theological Commentary on the New Testament.

C. K. Barrett. *The Gospel According to St. John.* SPCK, London, 1978 (2nd ed.).

Francis J. Moloney. *Belief in the Word: Reading John 1–4.* Fortress, Minneapolis, 1993.

Francis J. Moloney. *Signs and Shadows: Reading John 5–12.* Fortress, Minneapolis, 1996.

Francis J. Moloney. *Glory Not Dishonor: Reading John 13–21.* Fortress, Minneapolis, 1998.

Raymond E. Brown. *The Gospel According to John.* 2 vols. Doubleday, Garden City, N.Y., 1966–1970.

WATER

Photina Rech. *Inbild des Kosmos. Eine Symbolik der Schöpfung.* 2 vols. Otto Müller, Salzburg, 1966.

Rudolf Schnackenburg. *The Johannine Epistles.* Crossroad, New York, 1992.

Rudolf Schnackenburg. *The Gospel According to St. John.* Trans. David Smith and G. A. Kon. Crossroad, New York, 1982, esp. vol. 2, pp. 151–57.

Hugo Rahner. *Symbole der Kirche. Die Ekklesiologie der Väter.* Otto Müller, Salzburg, 1964, esp. pp. 177–235.

VINE AND WINE

Besides the abovementioned commentaries on the Gospel of Saint John and the work by Photina Rech, I should like to refer especially to helpful articles by Peter Henrici, Michael Figura, Bernhard Dolna, and Holger Zaborowski in *Internationale Katholische Zeitschrift Communio* 35, 1 (2006).

On Isaiah 5:1–7: Otto Kaiser, *Isaiah 1–12: A Commentary,* trans. John Bowden (Philadelphia, 1983).

BREAD

Christoph Schönborn. *Weihnacht—Mythos wird Wirklichkeit. Meditationen zur Menschwerdung.* Johannes-Verlag, Einsiedeln, 1992 (2nd ed.), esp. pp. 15–30.

C. S. Lewis. *Surprised by Joy.* Harcourt Brace Jovanovich, New York, 1942, esp. pp. 223–24.

THE SHEPHERD

Joachim Jeremias. "Poimen ktl." In: *Theological Dictionary of the New Testament.* Eerdmans, Grand Rapids, Mich., 1968, vol. 6, pp. 499–502.

Karl Elliger. *Das Buch der zwölf Kleinen Propheten,* vol. 2. Vol. 25 of *Das Alte Testament Deutsch.* Vandenhoeck & Ruprecht, Göttingen, 1964 (5th ed.), pp. 168–77.

Frits van der Meer and Hans Sibbelee. *Christus. Der Menschensohn in der abendländischen Plastik.* Herder, Freiburg, 1980, esp. pp. 21–23.

Chapter Nine: Peter's Confession and the Transfiguration

Rudolf Pesch. *Das Markusevangelium. Zweiter Teil.* Herder, Freiburg, 1977.

Karl Jaspers. *The Great Philosophers,* vol. 1. Trans. Ralph Manheim. Harcourt, Brace & World, New York, 1962.

Pierre Grelot. *Les Paroles de Jésus Christ.* Introduction à la Bible, Nouveau Testament, 7. Desclée, Paris, 1986, pp. 174–205.

Bernhard Welte, ed. *Zur Frühgeschichte der Christologie.* Quaestiones disputatae, 51. Herder, Freiburg, 1970. Of particular importance here is the article by Heinrich Schlier, "Die Anfänge des christologischen Credo," pp. 13–58.

Jean-Marie van Cangh and Michel van Esbroeck. *La primauté de Pierre (Mt 16:16–19) et son contexte judaïque.* In: *Revue théologique de Louvain* 11 (1980), pp. 310–24.

Hartmut Gese. *Zur biblischen Theologie. Alttestamentliche Vorträge.* Chr. Kaiser, Munich, 1977.

Jean Daniélou. *The Bible and the Liturgy.* University of Notre Dame Press, Notre Dame, Ind., 1956.

Harald Riesenfeld. *Jésus transfiguré. L'arrière-plan du récit évangelique de la transfiguration de Notre Seigneur.* Munksgaard, Copenhagen, 1947, pp. 188f.

Since this book is dedicated to the figure of Jesus, I have deliberately avoided offering a commentary on the statements regarding primacy in the context of Peter's confession. I refer in this connection to Oscar Cullmann, *Peter, Disciple, Apostle, Martyr: A Historical and Theological Study* (Philadelphia, 1953).

Rudolf Pesch. *Simon-Petrus. Geschichte und geschichtliche Bedeutung des ersten Jüngers Jesu Christi.* Hiersemann, Stuttgart, 1980.

Rudolf Pesch. *Die biblischen Grundlagen des Primats.* Quaestiones disputatae 187. Herder, Freiburg, 2001.

Joachim Gnilka. *Petrus und Rom. Das Petrus bild in den ersten zwei Jahrhunderten.* Herder, Freiburg, 2002.

Martin Hengel. *Der unterschätzte Petrus. Zwei Studien.* Mohr Siebeck, Tübingen, 2006.

Chapter Ten: Jesus Declares His Identity

Ferdinand Hahn. *The Titles of Jesus in Christology: Their History in Early Christianity.* Trans. Harold Knight and George Ogg. James Clarke & Company, London, 2002.

James M. Robinson. *A New Quest of the Historical Jesus.* SCM, London, 1959.

Rudolf Schnackenburg. *Jesus in the Gospels: A Biblical Christology.* Trans. O. C. Dean Jr. Westminster John Knox Press, Louisville, 1995, pp. 52–60 (regarding the Son of Man).

Rudolf Schnackenburg. *The Gospel According to St. John.* Trans. Cecily Hastings et al. Burns & Oates, London, 1980, esp. vol. 2., pp. 79–89 (the origin and meaning of the *ego eimi* formula) and pp. 172–86 ("The Son" as Jesus' self-designation in the Gospel of John).

Heinrich Zimmerman. "Das absolute 'Ich bin' in der Redeweise Jesu." In: *Trierer Theologische Zeitschrift* 69 (1960), pp. 1–20.

Heinrich Zimmermann. "Das absolute *ego eimi* als die neutestamentliche Offenbarungsformel." In: *Biblische Zeitschrift* NF 4 (1960), pp. 54–69, 266–76.

Regarding the context of biblical and conciliar Christology, I refer to the seminal work by Aloys Grillmeier, *Christ in Christian Tradition,* vol. 1: *From the Apostolic Age to Chalcedon (451),* trans. John Bowden (New York, 1965).

INDEX